From their Perthshire farm,  Argaty Red Kites, an award-... have played a key role in the restoration of kites, red squirrels and beavers to Central Scotland. Tom is a journalist, public speaker and rewilding advocate. His previous book, A *Sky Full of Kites: A Rewilding Story*, was shortlisted for the Saltire Society First Book of the Year award.

Praise for *A Sky Full of Kites*

'A wonderful book'
BBC's *Landward*

'An inspirational real-life story'
Scots Magazine

'Imbued with the author's passion for nature, and his desire to dedicate his family land to conservation'
The Bookseller

'An environmental story that gives hope'
Dundee Courier

'The story of how a farm was turned into a private wildlife reserve . . . hopefully more farmers will start to see wildlife as an asset, as this farm did'
Birdwatcher Magazine

WATERS OF LIFE

Fighting for Scotland's Beavers

Tom Bowser

BIRLINN

This edition first published in Great Britain in 2025 by
Birlinn Ltd
West Newington House
10 Newington Road
Edinburgh
EH9 1QS

wwww.birlinn.co.uk

Copyright © Tom Bowser 2025

The moral right of Tom Bowser to be recognised as the author of this work has been asserted in accordance with the Copyright, Designs and Patents Act 1988. All rights reserved. No part of this publication may be reproduced, stored or transmitted in any form without the express written permission of the publisher.

ISBN: 9781780278674

Typeset by Initial Typesetting Services, Edinburgh

Papers used by Birlinn Ltd are from well-managed forests and other responsible sources

Printed and bound by Clays Ltd, Elcograf S.p.A.

For Sarah, Rowan and Ellie, with all my love

Contents

Preface	9
Introduction: An Unexpected Call	17

Part One: Beavers and Bureaucracy

1.	They Were Once Here	25
2.	Small Reasons for Optimism	43
3.	#MoveDontKill	56
4.	Going Public	63
5.	A Test of Faith	71
6.	Time to Buckle Up	84
7.	Flood on the Tracks	91
8.	Two Sides of the Story	97
9.	Fighting Back	112
10.	Holding Back the Beaver	118
11.	Trees for Life, Take a Bow	131
12.	Beavers!	137

Part Two: Living with Beavers

13. Thinking Like a Beaver	149
14. The Common Cause	157
15. Shifting Baselines Back	167
16. Drought	175
17. Bamff	182
18. Different Species, Same Story? Sleepless Nights and Worry on Eagle Island	193
19. 'The Word "Whore" Gets Used a Lot'	212
20. All Roads Lead to Roy	222
21. Fig	234
Epilogue	245
Postscript	253
Notes	257
Select Reading	261
Acknowledgements	263

Preface

I couldn't have predicted how they'd change my life. I couldn't have predicted, couldn't have known. Their coming, on to my farm, into my world, was not unlike the arrival of a baby into one's home. One moment things were calm, quiet, easy, and if our days were also somewhat static, perhaps just a little bit dull, then we scarcely noticed. We knew no better. Then they came and they turned everything on its head. They brought anguish, sleepless nights, their own kind of order (which from the outside looked very much like disorder). But like that metaphorical baby, they brought other things too – colour, noise, joy. They brought life.

From the moment that these waters were given back their beavers, I knew that I would never wish to return to the time when they were without them, when the ponds and burns had forgotten their presence and the landscape was a grey and idle beast: old, tired, incapable of change. From the moment that these waters were given back their beavers, there was no going back.

Just as great as the changes they made to the landscape were the changes they made within me. I started this journey a moderate and ended a radical. I turned my back on a life of peaceful, placid pacifism. I lost some friends, but made many, many more in return. And together we brought beavers to safety here.

This is the story of a fight for Scotland's beavers. I write it for my daughters, Rowan and Ellie, for the years to come when they are old enough to read it. I write it for my wonderful wife, Sarah, who shouldered so many burdens in these years. I write it for anyone who wishes to know how we did this and why, what it took from us and what it gave.

Is 'fight' really the best word to use here? Ought I to substitute it for something more inclusive and less provocative? I could, but I shan't. To water down words is to dilute the truth. At its heart, the question of whether or not we restore nature *is* a battle between people with wildly different beliefs and priorities. Anyone who claims otherwise has not had to dirty their hands. They do not know.

And so, I use the word very deliberately, but it is important to stress that this is the story of *a* fight (rather than *the* fight) for Scotland's beavers. The latter began long before me, before my family and friends and the things that we did. Others have strived harder, and for longer, to see these incredible creatures restored across this country. They have their own tales to tell, and I would not presume to step into their space. This book might thus be best considered a chapter of that larger story: *the* fight for Scotland's beavers. I write it in the hope that it has some small influence on the ones that will follow.

More widely, this book is about a word that has come to mean so much to so many, a word that has become more than just a word. This book is about rewilding. This growing global movement has attracted many supporters, and some detractors too. Within these pages we'll meet members of both camps. But why does 'the R word' incite such passion? Why does it unite people and why does it divide? To lovers of the natural world, rewilding offers a chance to restore missing species, repopulate remote areas, arrest nature's decline. Its approach to ecological recovery seems so much bigger, more progressive, and frankly more exciting than any conservation movement that came before it.

But not everyone sees it this way. Some view rewilding as a threat. When they hear the R word certain Scots envisage change, usually forced upon them by outsiders, and the irreversible losses of tradition, ways of life and control. And when they see this threat, they rally against it.

The fact that even supporters of rewilding sometimes disagree on what the word actually means does little to narrow the divide or dispel the fears. (It is hard to claim that the criticisms are inaccurate, that rewilding is about none of these things, when we still argue over what it *is* about.) Some proponents claim that rewilding must involve keystone species* (especially carnivores) and be carried out at landscape scale. Anything else, they say, is merely tinkering. Others argue that this definition is too prescriptive and exclusive to be workable. By their less hard-line definition, rewilding means nothing more than working with nature rather than against it, bringing some wildness back so that ecosystems have space to function.

However we define it, whatever our feelings about it, we can all agree that the R word is really about a C word. Change. Perhaps this is why it divides people. Rewilding forces us to see the fault lines that run through our society, the questions that have no obvious answers. Who, if anyone, do the land and seas belong to? Who deserves a voice in their governance? What is their primary purpose: food production, recreation, nature conservation or all of the above? How do we strike the balance between our needs and those of plummeting wildlife populations? Rewilding brings these debates into sharp focus.

While we might continue to debate these points for a long time to come, I hope that we won't always argue about the merits of

---

*Keystone species are those that bring disproportionately large benefits to their environment relative to their abundance. They are seen to hold an ecosystem together.

restoring functioning ecosystems. Whoever we are, whether conservationists or farmers, gamekeepers or shopkeepers, whether we live in the countryside or a city, we all need clean air, clean water, healthy soils, healthy ecosystems. Our health is dependent upon our planet's health. For all that divides us, I'd hope that everyone could agree on that. If we can, then this nebulous R word need not drive us apart. Instead, we could unite around it.

Let us return to definitions. Providing examples of what rewilding means to other people is easy enough. The harder job is explaining what it means to me. In the past I've played fast and loose, using it freely without ever considering what I meant by it. Haggling and agonising over terminology was a job for bystanders, not for doers; that's what I believed. Part of me believes it still. But I also know that words must be properly defined if they are not to be misappropriated.

To me, rewilding is a process. It involves handling nature with a light touch, letting it take control and intervening only when there is sound reason, only when the ecosystem has been so badly beaten by human beings that it cannot continue to function or hope to repair itself without our help.

This process has a philosophical dimension too. This is about reparation, giving something back to the world to compensate for all that we have taken and continue to take from it. This view was first expressed to me by Pete Cairns, director of Rewilding at the charity SCOTLAND: The Big Picture. 'Those who are passionate about rewilding,' he said, 'are often driven by a profound sense of righting historic wrongs, correcting injustices on behalf of humanity.' In time I would come to see it that way too. The beavers would lead me to this belief.

When it comes to our farm, and trying to explain what any of this theory might mean in practice, I see rewilding as the evolution of a thought that began not in my head but in my father's. In the early 1980s he took over running Argaty – the 1,400-acre

Perthshire estate which has been home to our family since 1916. He did battle with every inch of this land, realising only through painful experience that steep, stony hills would never be worth ploughing, that gorse would always want to be gorse, bogs would always want to be bogs.

'I thought I was farming,' he'll say ruefully now. 'In reality, I was just fighting.' He abandoned the fight and chose a new course instead: farm the best, do something else with the rest. Native trees were planted on the stoniest ground, ponds dug in the wettest, the gorse was left to roam wheresoever it wished. With these small interventions (or non-interventions, in the case of the gorse) he began a journey to restore some wildness to this place. Then came red kites. In 1996 these majestic birds of prey were reintroduced to Central Scotland. When they arrived on Argaty, began to roost and then to nest here, they opened our eyes to the possibility of restoring missing species to our landscapes. Scores of birdwatchers flocked here in their wake, desperate for a glimpse of the then-rare raptors. At the time it felt quite overwhelming, but my parents took the bold step of embracing change. They built a viewing hide, employed a wildlife ranger and opened our doors to the public. Since then, we've worked hard to make our home a better home for wildlife, creating ponds, planting hedgerows and more. Today we run nature tours and evening talks, we've won an award, featured on television a few times (it's true, they really do let anyone on the box these days). This conservation work, which began as a pleasant sideline, has become a way of life. Beavers would be the biggest and boldest step in our rewilding journey. For years, Argaty had been growing wilder. With beavers here we hoped it would become wilder still.

Attempting to restore a wild species to our own wild space opened my eyes to some sad truths about the world. Like most of us, I am fully aware that our environment is ailing, but it was only when I tried to do something to help that I truly understood why.

Only then did I encounter the kinds of people, organisations and systems that make it so very hard to turn things around.

But it was not all doom and despair. Quite the reverse. Although this journey demanded much from me, it also gave me that most priceless of things – hope. Hope that the world might not always be so troubled. Hope that we can still make the situation better. All of this was thanks to the many good people who helped us along the way. Where there are good people, there will always be hope. We must remember that. Hope – more than anything else, I suppose that is what rewilding is truly about. I suppose that's what this book is about too.

An exploration of rewilding would be nothing without meeting the movement's protagonists. When our battles were over and my tale had reached its apparent end, I came to reflect upon those feelings of joy and despair, hope and hopelessness, and I thought of those who'd walked this path before me, who'd fought much greater fights. I felt an urgent need to meet them, to learn of the things they'd done and the challenges they'd faced, to see if bruises faded, given time. And so, just as one chapter ended a new one began, and I set out to hear their stories, to look them in the eye and know them.

The wonderful characters that I met are some of the greatest defenders of wildlife of our age. Indeed, given the troubles the environment faces today, they may be *some of* the greatest of any age. Some of... these words are crucial. Rewilding is a broad movement of individuals and organisations doing amazing things for nature. I wish I could have told more people's stories, but it would have made this quite a different book to the one I set out to write. So, while those included here are doing important work, they are only *some of* the people out there of whom this could be said. I share their tales to provide examples of the sort of highs and lows that environmental campaigners face, to show how very hard ecological restoration really is.

Perhaps I ought to say a few words on why I approached those that I did. Although in some respects they are very different, in others they are remarkably similar. Each is a well-known face in Scotland's rewilding story, a notable advocate for the rights of wild animals and wild places to exist. And while each has had to battle (and often to suffer) for their cause, each has also enjoyed huge successes. It is perhaps revealing that, when I asked various friends working within the field who they felt fitted the criteria listed above, all listed the same names. These rewilders, and their achievements, were so notable that they were, in a sense, self-selecting.

Personal preference may, I confess, also have influenced my choice. None of my interviewees has followed the road most travelled. Their routes into this profession have been unusual and that interested me. After all, wouldn't life be terribly dull if everyone walked the same line? I confess this too: I gravitated towards them because, in one crucial respect, I thought we might have something in common. My family's rewilding project had been running for several years by the time I returned home in 2009, and my role in it would, for many years thereafter, remain a bit-part. Most of my days were spent helping my father with farm work or else chopping and selling firewood. Occasionally, I'd run the kite tours too, but that part of the business was the domain of our ranger, Mike. When new jobs took him and his family south in 2017, the project fell into my hands. Only then did I take my first tentative steps into a career in rewilding. My life has taken its share of twists and turns and I've always been drawn to those who could say the same. These, however, were not the key reasons for approaching these people. The real one was very simple: I chose them because I admire them and the work that they do.

Of course, at its heart this book is about something more important than rewilding or rewilders, more important than any one person or movement. This book is about the Eurasian beaver,

Castor fiber. It is a window on to these animals' lives, a first-hand account of the ways that they reshaped a farm, of the worlds that they created, the many lives that those worlds supported. It asks the question: if this is the difference that they can make to a few ponds on one farm, what benefits might they bring across a whole tributary, river or country?

In these times of environmental decline, beavers are a symbol of hope. They are a small flame still burning as, one by one, other lights are snuffed out. Across the world ecosystems are crashing. In few places is this more obvious than in Britain. This island suffers the ignominy of being one of the most nature-depleted places on earth. (In analysis conducted by the Natural History Museum, Scotland ranked 212th, Wales 224th, Northern Ireland 228th and England 233rd of 240 countries assessed for intactness of biodiversity. Collapse is not just imminent, it is well and truly upon us.

But back in our midst is a creature that can help to reverse so many of these declines and breathe new air into the lungs of old, failing lands. And if rewilding has become more than just a word, then beavers are certainly more than just an animal. They are one of the most important allies that we have. This book is a celebration of them and of their return to Scotland's waters.

They matter. More than we know.

Tom Bowser
Argaty
January 2025

Introduction

An Unexpected Call

The phone call came one day in January 2020.

'Tom, it's James Nairne. Do you have a minute?'

We rambled through the usual polite preamble and nothing seemed amiss until he said: 'Listen...'

His voice trailed away.

'Go on,' I prompted.

'There's something I need to ask you. It's...' Again he faltered. And by some trick of paradox, as his sentences stuttered, the conversation's invisible heartbeat seemed to quicken. 'Erm... it's probably better... if I speak to you in person.'

More than a little intrigued, I set a date and ended the call.

At that stage I'd known James just six short months, since the time the previous summer when he'd paid me a visit, seeking advice on sowing wildflower meadows. I'd known *of* him for much longer than that, however.

A trustee of the Scottish Wild Beaver Group charity, he'd been quoted in several newspaper articles, extolling the environmental benefits that beavers brought and expressing dismay at the numbers being shot in Scotland. I knew that he had turned his back on a legal career overseas to return home, that he owned land near Comrie, some 24 miles north of Argaty, and I had always had the sense that we would one day gravitate towards one another, as likeminded people in this small country somehow always do. Where any of us draws the line between seeking a friend or a mirror is another question for another time, but in James – a fellow Perthshire boy who'd veered away from the country lifestyle of field sports, conservatism (upper and lower case) and *the set* he might easily have joined, who'd worked his way to this very different destination – I'd soon find both.

That cryptic phone call left an impression on me. I had the very clear sense that he was fishing for something, although what that might be remained unclear.

Later that week he found me on the boardwalk to our red kite viewing hide, nursing a cup of rapidly cooling coffee. High above us the kites were sketching gentle circles in the sky as they gathered for their winter roost. We leant on the railings like supporters on the terraces, taking in the scene as breath and coffee steam met the sharp edge of the winter air and were quickly diced to nothing.

Hunted to extinction in Scotland and England, largely by gamekeepers who wrongly believed them a threat to pheasants and grouse, kites were reintroduced to locations around Britain from 1989. Between 1996 and 2001 RSPB Scotland released 105 German chicks on to the two estates immediately to the west of Argaty. They swiftly took up residence on our farm. From that time to this, we'd provided them a small daily feed and run tours; people from around the world had come to see them and learn their story.

'So, James,' I said, watching the birds turn another arc in the sky.

'So,' he replied. 'Tom ... I need to ... pick your brains about something.'

Though my eyes were still fixed skyward, I knew that he was eyeing me carefully. And after a further pause he asked me a question which would change my life forever.

'Do you know of a landowner near here who might be willing to rehome beavers that might otherwise be killed?'

A long exhalation left my lips.

An Unexpected Call

Having escaped from private enclosures in Tayside, beavers had returned to Scottish waters in 2001. Most people had welcomed them back, but others (farmers and landowners in particular) pointed to the unwanted impacts they could have and said they did not belong here. Because of such sentiments, because the idea persisted that they had been foisted upon land managers, possibly due to deliberate releases, untold numbers had been shot.

Were we to attempt to help, it would put us at odds with some people. I couldn't know quite *how* upset they would be, but from the very beginning the danger was apparent. In spite of that, I knew that I wanted to do this – very, very badly.

My mind drifted west, to Knapdale Forest in Argyll. Between 2009 and 2014 Knapdale had played host to the Scottish Beaver Trial, the first formal, government-sanctioned mammalian reintroduction in British history.[*] It was there, in August 2018, that I had first set eyes upon a beaver. Her wetland and the incredible array of wildlife it supported had remained imprinted on my memory ever since. To see it had been to understand what a truly wild space was, and how central beavers were to its creation.

From that moment I had known three things. That something very valuable had been lost all those centuries ago when Scotland lost its beavers. That we needed these animals back all across our country, restoring our dying wetlands. And that tomorrow would be too late – we needed them back now.

So, when James put his question to me, there was no doubt in my mind that we *should* attempt this. Of all the counter-questions that filled my head, this was the easiest one to answer. Beavers

---

[*]We should note that the trial did not mark the first beaver reintroduction, but rather the first *sanctioned* one. By the time of its commencement, the Tayside escapees had been loose for eight years. Scotland had at that time two beaver populations, an unauthorised one in the east and an authorised one in the west.

were vitally important and every year scores of them were being killed. Not to help would mean more deaths, and that would be unconscionable.

Could we do it? On the face of it that was a trickier question because I had no earthly clue how one might go about relocating them, what the process might be, whom we'd have to convince. The fact that nobody else, from big wildlife charities to wealthy philanthropists, had attempted it suggested that this might be a task too great for us. However, I backed myself to, at the very least, have a try. Self-confidence is so important. If you don't believe in yourself and your ability to see a plan through from the very outset, you'll quickly come unstuck when the going gets tough.

Of course, the *coulds* and *shoulds* of this situation were not what really mattered. The only question that meant anything was the one that James had implicitly asked: *Would* we do it?

Knowledge can be a harmful thing. The more I'd learned of the natural world, the more I'd come to see how much trouble it was in. Like many people, I'd spent much of my life wishing for a chance to help change that. Now, here I was, face to face with such an opportunity. If I didn't take it, would another ever come my way?

I thought again of Knapdale. I remembered an arrow of ripples shooting across the water, the gentle slosh as the surface was broken. I remembered a head emerging, eyes, nose and ears designed in linear perfection so that each remained above water as she swam by. My first beaver had been special. She would always be with me. Thoughts of her, and of those in trouble closer to home, filled my head.

If we were to attempt this, if we were to pull it off, we'd have achieved something special. This would be just the second sanctioned, unenclosed beaver release in Scottish history and the first ever on private land.* My ego, the insatiable pirate captain at the helm of this ship, upon whose orders so many actions are based, drew me closer. It whispered two words: 'Do it.'

Overhead the red kites were spinning and spiralling, tying the clouds in knots and bows. Watching them, I took a breath, allowed myself one last chance to back out, and passed it up.

Turning to the man I barely knew, who would go on to become one of the great heroes of this story, I said, 'Okay, James, how do we do this?'

*

But I see that I have rushed in, given plenty of specifics and not a great deal of context. All too often I get carried away when I start talking about beavers. It's a common trait in 'beaver believers' – as the animals' supporters are affectionately known. While this introduction has, with luck, served to explain *how* the events of this story came to pass, it's time to answer bigger questions. *Why* was James forced to approach us? *Why* had beavers come to face so bleak a fate: eviction or death? What had gone wrong?

Let us take a step back in time and explore their history; let us try to unpick this knot. Somewhere in that tangled tale lie the answers.

---

* For sake of clarity, that combination of caveats – 'sanctioned' and 'unenclosed' – must be stressed. To date, there had been legal releases of beavers to fenced ponds/lochs at three private Scottish sites (Bamff, Aigas and South Clunes), and there may have been illegal releases to unfenced ponds at other sites too. Never before, however, had there been an authorised release to unfenced ponds on private Scottish land.

Part One
Beavers and Bureaucracy

1

They Were Once Here

Across most of their global range, the history of beavers can be told in three simple sentences.

They were once here.

They were wiped out.

People brought them back.

Historically, beavers moved freely between the land masses we now know as Eurasia and North America via the Bering crossing, but when rising seas submerged the land bridge, animals were left to evolve separately on either side of the ocean. Today two species exist, the North American beaver (Castor canadensis) and the Eurasian (Castor fiber). From Frank Rosell and Roisin Campbell-Palmer's *Beavers: Ecology, Behaviour, Conservation and Management*, we learn that the Latin (*castor*) and Greek (*kastor*) are likely to have originated from *kasturi*, the Sanskrit word for musk. Fiber, meanwhile, is Latin for beaver. The Old English term, *beofor*, is thought to stem from the Old Teutonic *bebru* (meaning brown animal) and has morphed into the modern form, *beaver*.[1] Weighing up to 30kg (rare examples exist of even heavier beavers), they are the second-largest rodents in the world (after the capybara) and are the last surviving members of the genus Castoridae, a family that was once much larger, whose evolutionary origins can be traced back almost 40 million years.

From Siberia, the Korean peninsula and China in the east all the way west to Britain, from the Arctic Ocean in the north as far as Spain, Iran and Iraq in the south, beavers were once abundant. However, by the late nineteenth century they had reached the brink of extinction. An estimated 1,200 animals survived, scattered across Eurasia. People were responsible for this. We hunted them mercilessly. We almost wiped them out.

You might suppose that the beavers' problem was that they were considered a pest, but the opposite is true. They were too valuable for their own good. Across Eurasia they were hunted for their meat, for castoreum (an exudate from their castor sacs which was used in medicine and perfume) and for their pliable yet strong, weather-resistant pelts, which formed the basis of the global hat trade for several centuries.

Having pushed our beaver populations to the brink of collapse, we turned our attention to North America and its untapped resource of 'brown gold' (as beaver furs were colloquially known). From the 1600s, growing numbers of European colonialists set sail for the new world, where they would spend the following three centuries bringing the beaver population to its knees.

The job of trapping animals was usually undertaken by Native peoples, with furs traded for beads and brandy, tools and tobacco – items of considerably less value. Where tribes had formerly harvested some beavers annually, leaving enough that a viable population remained, now the hunting culture changed. Beavers were systematically trapped out, waterway by waterway. By 1900 a North American population once thought to number 100–400 million had been reduced to around 100,000. To paraphrase Grey Owl, the fur-trapper who saw the light and became one of the animals' greatest advocates, 'The wholesale slaughter' only came to an end 'for want of victims'.[2]

Had it not been for changing fashions (which saw declining beaver felt supplies displaced by materials such as silk), legal protections and a series of reintroductions, it's likely that beavers on both sides of the Atlantic would now be extinct. Instead, numbers are rebounding; recent estimates place the Eurasian population at around 1.5 million[3] and the North American at 15 million.

In three crucial respects, Scotland's beaver story seems no different to anywhere else's. We had beavers too. They were extirpated. They were reintroduced.

However, these headlines do not show the full picture. Frankly, we don't know many of the finer details of their history in Scotland – when they were killed off or how they returned to this country. Their story is riddled with unknowns.

Before we address these mysteries, let us focus on the one thing that we do know: beavers were resident here. In 'The History of the Eurasian Beaver *Castor fiber* in Scotland', authors Kitchener and Conroy state that the animals probably entered southern Britain 10,000 years ago, at the end of the last glaciation. Crossing the land bridge which once joined us to continental Europe, which rising seas have since buried, they would have moved north through England and into Scotland, colonising empty wetlands as they went. Although they are not known to have made it to the outer isles, physical evidence of their existence has been recovered from across mainland Scotland, from the border counties right up to Moray in the Highlands. Written and oral accounts place them in Aberdeenshire and Inverness-shire as well. Given the range of locations from which beavers are known or were reported to have been, Kitchener and Conroy deduce that they were once widely distributed throughout the country.

We have the drainage of peat bogs in Perthshire, Roxburghshire and Berwickshire to thank for uncovering much of the palaeontological evidence proving beavers' existence in Scotland. Of particular interest were the red deer and auroch bones, horseshoes and arrowheads found at Linton Loch, Roxburghshire, in 1843.

Perhaps the animals died of natural causes, but in her book *Beavers in Britain's Past*, Bryony Coles raises an alternative possibility: that they may in fact have been used as a votive offering.* Beaver remains have also been found in caves in Ayrshire and Morayshire, in a shell pile (again in Ayrshire) and in a midden in Edinburgh Castle. Most recently, in 2005, scientists discovered a drowned forest by Loch Tay's shores. Subsequent exploration produced evidence of gnawed wood and, possibly, of dams and lodges too. Some of Scotland's beaver evidence has been lost, and some destroyed during excavations, but radiocarbon dating of the surviving subfossil pieces places them variously at between 8,000 and 1,500 years before the present time.

While it is certain that beavers were here, the date of their extirpation has vexed historians. Primary accounts are thin on the ground, but one source suggests that they may already have been scarce from as early as the 1100s. 'In Scotland, or so they tell me, there is . . . only one stream where beavers live, and even there they are rare,' wrote the Cambro-Norman Archdeacon and historian Gerald of Wales in 1188.[4]

Beavers were not included in a 1424 Act of Parliament detailing all fur-bearing animals on which duty was to be paid and were also missing from an export duty list of fur-bearing mammals from the Port of Leith in 1482.[5] Writing in 1526, Hector Boece did, however, name them amongst the wildlife found in Loch Ness. The passage, as translated from Latin by John Bellenden, read as follows: 'Beside Lochnes, quhilk is XXIV milis of lenth, and XII of breid, ar mony wyld hors; and, amang thame, ar mony martrikis,

---

* However, the presence of horseshoes, notes Coles, confuses matters as the beaver bones date from a time prior to the arrival of domestic horses in Britain.

bevers, quhitredis, and toddis; the furringis and skinnis of thaim ar coft with gret price amang uncouth marchandis.'*

If Boece was correct and beavers were still present on Loch Ness by the 1500s, historians such as J. E. Harting have deemed it unlikely that they could have survived there in large numbers, due to their value to the fur trade. This calls Bellenden's translation into question. Was it merely pine martens that were abundant, or all of the area's wildlife, including beavers? The passage leaves much room for speculation. A final reference to beaver presence in Scotland comes from Lochaber, where oral tradition told that *dobhrán los leathan* (broad-tailed otter), as the Highlanders knew them, were once present. Bryony Coles hypothesises that this may have dated from the 1650s or perhaps earlier. Beyond this point they vanish from all record.

What the evidence, or lack thereof, would seem to tell us is that beavers may have been scarce in Scotland many centuries before they became so across the rest of their range; only by the sixteenth century had Eurasian populations entered steep decline. That we wiped them out so swiftly may be a consequence of being a small country on a small island. Once a mammal is gone, it cannot simply recolonise from adjacent countries, and in any case, England and Wales may already have eliminated most of their beavers by then. (When he wrote *The Journey Through Wales* in 1188, Gerald believed they only survived on one Welsh river and were extinct in England. A beaver-gnawed stick found in Northumberland has since been carbon-dated to the fourteenth century, however. A record also exists of a church warden in Bolton Percy, North Yorkshire, paying a bounty for the head of a beaver in 1789.) Perhaps the speed of their extermination in Scotland is also a

---

*In old Scots, martrikis were pine martens, quhitredis were weasels, and toddis, foxes. (J. Bellenden, *The History and Chronicles of Scotland*, p.33.)

reflection of our agricultural developments and the deforestation that accompanied them. Our woodland cover is thought to have reached a peak 6,000 years ago and to have declined steadily since. This will have reduced food availability for beavers. A mini ice age, which began in the late thirteenth century and continued intermittently until the end of the nineteenth, may also have impacted survival rates.

This was not quite the end for them in Scotland. The Marquis of Bute housed North American beavers in a walled enclosure in the 1870s; they are believed to have exhausted their food supply and perished.[6] Crowds of people also marvelled at the work of further canadensis families imported to Edinburgh Zoo in the early decades of the twentieth century. Their ceaseless attempts to dam are said to have kept zookeepers on their toes; the constructions had to be removed as soon as they were built for fear that their creators used them to escape over the four-foot-high walls. These strange exceptions aside, for at least 350 years, possibly longer, beavers remained absent from Scotland. Their dams broke down, their complex wetlands – arteries of life which must once have sprawled across our landscapes – disappeared. In their absence we've straightened rivers and filled in ponds. We've become increasingly adept at agricultural drainage, whisking water off the land as efficiently as possible.* In doing so we not only dealt our wildlife the cruellest of injuries, but turned our landscapes into a series of sinks without plugs, stripping them of their resilience to cope with the sort of weather extremes that we face today. And the beavers? We forgot what they were, forgot what they did – a fact perhaps best exemplified by C. S. Lewis's *The Lion, the Witch and the Wardrobe*, where a pair of talking beavers prepare a meal of freshly caught trout. Generations of children grew up reading such

---

* According to CREW (the Centre of Expertise for Waters), 60.9 per cent of UK agricultural land is drained.

stories, wrongly believing that these entirely herbivorous animals were in fact carnivores. As beavers slipped from living memory, reality gave way to myth; they became creatures of fantasy.

If details of their annihilation could be deemed hazy, then their reintroduction has been a murkier business still. Quite how or when they returned to our waters remains the subject of intense debate. Some say that captive animals escaped, others have suggested that activists, known in some quarters as 'beaver bombers', deliberately and illegally released them. Many people have claimed to know the truth. Few really do.

In *Bringing Back the Beaver*, Derek Gow – the man who has done more than almost anyone to restore the animals to Britain – finally shed light on the situation. Near the picturesque village of Comrie on the River Earn is a wildlife park. In 2001 beavers were imported by the park's then-owner, whom the author referred to as Nevin. Gow wrote:

> The beavers were settled into a small but robustly fenced enclosure where an internal mains hotwire packed a punch that would stun a tyrannosaur trying to breach its fortified bounds. It was safe. Very secure. All was well until one day when the keeper in charge of the beavers straddled the metal stile into their pen with a large bucket of carrots and discovered instantly, suddenly and very painfully that by placing a branch on the electric wire running around the internal fence the beavers had connected it to the stile. Her carrots went skyward. She screamed, and after hobbling over to switch off the fence went to bed weeping without telling anyone else.
>
> When she came back to work three days later the carrots inside the enclosure were still there; nothing had touched them and the beavers had gone.
>
> Nevin replaced them with others... and for a time no

one was any the wiser. He hoped the escapees were dead. They were not.[7]

*

A period of relative calm followed the jailbreak. As far as most people knew, there were no beavers in Scotland. Then in 2002, Hugh Chalmers of Borders Forest Trust took his family on a canoeing trip with friends. Departing from the town of Newburgh on the southern bank of the Tay they paddled upstream and onto the Earn. They were a mile or so from the confluence where the two rivers met when a furry head suddenly appeared in the water.

'My family was with me and a friend's family was in a second boat,' Hugh told me recently. 'When we first saw the head, they thought it was an otter. But I said: "That's no otter." It turned, slapped its tail and went down, and then went on the bank and it was definitely a beaver.'

Aware that Derek Gow was interested in beaver reintroductions, Hugh phoned to share the news. In turn, Derek called the wildlife park to ask whether their animals were still safely enclosed.

'And they said, "Actually ... no, a tree fell over the fence and they ... erm ... seem to have gone,"' Hugh recalled.

The park's owners were not perhaps the only ones keeping their heads down and hoping that nobody would spot the river's newest residents. Hugh's canoeing companion, Gus MacEwan, had friends at the national nature agency, known then as Scottish Natural Heritage (in 2020, SNH were rebranded as NatureScot).

'How did they react when he told them what he'd seen?' I asked.

'They looked at each other, shuffled their feet and said: "Nobody's supposed to know about that!"' Hugh said.

When, in 2006, beavers built a lodge and laid siege to ornamental trees in a fishery near Bridge of Earn, their existence could be denied no longer. The following year the Scottish Government contracted the Royal Zoological Society Scotland to trap and remove them. Though one was caught, its companion escaped capture.

'The other half of the duo dubbed "The Bridge of Earn Two" is still on the run,' wrote the news agency Reuters in a colourful tale of 'fugitive flat-tailed felons'.[8]

Further years passed. More fleeting sightings were reported. Quietly, the beavers bred, they spread and, aided by further escapees from private collections, their population grew. They began to establish on the Tay and on adjoining rivers like the Isla, where lies some of Scotland's most productive arable land. Trouble lay ahead.

In these flat parts of the country, where farming often continues to the water's edge and field drainage systems are designed to flush rainfall straight from the land to the river, the presence of a semi-aquatic rodent known to bend hydraulic systems to meet its own needs could, and occasionally did, cause people major headaches. Sometimes they dammed drainage ditches, raising water levels and flooding land. Sometimes they burrowed into the man-made flood banks that stood as the sole line of defence protecting farmers' ground from the river immediately beyond.* They even stole produce from arable fields, eating vegetables and packing oil seed rape into their dams. Important though they are, in certain situations beavers can be a perfect pain in the backside; the purpose of this book is not to deny that.

Though most conservationists agree that having beavers back in Scotland is beneficial, there is sharp disagreement as to whether

---

*On this issue, it should be noted that proving that a flood bank has collapsed because a beaver burrow weakened it is not always possible; the floods often wash the bank and all beaver evidence away. It is also important to note that many flood banks failed prior to beavers' return to Scotland. Between 1990 and 1997, 228 flood-bank failures occurred on the River Tay alone.[9]

the manner and location of their return was for the better or for the worse. Some feel that the animals reappearing where they did, in the way that they did, was a disaster. They argue that if beavers had arrived in places where the land was of poorer quality and the drainage less finely tuned, they'd have met with less opposition and attempts to reintroduce them more widely across Scotland would have progressed further by now. But because they arrived without any prior planning or consultation into one of the few areas of Prime Agricultural Land (PAL) that Scotland has, because their activities sometimes impacted livelihoods and rumours persisted that they had not escaped but in fact had been deliberately released, trust between land managers and conservationists was eroded, and positions became entrenched. Time and energy that might have been spent restoring the animals nationwide have instead been wasted trying to fix this mess. All that trouble and anguish could have been avoided had the beavers returned via proper routes to a more appropriate location, and fewer would have been killed along the way . . .

So this line of reasoning goes.

Others take a different view. Beaver reintroduction, they argue, has only progressed as far as it has *because* the oh-so-slow official routes weren't followed, because beavers escaped back into the wild and made it to the Tay, the longest river in Scotland. 'Remember how long it took to get a licence for the government-sanctioned release in Argyll,' they say, by way of evidence.

In 1992, Britain signed up to the European Commission's Habitats and Species Directive, which compelled members to consider the case for restoring extinct native species. Scottish Natural Heritage first commissioned work on the feasibility of a trial beaver reintroduction in 1995. Despite a successful 1998 national consultation, which revealed that around two-thirds of respondents were in favour, it took until 2009 before beavers were finally released in Knapdale, a site where there was little conflict with surrounding land use and where geographical features limited their chances of escaping back through Argyll and across the Scottish mainland. Had it not been for a change of government, the trial may never even have happened. A first licence application was rejected by the Labour government in 2005. Only when the Scottish National Party (SNP) came to power did the ball start rolling again. A second application was approved in 2008. One year later the Scottish Beaver Trial began at last; between 2009 and 2014, 16 Norwegian beavers were released in Knapdale.

Given that it took 14 years to reintroduce beavers via official routes and that all other attempts to restore them to other, better-connected watercourses were thwarted – largely by farmers, anglers and foresters – many people believe that beavers might never have returned elsewhere in Scotland had it not been for the Tayside escapes. They point to Scotland's land-use model, where 75 per cent of our land is used for agriculture, and conclude that wherever beavers were restored they would have the potential to impact farmland. Whenever that risk existed there would be someone with a gun who said 'No!' Just as there has been for white-tailed eagles, red kites or any medium-to-large reintroduced species, no matter how they were brought back.

'We'll never achieve consensus, the people with guns will always be there, but if we wait for attitudes to soften, for everyone to agree, these animals will never return. Though some may die, we will eventually get what we want: the widespread restoration of these species . . .' So this (alternative) line of reasoning goes.

This, as we shall see again and again, is the difficulty with Scotland's human–beaver debates. What is legal may not always have been moral, what is moral may not always have been legal, and though most people are not entirely right, most are not entirely wrong either.

While we might forever debate the particulars of this history, what cannot be denied is that the Tay acted as a super-highway, speeding beavers' recolonisation of Scotland. Further conflicts with farmers ensued and in 2010 SNH decided to take tough action. At a time when the nature agency were overseeing the trial reintroduction in Argyll, they announced that the Tay beavers would be trapped and removed to a zoo.

Incensed that SNH were promoting beavers in one part of the country and apparently trying to eradicate them from another, environmentalists fought for the animals' right to remain. Perhaps the most prominent voices belonged to Louise and Paul Ramsay, owners of the Bamff estate near Alyth. Long-term reintroduction advocates, by 2002 they had grown tired of waiting for the authorities to act and had released beavers into enclosed ponds on their land. Their demonstration project, as well as one established in 2003 by Sir John Lister-Kaye at the Aigas Field Centre in the Scottish Highlands, helped to educate thousands of people on the benefits of these ecosystem engineers. Quite how enclosed the Bamff ponds truly were has sometimes been questioned. To this day certain people still point to Paul as the original *beaver bomber*, the source of all of Tayside's free-living beavers – an accusation which conveniently ignores the fact that beavers were seen in the wild before Bamff even obtained any. As SNH stepped up their attempts to remove the flat-tailed fugitives, the Ramsays lobbied for their protection. They established the 'Save the Free Beavers of the Tay' campaign (which eventually morphed into the Scottish Wild Beaver Group). They enlisted the support of the Alyth Beaver group (the junior order of the local Cub Scouts). Dancers at a Perth nightclub donned T-shirts bearing the unforgettable legend 'Hands Off Our Beavers'. Continuing on that theme, at a rally outside the Scottish Parliament, to simultaneously denounce the then-US president and show support for the animals, protesters proudly displayed a banner reading: 'No to Bush, Yes to

Beaver'. While Paul went to exhaustive lengths researching beavers and the laws that govern wildlife protection, Louise took to the press, writing a series of fiery articles denouncing the authorities. Many of her works are still available to read online. Anyone wishing to know what true bravery looks like in action would do well to read them.

As for SNH, their trapping proved to be a classic case of locking the door after the beavers had already bolted. Of the estimated 100-plus animals living in the wild, they caught just one. Dubbed Erica (after the River Ericht, where she was caught), she became a symbol both for the beaver believers' campaign and of SNH's failure.* By that point the population had grown sufficiently large, and support for them sufficiently loud, that any attempt to remove them would have been nigh on impossible. In 2011, trapping was officially suspended. For the duration of the Knapdale Trial, the Tayside beavers would be allowed to remain in Scotland and their activities would be monitored. When the trial came to a close, the Scottish Government would decide whether the official and unofficial populations could remain permanently.

Time passed. Beavers spread into Fife, as well as through the Forth catchment. A pair took up residence on the Carse of Stirling, barely five miles from Argaty. Reports reached our ears of further sightings at Blair Drummond, of gnawed pencil-shaped tree stumps at Callander. The River Teith links these sites. One day animals would leave the main stem of the river and journey up its tributaries, towards the headwaters. The Ardoch and Argaty Burns would lead them to us. We crossed our fingers and waited for that moment to come.

In the meantime, academics had begun to prove what great benefits beavers were bringing to the British countryside. Working

---

*Erica met a sad fate, dying of septic shock in captivity due to a splinter of plant material in her leg which brought on an infection.

at Bamff, Nigel Willby, Alan Law and their colleagues at the University of Stirling discovered incredible biodiversity gains.[10] In a personal communication, Nigel explained their findings:

> In landscapes containing habitats created by beavers, there were almost a third more macroinvertebrate species than in those that lacked beavers. Macroinvertebrates feed fish, amphibians, bats and birds – they're the powerhouse of food chains.
>
> Plant life increased dramatically, too. Certain tall plants used to dominate the watercourses, but once beavers began to munch on their juicy rootstocks the wetlands were freed from their stranglehold. The site's flora increased by 148 per cent and the diversity of habitats on offer to other species also rose substantially. Over a twelve-year period an unassuming plot of drained land was utterly transformed by beavers.

Equally exciting was the work of Exeter University, which demonstrated that the animals could play a key role in natural flood management. Hydrological monitoring was carried out in beaver enclosures in Yorkshire, the Forest of Dean and Cornwall, as well as in an unenclosed wetland in Devon, where a free-living population, from origins unknown, had been living for several years. The studies showed that beaver landscapes slow the flow of water, even in wet and stormy conditions, greatly reducing the risk of downstream flooding.[11] Through another personal communication, Alan Puttock, one of the project's lead researchers, explained their findings to me:

> The intensive management of our anthropogenic landscape has led to reduced roughness, reduced infiltration/ water storage, etc. and increased run-off. The extreme

example of this would be something like a tarmac/concrete drive in an urban environment where nearly 100 per cent of rainfall hitting the drive will run off (and do so quickly). Our river management has also reduced lateral connectivity between the river and floodplain, but increased it downstream through channelisation and drainage. We call this longitudinal connectivity. To a lesser extent compacted or drained farmland can act in the same way. So, basically, when it rains we get water rushing off the landscape fast and increasing downstream flood risk.

In contrast beaver wetlands (or other types of restored landscape/natural flood management systems) not only increase water storage, but are more complex and rough, meaning water has to work harder and takes longer to travel through them. This can be a result of increased friction from woody debris, leaky dams, canals, etc. Critically, though, beaver dams and canals also increase that lateral connectivity, pushing water sideways back onto the floodplain, slowing the flow, promoting infiltration and creating wetlands.

When flooding and flood management already costs the UK an estimated £2.2 billion every year[12] ... When both the problems and the costs stand to rise as climate change intensifies ... When the cement and concrete industries emit more carbon dioxide than any country in the world other than the United States and China[13], rendering man-made flood defences simultaneously a fix to today's flooding problem in one place and also, perversely, a contributor to tomorrow's issue somewhere else ... When all these troubles are mounting, beavers are waiting in the wings, ready to help.

As an added bonus, both the Stirling and Exeter scientists found that dams trap sediment and agricultural run-off, thus purifying water below the dam. One Stirling study recorded a 50 per cent decrease in phosphorous and 44 per cent drop in nitrates below the dam compared to above it.[14] This research highlighted the potential of the wetlands to act as diffuse pollution sinks, bringing downstream benefits for all the many species that depend upon clean water, including fish, amphibians, freshwater invertebrates and, let us not forget, people.[15] All of this added to a growing global body of evidence proving just how vital the animals are and will continue to be, just how deserving they are of their reputation as ecosystem engineers.

Having delayed on a decision for years, in November 2016 the Scottish Government announced that the beavers in Tayside and Knapdale would be recognised as native and thus allowed to remain in Scotland. Most importantly, they would be afforded the greatest possible level of security wildlife can receive under UK law, becoming a European Protected Species. Thereafter it would be illegal to capture, disturb or kill them, except in very specific circumstances, all of which would require a licence from SNH.

Delivering the news, Roseanna Cunningham (then Cabinet Secretary for Environment, Climate Change and Land Reform) said, 'Today's announcement represents a major milestone in our work to protect and enhance Scotland's world-renowned biodiversity. But I want to be absolutely clear that while the species will be permitted to extend its range naturally, further unauthorised releases of beavers will be a criminal act. Swift action will be taken in such circumstances to prevent a repeat of the experience on Tayside.'

It took 18 months for protection to come into force, and as that deadline approached those opposed to the decision are believed to have stepped up their efforts to eradicate beavers before the new legislation made things onerous.

James Nairne recalled voicing concerns to SNH about the extent of the killing. 'So many dead beavers were being found,' he told me. 'In one particularly awful incident a family had seen one that had clearly been badly shot fighting the current as it was washed downriver.'

Initially SNH seemed minded to downplay his concerns, but James was persistent, and their beaver project manager agreed to go for a walk along the River Earn to discuss the matter. Within an hour they had stumbled across two bullet-riddled bodies.

At last protection came in May 2019 and those who had long campaigned for it breathed a sigh of relief. But what seemed like a red-letter day was not to be. The Conservation (Natural Habitats, &c) Regulations 1994 contained a provision whereby lethal control licences could be issued for specified purposes, including preventing serious damage to crops. SNH, who would issue the licences, had themselves identified over 100,000 hectares of core woodland habitat throughout Scotland, currently unoccupied but suitable for beaver colonisation. However, government policy forbade translocating (trapping and relocating) beavers to more suitable sites when their activities brought them into conflict with humans. The only ostensible change protection had brought beavers was that farmers now had a piece of paper authorising their shooting. The killing continued.

Campaigners hit the trail again, demanding change, and in a meeting of the Scottish Beaver Forum* the government announced that if beavers were already living naturally nearby, a willing landowner could apply for a licence to have animals translocated to their site from areas where lethal control licences had been issued.

Listening intently to this announcement was the Scottish Wild Beaver Group's representative at the meeting. He sped home to

---

*Chaired by NatureScot, the SBF was established so that interested parties from the conservation, land management and fisheries sectors could meet to discuss beaver management. It ran from 2017 to 2022, at which point it was replaced by the Scottish Beaver Advisory Group.

discuss possible candidates with his fellow volunteer at the charity, Elliot McCandless. Together they studied maps, seeking a site that met three stipulations: it must be within beavers' existing range, with watercourses suitable for long-term occupation, and landowners well-disposed towards the animals.

Days later my phone rang.

'Tom,' the caller said. 'It's James Nairne. Do you have a minute?'

2

Small Reasons for Optimism

Every beaver believer has a story. Each of us has experienced that moment of clarity when you see for the first time exactly what these animals mean to the health of our planet. My moment came with that visit to Knapdale in Argyll in August 2018. I will never forget it.

I was halfway through writing my previous book, which told the history of red kites and of the project to restore them to Central Scotland, and had determined to include beavers in it. Should anyone have asked what beavers living on Scotland's western frontier had to do with kites in Perthshire, I'd have been hard pushed to answer. All I knew was that one seemed important to the other somehow, and that by making this journey I hoped to discover why.

The hills of Knapdale forest stood towering over us as my friends and I drove over the Crinan Canal in the late afternoon sun. That sharply rising terrain represented a dividing line. One of the reasons that the Scottish Beaver Trial had taken place here was that the land was too steep for the animals to ascend. They were, in effect, enclosed; their impacts could be monitored, and they could not escape and wreak havoc across the country, as some feared they would.

The road climbed the hills, taking us closer towards them. To our right, ancient Celtic rainforest stretched down to rocky beaches.

Worn by years of salt air and spume, those stunted, gnarled trees looked like broken-backed geriatrics taking a final walk to the sea. To our left, non-native conifer plantations stretched in an apparently endless expanse.

Deep in the heart of that dark woodland lay our destination. Hidden in the floor of a glen was a body of water fringed with tumbledown, moss-covered boulders and further remnants of rainforest. The lochan had no official name – at least, none that cartographers had troubled to record – but the locals knew it as Lily Loch.

Having parked up, we made our way to the water's edge. Pencil-shaped stumps stood all around. Although they'd been chopped at the ankle, the trees were somehow regrowing. A low wall of mud, stick and stone lay across the lochan's outflow stream. Against all odds this fragile-looking dam had stemmed the water, causing it to rise and swell. Now trees that once stood on dry land were being taken by the incoming tide. More striking than any of these sights was the sound. The air thrummed to the tune of thousands of insects, drawn in by the deadwood and the impounded water. Fish rose again and again to feed upon them. Birdsong filled the surrounding woodland. The whole place was bursting with colour and noise the like of which I'd never experienced before. The beavers had created a new world, a birthplace of life.

But perhaps 'new' was the wrong word. Although I was stepping into a scene unfamiliar to most modern-day Scots, what lay before me felt like a vision of some forgotten past. I could picture the first hunter-gatherers traversing this country. They would have made for wetlands such as these, used the beaver-gnawed branches with their spear-sharp points as weapons or in fortifications designed to keep predators at bay. They'd have hunted the birds and fish that made these pools their home. They'd have hunted the beavers too, eaten their meat, worn their pelts, used their teeth for tools. They may have learned how to dam water and to coppice (cutting trees so that they regrow rather than die)* here as well. Wetlands like this would have been as familiar to past generations as they were foreign to present ones.

Seeing that place changed me. Until that moment I'd thought that Scotland's countryside was rich and diverse. I'd thought it was the way it should be. I'd been a victim of 'shifting baseline syndrome', accepting the nature-depleted world around me as normal because I knew nothing else, could not see beyond my own horizons, had no means of travelling back to a time before humans had exploited nature – a time when wolves and bears roamed our lands, when lynx prowled our forests and beavers shaped our watercourses. In that long-lost yesteryear our ecosystem still functioned as it should; animal populations were at their true baseline. Normal? Modern Scotland was anything but. The beavers taught me that.

Like some amateur sleuth who stumbles across the clue that unlocks the mystery, I also understood the connection between them and kites too. Different though they were in almost every respect, both were part of the same continuum: the journey towards a wilder Scotland. Could reintroduced beavers have been accepted back into our countryside had raptors like kites and sea eagles not been successfully restored and (by and large) reintegrated first? Would we have been ready for the upheaval they brought? Perhaps the birds had softened our hearts and prepared them for beavers' return. And if we could allow beavers back into our lives, might those same hearts prove big enough to allow other missing species back? Britain enjoyed the unfortunate distinction of being one of the few countries in the world not to have an

---

*The trick, as ecologist Duncan Pepper recently explained to me, is cutting trees at an angle similar to the pencil-shaped stumps that beavers leave when they gnaw. This allows rainwater to run off the wood, rather than pooling and rotting the stump.

apex terrestrial predator.* Their absence left our ecosystem fatally unbalanced. It struck me that evening, as it has often struck me since, that beavers mattered not just for the worlds they created, but for the doors they might unlock. Only once these herbivorous mammals had been widely accepted across this country could we hope to bring predatory mammals back.

Later, as the light was fading, bats took to the sky, swarms of midges mined blood from our faces and arms, and I saw my first beaver. A trail of bubbles foretold her coming. Breaking the water's surface, she glided calmly past, metres from where I sat, paying me no heed. What was I to her anyway? Just another human, drawn – as humans had been for time immemorial – to these waters of life.

I watched her as she dived and disappeared from sight, little imagining that this would be but the first of many beavers I'd know in my life, that very soon they'd come to play a major part in my story and I, perhaps, a small role in theirs.

Every beaver believer has a story. That was mine.

*

I am, by nature, a fanatic. An intense boy grew into an intense man. I chase goals with single-minded purpose, always certain that contentment lies just over the horizon. That night in Knapdale I joined the ranks of the beaver believers. The fire of obsession was lit, and it would never be extinguished. James's suggestion was fuel to the flames. From that moment, my mind would be gripped by the thought of bringing beavers to Argaty. Those animals came to represent the greatest obsession that I had ever known.

Filled with enthusiasm following James's visit, I rushed home to share the idea with Sarah.

Sitting in her swivel chair at the office computer my wife heard me out in contemplative silence.

---

*The badger remains Britain's largest land predator.

'So, what do you think? Should we go for it?' I asked, eyeing her with manic enthusiasm.

'Of course I'm up for it,' she said. 'Good luck convincing your parents, though!'

I managed nothing more than a grunted 'Hmmm' in response.

In an email sent the following morning, James also urged caution:

> All translocations are governed by The Scottish Code for Conservation Translocations, a document which strikes me as having the primary purpose of making translocations extremely difficult, if not impossible. Approaching Scottish Natural Heritage may just be the first step on a long road, and you need to be prepared for that. I wouldn't be surprised if beavers get to your ponds on their own before any government-sanctioned translocation occurs. Still, nothing ventured, nothing gained.

These comments set my giddy high spirits wavering. I hadn't so much as considered my parents' thoughts on the matter. Nor had I given much thought to the bureaucratic hurdles we might have to jump in order to do this. My head was already at the finish flag, though my feet remained planted on the starting line.

Now that I *did* stop to think, I felt that Sarah was correct. Though farmers never really retire, my parents had at least stepped back on some fronts in recent times. In 2017 I'd taken over steering our rewilding work; our excellent contract farmers, Mark and Harriet Donald, had taken charge of the livestock management. The last thing my parents needed at this stage was a beaver-fuelled fall-out with our neighbours. Fully expecting the worst, my heart already heavy with grief for an idea-not-yet-dead, I sat them down the following morning and put the proposal to them.

They listened in the same pensive silence as Sarah had.

'They're going to get here anyway, aren't they?' my father asked, once I'd concluded my pitch.

I said that I believed they would.

'And they'll be killed if they're not moved?'

'Quite probably,' I said. 'They'll be coming from farms where cull licences have been issued anyway.'

'Well, then ...' he said, and the subsequent moment's pause seemed to last forever. 'If you want to go for it – go for it.'

My mother, sitting alongside him, nodded in agreement.

'Are you worried about what the neighbours will say?' she asked.

'If we manage this, we'll make more friends than we lose,' I replied. 'Are either of *you* worried?'

'Some of them will do the sensible thing,' said Dad. 'When they find out that beavers are coming, they'll learn what impacts they might have and prepare for that.'

'And the others?' I said.

'The others will complain like hell, do nothing to prepare and then complain like hell when they arrive,' he replied.

'I started to take the whole idea a little more seriously after that conversation,' Sarah would later tell me. 'And you know, I don't think I was entirely wrong to think they might have said "No."'

I couldn't argue. My working life had begun with a series of false starts and screw-ups. I'd been like a flighty bird, unable to settle anywhere. Of all the many embryonic ideas my mind hatched, none were ever reared to the point of fledging. My parents would have been mad to trust me in those days. Recent years had brought a change in me. I had begun to take life seriously. I'd committed to it. Perhaps their support was a recognition of that.

While we'd had no ultimate need to worry about their reaction, James's concerns would prove very well founded. When I'd said 'yes' to his idea, I'd felt as though I was stepping off the ledge, taking a great leap into the unknown, uncertain whether I would fall or fly. Having made the jump, I had hoped to learn swiftly whether I was destined to soar or sink. Instead, I found myself floating in limbo for many months.

The trouble was that nobody knew how to apply for beavers. Nobody had yet attempted it; there was no clear path to follow. The first move, I supposed, was to establish whether our watercourses were even suitable for colonisation. My friend, the author and wildlife rehabilitator Polly Pullar, is a trustee at the Aigas Field Centre, the second Scottish site (after the Ramsays at Bamff) to host an enclosed beaver trial. If anyone would know how to progress this, said Polly, it was Aigas owner Sir John Lister-Kaye.

Through Polly, John's reply was relayed: If I was serious about pursuing this, I should contact Roisin Campbell-Palmer. Bureaucratic minefields surely lay ahead, however. John was quite clear about that.

Everybody warned me. Looking back, I recognise that. At the time I was deaf to all protestations, imbued with a belief that I was different, that I could succeed where others had struggled. I was younger then. I'm older now. All that I can say in my own defence is that few of us could imagine how difficult it is to reintroduce, or in my case to relocate, a polarising species. The only way to learn is to do it. Then you'll never forget.

Dr Roisin Campbell-Palmer is widely regarded as Scotland's top beaver expert. That we had never previously met seemed strange to me, for it transpired that we had many mutual friends. The explanation as to why our paths had never crossed was very simple, though. To that point, I had merely hovered around the fringes of rewilding, doing my own thing on my own small patch, far away from the coalface, where people like Roisin were to be found. Nominally, we worked in the same field. In reality that field was large, and I was standing on the edge of it.

Having worked as the field operations manager at the Scottish Beaver Trial, she had since become an independent contractor, working for SNH to provide mitigation services and advice to people experiencing unwanted beaver impacts. When issues grew too great for some landowners to endure, she performed her most vital role: trapping animals and relocating them to safety in English and Welsh enclosures, massive wetlands surrounded by beaver-proof fencing. England already had an estimated 500 free-living beavers, and Wales a smaller population, thought to number less than 50 – all the suspected result of further acts of beaver bombing. However, at that time, it was illegal to release them into the wild in either country. Enclosures were beavers' best bet. (Public and political support for reintroductions has since grown, and in March 2025 the first sanctioned wild release in English history took place at Purbeck Heaths nature reserve in Dorset. As more releases happen and enclosure fences are taken down, Roisin's Scottish refugees will become the founders of free-living populations across Britain. The beavers owe her a great deal. We would come to owe her too.)

We fixed a plan to meet, but three months would pass before we'd actually be able to do so. In late March 2020 the coronavirus global pandemic brought society to a standstill.

It is hard now to emphasise how very strange those times were. At first many of us assumed that the virus would disappear as swiftly as it had arrived and normal life would soon resume. How wrong we were. Covid did not go away. Lockdown continued.

Looking back, I wonder what my daughter, Rowan, aged six at the time, will remember of that period. Will she recall everyone wearing face masks and keeping a two-metre distance from one another, only seeing her grandparents in outdoor settings and being forbidden from hugging them? Will she remember her parents frantically washing and disinfecting any item of shopping before it came into the house?

Those were terrifying times. As a family, however, the isolation was kind to us. Never had we been so aware of our privilege. Our time was spent wandering Argaty, uncovering the many secrets that this old estate had been hiding. Memories of those days will remain with me for life. I see a mud-caked Rowan, dressed in an eye-catching combination of bobble hat, over-large welly boots and luminous pink tutu, crouched beside streams, blocking the water's flow with beaver-like mud and stick dams. I see her searching beneath rocks for insects, climbing trees and gates. She was utterly wild, utterly at one with her world. And I remember thinking how very like cuckoos people are, farming our young out for others to raise. Although we have good reasons for doing so, enforced home-schooling being a special form of torture for you and your offspring, I was sorry nonetheless. I felt that I'd gone against the laws of nature and taught Rowan very little. I was glad to have the chance to address that, glad of those stolen days with her and with Sarah, getting to know them better than I ever would have done had one been in school and the other at work. How lucky I was to have them. How lucky to have the room to roam and to think of family, of life, and in the quiet moments, of beavers.

As human society ground to a halt, the natural world earned a much-needed reprieve from cars, planes and the many other weapons we attack it with. Left to its own devices it tended its wounds; they began to heal. Choirs of birds serenaded the otherwise silent city streets. People began to notice the small things that the hustle and haste of modern life had blinded them to. In those, the very hardest and strangest of days, there were small reasons for optimism.

*

June came, the days stretched out, the land lay basking in the summer sun. Coronavirus restrictions were eased, outdoor meetings permitted, and so I met with Roisin.

As she got out of her van, I saw that the picture I'd mentally sketched of what a beaver expert might look like, which amounted to nothing more considered than some lazy stereotype of a scientist, bore little resemblance to reality. Her jumper was so riddled with holes it looked as though it had lost a fight with a beaver. Something in her appearance, the dark eye shadow and just-visible arm tattoos perhaps, suggested that she might enjoy heavy rock music. This impression might be very far wide of the mark; it occurs to me now that I've never asked. (These days I can divide my friends into two categories: BB (before beaver) and AB (after). The members of the former group are the ones I have known longest and also the ones I now see the least of. The people I've met since James's visit, who have become the more regular fixtures in my life, are no less dear to my heart, but they are a different sort of friend nonetheless. I know little about their private lives: what their partners do for a living, the names of their children, any of the usual things one might be expected to know. Beavers are the glue that binds us together, the topic to which our conversations instantly and inevitably turn. Roisin was the first of many AB friends I would make.)

Her superficial air of toughness did not mask a subcutaneous fragility. Though she swore like a sailor in glorious streams of Belfast invective, she kept her guard high, weighing her words carefully before imparting them. She was an intriguing mix of things and I liked her very much.

We set off on a tour of Argaty's watercourses. Until that point I had been unshakeably proud of each of our ponds and the life they supported, but my opinion of several was set to suddenly change.

'Banks are too stony for burrowing.'

'Not enough trees.'

'Trees are too far away. They'd never stay.'

Roisin wasn't slow in pronouncing judgement. Several of the spots I'd hoped would prove *most* suitable were batted away in the blink of an eye.

But there were others that did meet with her approval: deep, dark pools edged with willow and flag iris, alder and rowan, where tangled trysts of brambles overhung the water. (I learned from Roisin that, thanks to a mucus lining in their stomachs, the beavers could eat brambles, thorns and all, and suffer no discomfort.) Some of the ponds had steep banks, others did not, but their soils were friable. On the former beavers might burrow, on the latter they'd build a lodge. Whether they made their homes by digging a series of underground chambers known as burrows, or by creating a lodge (with some 'wet' chambers dug below ground at water level, and mud-walled sleeping rooms filled with beds of bark, grass and wood shavings built above ground) was, I learned, largely dependent upon water depth and bank profile. Where water was deep and banks steep, they usually burrowed; where banks were flatter, they tended towards lodges. Either way, they needed a dry chamber to sleep in and would build upwards if they had to.

While we walked, we discussed the big news from the beaver world. In May, SNH had released a report detailing the management actions it had licensed from May to 31 December 2019. It had sent shockwaves through the wildlife community. At least 87 beavers had been shot under licence in that period.

Some context may be useful here, to show just how significant that number was. In Bavaria 12 million people live alongside 23,000 beavers. Norway has 5.4 million people and an estimated 80,000 beavers. In 2019, Scotland had 5.6 million people and approximately 450 beavers. And in the first year of apparent protection one in five of the animals had been shot. Of the 45 licences issued, 21 were given without a visit being undertaken by SNH or their agents in the previous six months. In those cases, nobody had checked that problems really existed which could not be sorted through non-lethal mitigation measures.

One silver lining in the SNH report was the lines: 'We will work with licence-holders to maximise potential for live trapping as an alternative to lethal control ... We will consider conservation translocations of beavers from high to low conflict areas within existing catchments to improve the resilience of existing populations.'

That sounded positive to me. With the translocation embargo officially lifted other applicants would surely step forward and spare further beavers the bullet. Roisin did not share my optimism.

'The conservation world will applaud you doing this, but wait and see how many of them apply for translocations themselves,' she said.

She had the air of a soldier who had been in the trenches too long, who'd seen too many deaths, watched too many politicians and conservation generals come, make great promises, fail to deliver and then go. Next to her I was like a bouncy puppy, full of youthful enthusiasm.

It now pains me to recall that I teased her for her negativity during that first meeting. Years later she'd tell me that she thought I was 'overly positive' and laugh about how 'reality had subsequently ground me down'.

With the benefit of hindsight, I can't help but feel that she won that one.

*

After three months of isolation, things were set to change.

It started with another easing of lockdown restrictions. We reopened our doors and welcomed visitors back to Argaty. Rain or shine we ran all of our red kite tours outside, and whether sunburned or soaked, people seemed thrilled to be there, to see other faces and enjoy some semblance of the old world again. By then I'd developed a second shadow. Throughout lockdown Rowan had followed me wherever I went; post-lockdown she stayed with me. What joy it brought to see her charging around the farm with visitors' children, kids she'd never met before and would never see again but with whom she shared some fundamental understanding that a great and terrible storm had temporarily abated, and that now was the time for games, for companionship, for happiness. I can still hear their high, wild laughter as they chased one another around dusty paths in the late summer sun. The sound of their footfall still runs through my mind. Strange and hard times lay behind us, outrun for the time being; ahead lay new roads to very different futures. Theirs were the first feet to grace them.

3

#MoveDontKill

'Translocate protected beavers to reduce licensed killing,' read the title of Petition 1815. Lodged by Steve Micklewright, CEO of rewilding charity Trees for Life, it asked the Scottish Parliament to urge the government to initiate a programme to translocate beavers to suitable habitat across the country, to minimise the need to kill animals adversely impacting arable farmland.

The petition had been brewing like a storm for many months. I'd first heard mention of it back in March, just before the madness of lockdowns had begun, at a meeting of the Scottish Rewilding Alliance. The SRA were a recently convened coalition which sought to bring the environmental community together to coordinate advocacy work and enable rewilding at scale. That March gathering had been my first meeting and had proved an uncomfortable experience. I'd never really known where to put myself when in the company of either farmers or rewilders. Surrounded by farmers I felt like the most radical person in the room; surrounded by rewilders, the most conservative. When I'd looked around that meeting, my first thought had been how very different I was to everyone else there; how very far from the farm I was. They talked openly of land reform and lynx reintroduction, causes that I supported but which others in my social circle opposed vehemently.

The sense of unease had intensified when Steve Micklewright – who, on top of his Trees for Life duties, served as convenor of the SRA – shared news of the upcoming beaver petition and asked the members to help promote it when the time came.

The consensus was that the situation couldn't continue. The public wouldn't stand for the current level of killing. At some point those politicians, bureaucrats and farming representatives responsible for the lethal control policy would have to come to the table.

My heartbeat quickened from a canter to a gallop. As a family and a business, we had always kept away from the tired old battles between farming and conservation. Were we to proceed with our beaver project, I'd hoped we could stay in lane and not be seen to take a side. Should the petition catch the public's imagination, and the debate become a shouting match, the chances of remaining neutral would be slim; to the most inflexible of thinkers, any pro-beaver move would automatically be construed as anti-farming. Herein lay the danger for us. While the rewilding side of our business was the part dearest to my heart, it was farming that kept a roof over our heads. Were it not for sales of livestock and of sheep-handling equipment, we could not have afforded to do the environmental work that we did. Farming is a small community, with strong values. People buy goods from those that they know and trust. If we came out too strongly in favour of the conservationists and against the farmers, would those farmers still buy from us? Or were we, financially, slitting our own throats?

I left that meeting wondering if I could really afford to attend another, shoved the petition to the back of my brain and hoped never to think of it again.

For several months I would succeed in that aim. Lockdown ended, Argaty reopened, life moved on. But then August arrived and, as petition-related emails flooded my inbox, the topic became impossible to ignore. A dark day loomed on the horizon.

From 16 August, young beavers would no longer be reliant upon their parents for survival; the licensed culling could resume. Eight thousand people had thus far signed the petition. With it due for submission at the end of the month, Steve was orchestrating a major push to gain more publicity and more signatures. A hard-hitting social media campaign was planned. On Monday, 17 August the SRA would launch a Twitterstorm based around the hashtag #MoveDontKill. Associated images featured beavers in rifle crosshairs. People were asked to log on to Twitter (as the social media platform was then known), share the images and slogan, and drum up publicity for the petition.

#MoveDontKill would be the most contentious campaign of the SRA's young life. Three of the alliance's largest member organisations argued that the slogan presented an oversimplified dichotomy between moving and killing animals, which conflicted with their positions on the culling of other species. The images were felt to be divisive and inflammatory. They also called (with some justification) for a clearer sign-off process for SRA campaigning. To the surprise of many, however, these charities not only refused to support #MoveDontKill, but left the alliance entirely.

Some feared that this might spell the end for the fledgling group. Instead, it had the opposite effect. The SRA existed to push boundaries and enable rewilding at scale. Everyone who remained in the tent accepted this as the price of entry. I did too, and so I swallowed my qualms and committed to both the cause and the alliance.

As convenor, Steve (someone unafraid to poke government, bureaucrats and any other big organisation in the eye if doing so would deliver meaningful change) was the perfect embodiment of the SRA's ethos. This trait, which had made me a little wary of him at first, would become the thing I liked most about him. Wildlife conservation is full of gentle, well-meaning people who hate to fall out with anyone. While these are generally commendable traits, we need people like Steve who will not (perhaps cannot) keep their mouths closed when they see nature being harmed.

The Twitterstorm went ahead, attracting major newspaper and radio coverage. By the time it closed on 27 August a staggering 16,750 people had added their names. It is believed to be the most signed petition in Scottish Parliament history.

I've often wondered what it was about #MoveDontKill that led those charities to quit the alliance. I could (just about) understand withdrawing from one campaign, but leaving the alliance entirely ... That choice puzzles me. Everything that follows is mere conjecture, but I think this story hints at a wider divide that exists within the conservation world.

I saw this as a clash between two very different types of wildlife organisation, with wildly different ways of operating. On one side we had the older, larger charities; on the other a new breed of small rewilding ones. The former group had many strengths. They were established and well-respected. They had money and large membership lists, and this gave them lobbying power. But the heads of those organisations faced a problem. The larger their charities grew, the hungrier they became, the more human and physical resources they needed. Their money came from membership sales, legacy bequests, and government and nature agency grants. Stoke too much controversy and they risked upsetting people, losing funds and having to shed the employees, infrastructure and assets they had worked so hard to gather. Walking that tightrope must be one of the hardest tasks in the world.

To further complicate matters, the older charities now faced another challenge, with the rise of rewilding ones. These new rivals did not have the income or power of the bigger charities, but being small was not always a weakness. With fewer overheads came less jeopardy. Their chief executives didn't risk hundreds of jobs every time they courted controversy. Quite the opposite.

They had a mandate to push the boundaries because their supporters demanded it.

How the future will play out – which of those old or new guard will still be here in 50 or 100 years – is anyone's guess. But I wonder if some of the larger charities may struggle to balance the competing demands of remaining both financially afloat and relevant in this changing world. I think that the decision of those three organisations to leave the SRA rather than back the beaver campaign was a reflection of that struggle, of them picking their fights. I think they made a mistake. Like political dissidents, or the free press, conservation organisations must always be prepared to speak truth to power when it fails to protect nature. If they can or will not do so, something has surely gone wrong.

Those are my thoughts on the matter. Steve Micklewright would express his rather more emphatically.

*

Recently, he and I had sat down to share recollections of #MoveDontKill. So comfortable am I with him today, so much do I like him, that it amuses me to recall how terrifyingly radical he, as the leader of the SRA, seemed to me when we first met. Little about rewilding or rewilders feels radical to me now. As humans send the world spiralling closer and closer to total ecological collapse, the radicals are not the ones striving to change our course but the ones still steering us onwards.

Steve is a quick thinker and even quicker talker. A machine-gun blast of theories and ideas fire from him as he speaks. While this makes for a highly engaging interview, transcribing his words is tricky, for it is impossible to know where a full stop might belong in his sentences. Ultimately, I would conclude that to accurately replicate his voice, full stops were in fact very rarely required.

'Why did we get involved with beavers?' he said, repeating my opening question back to me. 'Because we were just not happy with the way the Scottish Government were dealing with the Tayside situation... We were dismayed with 20 per cent of Scotland's beavers being shot, and frustrated because bigger eNGOs [environmental non-governmental organisations] that should've been championing them weren't prepared to push the situation hard to get a change. And it was James Nairne's idea that Trees for Life led on this... Somebody needed to put their head above the parapet, and that's what we decided to do.'

How did he feel, I wondered, when some chose not to back the campaign? As I asked the question, I could almost sense a still-held indignation flaring within him. Already, I knew how he'd answer.

'There needs to be an organisation or body that's prepared to say the hard truths about what's going on in Scotland,' he said. 'We were trying to get people upset about beavers because we felt what was happening was wrong, so we went down the emotive, hard-hitting campaign route ... And it's clear to me that those organisations, for whatever excuses they gave, just weren't prepared to stand up and be counted. That's how I felt about it, and I thought: "What, for fuck's sake, are you doing then?" Very honestly, it really tarnished my view of them, which has only got worse since then.'

Our conversation turned to the Twitterstorm, when social media went beaver-crazy. Celebrities, campaigners and members of the public took to Twitter, retweet followed retweet, petition signatures skyrocketed. For Steve, it felt like a moment of validation.

'It told me that people really cared. We were right to make a fuss about beavers,' he said.

Despite his choice of words, Trees for Life's motivations went far beyond simply making 'a fuss'. This was also about redressing a balance. In 2017 beavers were discovered living on the River Glass near Beauly in Inverness-shire. As in Tayside, they were believed to have escaped from private collections.

Hoping that it would kick-start conversations on wider reintroductions across the country, to areas like Glen Affric – where Trees for Life have been restoring native woodland for 30 years and the potential for conflict with people was low – they decided to inform Scottish Natural Heritage about the Beauly animals.

The plan backfired. At that time the Scottish Government were under huge pressure for having allowed the Tayside beavers to remain, and Environment Secretary Roseanna Cunningham had announced that further releases would be considered a criminal act.

'SNH probably already knew beavers were on the Beauly, but didn't want to act,' Steve said. 'As soon as we made it formal, they had to respond by removing them.'

Three were caught. Two died in captivity.

Years later, the memory of that incident still lingered. 'I think that was part of the spur of us getting involved at a national scale on beavers,' Steve said. 'We saw on the ground the absolute absurdity of government policy. It was morally wrong. Beavers weren't causing problems just by being there … Them getting trapped and then dying – that was just an insane situation … We'd made a massive error. We owed beavers something for causing them to die.'

If there was a debt to pay, and there's a strong case to say that there wasn't, it being the Scottish Government who ordered those animals' removal, Trees for Life would more than settle it in the year that followed. #MoveDontKill was just the first step in their campaigning. Much bigger things were to come.

4

Going Public

'How was it?' I asked Rowan as we left the playground at the close of her first day back at school.

'Good,' she replied. 'Although at break a strange thing happened. A boy came up and asked me to say the word "cuff" backwards.'

'And you said . . .' I prompted, apprehension rising in me.

'I told him he'd spelt it wrong,' she said sweetly.

The sound of my laughter travelled the length and breadth of Doune.

Over the summer months coronavirus cases had continued to fall and schools had reopened for the new term. Our nerves fraying, Sarah and I sent Rowan back in. She needed to be with her peers, receiving (and dishing out) a proper education. These things had been too long denied her. We knew that. But we also saw that there'd be little protection from the virus now. Being alone and away from everyone, the one thing that had kept us safe was the one thing everyone now had to forsake.

With progress came apprehension, on more than one front. Roisin had drafted a feasibility study showing the suitability of our ponds for beaver colonisation. The time had come to put the proposal before the agency now known as NatureScot (the name Scottish Natural Heritage had recently been dropped). In the long months since James had first mentioned rehoming beavers, the idea had morphed into different and contradictory things for me. It was the skeleton in the closet which, if discovered, might ruin my life. It was the five-pound note that had to be spent before it burned a hole through my pocket. For better or worse, it had to come out. Heart thudding to the beat of a nervy but excited drummer, I sat down and typed out the email.

In the closing days of September, I met online with their beaver project manager, Jenny Bryce, and Tayside area manager, Denise Reed. (The latter had the unenviable task of chairing the Scottish Beaver Forum, a job that sounded not unlike refereeing a bare-knuckle boxing match.) I felt we had a solid proposition. Some neighbours might not like the idea of us moving beavers to Argaty, but as animals were already living wild mere miles away and would disperse to all our waters anyway, given time, it was surely better to know when that moment might arrive. Hitherto, in other parts of Scotland, most people had had no such warning. They were thus caught unawares when the animals came, felled trees, built dams and did all the many things that they do. Our project could be different. This needn't be a reactive situation. Across Europe and North America, mitigation measures against most unwanted beaver impacts had been well trialled. If everyone knew in advance that beavers were coming, they would have time to learn what issues might arise and which mitigation measures might help fix them. There were many options to try before anyone need reach for the gun.

Feeling for the first, but not the final time as though I were inhabiting the role of a salesman, I laid all of these thoughts out like goods on a market stall for NatureScot to inspect. And did I imagine it, or did I sense relief from them? Politicians made the policies; the nature agency tried to make them work, even if they were, at times, unworkable. Beavers having legal protection, but also somehow not having it, was the ultimate, tragic example of this. Since the previous year's cull numbers had been published, the press had been gunning for NatureScot. The idea that, sitting like a pot of gold at the end of a rainbow might be that rarest of treasures, a positive, non-lethal solution to human–beaver conflict, must have been of interest to them. As I brought my sales pitch to an end, I felt it had been well received.

That this was merely the beginning, that nobody quite knew how we might reach an end, was very apparent. Roisin had removed beavers from arable land in Tayside and taken them to Knapdale, where the population had begun to falter (perhaps because of in-breeding, the harsh west coast climate or predation of kits by otters, but most likely due to the land-locked nature of the site, which forced young beavers to disperse out to sea, where many are thought to have drowned[*]). With increasing regularity, she was relocating them to enclosed English and Welsh wetlands too. Nobody had yet attempted to move them to a new, unenclosed site in Scotland, however. I would be the first and (it would transpire) only applicant wishing to do this. Together, NatureScot and I would have to travel in good faith, moving forward on the understanding that we were all charting new waters and would work out how best to steer this ship as we went. Mistakes were bound to be made, but we would learn from them. Although some would later criticise our collective errors, though I too would find reason to fault NatureScot's handling of certain things, I hope that I never lost sight of that original, unspoken pact.

Later in the meeting, when discussing possible next steps, it was suggested that I approach Martin Kennedy, of the National Farmers Union Scotland, for an informal chat. Then Vice President, soon to be appointed President, Martin was one of the NFUS's leads on beaver negotiations. As if to demonstrate the

---

[*] Beavers are freshwater animals. Prolonged exposure to saltwater can make them sick or even kill them.

divide between farming and conservation, most farmers I knew thought he was fantastic, while most beaver people believed him highly obstructive.

I didn't see the purpose and said as much. To my knowledge NFUS had never said anything positive about beavers. What hope did I have of changing their stance?

Even in an online meeting one can sense the moment that an atmosphere begins to strain. Without knowing why, I feared that if I failed to pick the ball up and run with it, it might be kicked into the long grass.

Steeling myself, attempting to ignore the pool of dread that sat festering in my stomach, I called him a few days later.

You may wonder, with good reason, quite where that fear came from. All I wished to do was move a few animals to a place they were certain to reach anyway. Who could object to that? Hard as I tried to keep this in mind, that fear remained very real.

Although I know that they can cause issues, I think that beavers can be farmers' friends. I believed it then. I believe it now. Farming relies upon a healthy, stable environment. Without that, producing food becomes a highly unpredictable, if not impossible practice. Beavers improve the health and stability of our environment; hence, I view them as an agricultural ally. To some farmers, however, that argument would make no sense. Tomorrow's concerns pale into insignificance when you fear being hit in the pocket today, and in the absence of any schemes to incentivise people to accommodate them, beavers probably seem like just another thing that makes the job harder.

Just as some farmers might struggle to see any good in beavers, I know some conservationists who cannot understand how that could possibly be. It comes down, I think, to this: As a farmer or land manager, your land is your own small nation. You are responsible for its governance. You seldom look beyond your borders. You have no influence there. Your world is all that really matters.

You wish simply to see it flourish, to feed your family and one day hand control to them.

Keep that in mind. Now imagine that you are a farmer. Someone wants to do something that could impact your land and, by extension, your livelihood. They talk of the societal gains their proposal will bring, but all you can see is local pain ... Your own fields impacted, your own income hit. How would you react? And yes, climate change is a threat, but to you as to most other people it seems distant – something that will happen in the future. You are not a politician. Nobody pays you to fix these things. Why should you foot the bill for society's problems? Our collective inability to find an answer to that question is the main reason why Scotland's beaver conflicts persist to this day.

I had no answer to it either, and I dreaded calling Martin Kennedy because of that. But there were other reasons for my discomfort, and these cut deeper.

In 2017, I gave up on the career that I'd been lined up for. I quit farming. My parents hired contractors to look after our livestock so that I could launch, gamely, if somewhat blindly, into a career in conservation. Because of that choice, the skills and knowledge my father gained in his working life would not be passed down. Each generation of our family would know less about the work than the previous one did. Our hands would grow softer, our backs weaker, that particular tie to the land would strain, fray and eventually snap. The line of succession was broken on this farm when I turned away from that life. I carried that knowledge with me. Many of the beaver interactions I would have, with farmers and their representatives, would be coloured by it.

Already I had taken one step away from the farming world. Now I was set to take another, and this one felt even more decisive. As the UK moves further from its industrial past and into its service-sector future, the workplace bonds that once held people together grow slacker all the time. Farmers are perhaps the last survivors of that bygone era. They remain a community, represented by a strong union. When you grow up in the farming world you come to realise how valuable that sense of belonging is; you know how important it is to have a union fighting your corner. You also see that the same external forces that did for the likes of the miners could easily do for your people too. Strength lies in solidarity. You know this. You understand it without ever having to be told.

Perhaps you see now why my heart began to race as I made that call. In a matter of moments I would do the one thing we spend our entire lives trying not to do: break ranks.

*

Martin Kennedy was perfectly decent to me. He gave me a fair hearing, allowed me to say my piece. I saw that he was a shrewd negotiator who fought hard for his members and I liked him well enough. The fear remained with me all the time, however. It was not Martin himself who induced it so much as what he represented: a strong community united (in the most part) in their scepticism about reintroductions and rewilding.

I can't pretend that we agreed on everything. With heavy emphasis on the penultimate word, he stressed that we lived in a 'managed' countryside. I felt that the countryside might be less stressed if we managed it a little bit less. Small examples of a wider divide. No doubt a workable way forward lay somewhere between our approaches.

We chatted for an hour and I set out my stall, just as I had for NatureScot. This was not an anti-farmer move. I wanted him to know that. I simply believed that the environmental crisis would do more harm to farming than any number of beavers could. He listened, told me that he saw where I was coming from, though whether this was true or not I couldn't say. Whenever I find myself politely disagreeing with farmers, I wonder if the farmer in question thinks me a daft wee laddie, another deluded conservationist who doesn't really understand how the countryside works. As we must when we see no realistic hope of receiving an answer, when continued speculation can bring us nothing but harm, I put these thoughts to bed. Some questions are better left undisturbed.

Having heard me out, Martin explained the Union's position.

Adaptive management measures, which I understood to mean a suite of options, including lethal control, had to remain in place so that people could manage their land effectively. I didn't fight him on this. Across Europe, in countries with far greater numbers of beavers than we had, a certain number were culled every year. There were places where, in the modern, human-modified world, beavers could not be, where they risked impacting essential infrastructure or agricultural land, where no mitigation measures worked. The idea of shooting them for this was awful, but I accepted that sometimes it might be necessary. My issue was not the killing, but the excessive level of it in Scotland. So often it seemed a first rather than last resort. But I did not put this to Martin, for my job was to listen, not to attempt to change a mind that was likely not for turning.

Mitigation schemes, he continued, must be sufficiently funded, so that farmers weren't forced to shoulder the capital costs of having beavers on their land.

That sounded perfectly reasonable to me.

Funding, he added, should not come from the AECS budget. That would be deeply unfair to farmers.

Again, I could find no fault with that. The Agri-Environment Climate Scheme (known to all as AECS) is a Scottish Government fund aimed at promoting farmland management practices that improve Scotland's environment. Highly competitive, AECS tends to favour large farms and disadvantage smaller ones (the larger the landholding, the more projects it is capable of running, the more points it can accrue. Points win prizes. Those who accrue the most are the likeliest to have AECS applications accepted). I had no more wish to see the budget further stretched and smaller farmers excluded from mitigation funding than Martin did.

As a final point, I learned that the Union could not support my proposal unless all the local farmers were in favour. We both knew that there was no chance that they would be. Although the distance from us to the nearest beaver territory was vanishingly small, though the animals were coming our way regardless, this small translocation might be a foot in the door. Should we succeed, others might attempt more ambitious relocations. And if beavers were accepted back across Scotland, who knew which other missing species might be brought back next? 'Beavers today, wolves tomorrow?' The farming community is always on a state of high alert, fearful of unintended consequences. They would seek to slam the door shut on us. And if the farmers said 'No'? What would happen then?

A memory came to mind of my father returning, exhausted, from fractious meetings in the days when he'd chaired the NFUS's Forth Valley branch. I recalled his warning: 'You know the difficulty with being a Union rep? You're only ever one step away from anarchy. Anger the members and it's: "NFU: No Fucking Use". Then you're in trouble.'

If the farmers said 'No', the Union would follow suit.

Promptly on the hour mark, Martin thanked me for the call.

Reflecting on the conversation, I could only conclude that I'd made no real impression upon his position, and he very little on mine. Neither of us had softened our stance. Perhaps we'd never been likely to. I was where I was, he was where he was, and that was fine. I felt that I understood his reasoning, however, and hoped that he understood mine. More than anything, I fervently hoped that we could respect one another, agree to disagree, and that relations would remain cordial.

In the months to come I'd look back wistfully on that call, recognising it as the high point of our interactions with NFUS.

5

A Test of Faith

Here's a fact that all aspiring beaver believers ought to know: in the darkest depths of a Scottish winter, when the rain falls without remorse and not a flower is in bloom, nor an insect in flight, your faith in these animals will be tested. In those sodden, weather-beaten weeks, you will wonder why you ever believed that a creature that *increases* volumes of water being stored on the land could possibly have been a good thing. I know this because in late November 2020 it happened to me.

*

'What do you think?' asked James.

With a mounting sense of horror, I cast my eye from right to left, near to far. The scene was not unlike the aftermath of a student party where too much rum went into the punch. Aspen trees lay in various stages of inebriation all around us. Some were hanging, relying on their friends to keep them upright. Others were down on their hands and knees. The worst affected were passed out on the floor, woodchips piled like something unspeakable at their feet. Underlayers of wood the colour of sickly pale-white skin had been exposed where their bark had been gnawed.

I took in the atrocity exhibition again. There was no colour in the scene, save for the grey of water and sky, and the sodden green-browns of the banks; no sound but the pounding of water, which seemed to be flowing everywhere.

I could think of nothing to say in reply except: 'It's really wet.'

James's answering laugh sounded a little too nervous for my liking.

Taking a bracing breath, I muttered two words which had become something of a mantra in his presence: 'Oh shit.'

What had I let us in for?

*

Earlier that day I had passed north through the village of Braco and taken the Langside Road, following its many meanders towards Comrie. Kestrels and buzzards made occasional passes overhead, but my constant companions throughout the journey were red kites. Since their reintroduction those birds had climbed this central spine of Scotland, colonising its plunging valleys, hunting and scavenging on its wide, empty moors. Where there are mature trees to nest in and unimproved grasslands to plunder for food, the ever-adaptable kite will fare well.

Rounding another corner, I began the descent that would lead ultimately to Comrie. I was nearing the cradle of the revolution now, the wildlife park from which the first beavers were said to have escaped. And still a kite hung above me. They had been the regular companion of writer Jim Crumley, who stalked the upper reaches of the River Earn researching beavers for his book *Nature's Architect*. The sightings led Jim to speculate on the relationship between the two and to reach the sad conclusion that both were likely to meet the same fate at the hand of man. He wrote: 'An awareness of killing . . . is surely as deeply ingrained in the DNA of the reintroduced beavers as it is in the DNA of the red kite. That is the nature of the relationship between them.'[16]

That passage had stayed with me, mingling with my own ruminations on the unlikely connections between the two. At first glance, bird and beast seemed very different characters from very different realms. One glided above and aloof from their world, both a part of it and somehow apart from it. The other was always involved in the politics of its locality. It was a shaper and driver of its community, an interventionist, forever meddling, aware that they who control their surroundings retain power over them. But appearances can deceive and beneath the surface there was much to link kite to beaver, beaver to kite. Both were former residents of this country, both were extirpated (beavers probably killed off by humans, kites definitely). Different personalities from different realms perhaps, but they had known (and continued to know) the same troubles, just as Jim said.

However, there were happier associations to be drawn. Kites were brought back by humankind. Beavers too ... in a haphazard way. And despite the best efforts of the few that opposed them, populations of both were growing apace.

I had my own reasons to connect them as well. In a sense it was kites that had sent me both on today's trip to visit James and learn more about beavers, and on this wider journey to attempt to bring them to the farm. Kites had come to me at a formative stage of my life. When they were reintroduced to our neighbours' estates and quickly flitted across the border to Argaty, I was still a child, on the brink of my teenage years. I accepted their return (and the broader concept of bringing back lost species) without question, without even realising that others might think it odd, or even undesirable. Had a flap of the wings or a turn of the breeze taken those first birds in another direction, had they not come to Argaty and to me in that precise period of my development, would I have any interest at all in beavers?

With that in mind, my thoughts turned again to today's mysterious mission. Not for the first time, I wondered quite why I was Comrie-bound. James's reasons for wishing me to come were as inscrutable as had been his motive for visiting me at Argaty ten months previously.

In a phone call earlier that week he'd made vague mention of *'preparing* me for having beavers' on Argaty.

Curiosity piqued, I'd agreed to go.

He lived in a charming white-walled farmhouse, west of Comrie. On the opposite side of the road was Dunira estate, where, to further illustrate Jim Crumley's point, gamekeepers had killed 30 kites in 1809. An awareness of killing must surely have been ingrained in the DNA of keepers during that miserable era.

When I pulled up onto the gravel driveway, James was already at his door chatting with Andrew O'Donnell, our filmmaker friend who'd come to join us for the afternoon.

Together we crossed the fields adjacent to the house, walking towards the River Earn, which lay churning in the distance. These fields were once the site of an old mill, its wheel powered from a lade that ran off the Earn. Though the mill was long gone, the stream still ran, filling an elongated pond before curving back to rejoin the river. Surrounding the pond were several tall enclosures, roofless cuboid pens fashioned from deer posts and stock wire.

'I wanted to show you these,' James said.

Within each enclosure stood shoulder-high aspen trees.

Aspens are high in calcium and phosphorus; beavers love browsing on them. Upon arriving on my aunt's farm on the River Dochart, west of Killin, they had gone through the riparian aspen grove like chainsaw-wielding maniacs. Alongside poplar, these trees were perhaps their favourites (although they wouldn't pass up a good willow, birch, cherry, hazel or hawthorn either).

Running a hand over the fencing wire, James explained the purpose of the enclosures. The smell of aspen would entice beavers to the pond, but the 'little pens' would protect the trees until they'd grown a bit more.

Fighting down the urge to smile, I surveyed the 'little pens', thinking that Fort Knox was less well-guarded than these trees.

'I might have gone a bit overboard,' he said, intuiting my thoughts.

'You might,' I agreed, allowing the grin to escape.

'Have beavers visited?' Andrew asked.

It transpired that they had. Though many animals had moved east from these parts, along the Earn and into the Tay, others had made their way west.

One evening in the summer just past, James had come down to the pond for some solitude. 'I was thinking about my dad, missing him, feeling a bit down,' he explained. (I'd never been told that his father had passed away, but James's tone told me all too plainly.)

As the sun was setting, a beaver suddenly appeared and swam around in the golden water for 20 minutes or so. There were no tail splashes or alarm, just the calm reclamation of a water channel that they had probably been absent from for half a millennium. After all the effort campaigning for protection James and colleagues had been involved in in 2019, it felt like 'a spiritual moment'.

'And that was my pond's first beaver,' he concluded with a smile that was both happy and sad.

Beavers had been the favourite animal of his father, David, who fell in love with them while reading Grey Owl's *Pilgrims of the Wild* as a boy. Nairne senior had encouraged his children to choose their favourite creatures too. The appearance of that beaver, in that moment, had been a wonderfully fitting tribute to a man who'd adored them so, who'd kindled that flame of interest within his son.

Walking the rest of the riverbank, we noted the places where animals had gnawed branches and then moved on. Although he still saw them periodically, they mostly proved elusive; there'd never been another prolonged interaction like that first one.

I could well believe that. The average size of a river-dwelling beaver's territory is 3km of shore length, and they tend to forage upstream from their lodges or burrows, using the current to float branches home. Combined, these behaviours make them hard to pin down on large bodies of water.

'If you've time,' James said when we arrived back at our vehicles, 'there's somewhere else I'd like to take you.'

Back in the car I followed Andrew's van, which in turn was trailing James's Land Rover. The skies had darkened; rain was tapping a drumbeat on my windscreen. The further we drove, the heavier that beat became. Soon the road began to climb as we left the glen's floor and slowly scaled its walls, moving into upper Strathearn. Our destination was a large chalet of continental design, which must have looked positively other-worldly when introduced to these parts several decades earlier. The first sound that we heard upon arrival was a roaring. The cause of the commotion might previously have been described as a burn. Today that word seemed inadequate. That once-small stream was now a tumbling, plummeting explosion of water which dived past the chalet into a culvert and disappeared downhill in a volley of gunfire.

Maintaining a safe, dry distance from the bulging, bursting stream, we followed the waterfalls towards their source.

'This is what I really wanted to show you,' James said as we crested the hill, and the world of water and fallen aspen met my eyes. 'What do you think?'

*

Now that I held my convictions up to the light, I saw how very full of holes they were. My belief in the importance of beavers was based, not upon a lifetime of study and contemplation, but upon a few scientific articles read, a few short hours spent in their company two years earlier. That serene summer's night at Knapdale, when beavers had conducted that orchestra of buzzing insects, rising fish and chattering birds, did not feel real to me now. That place was nothing like this. Nothing. Here, everything was silent except for the pounding of water, which filled my ears as I surveyed the scene, struggling to take it all in. I was not so naive as to believe that beavers were a silver bullet that could save us from environmental ruination. It has taken many centuries of concerted effort to get to this point and it will take more than an animal to rescue us from it. Nonetheless, they had come to seem like one of the greatest hopes that we had. But had I been too eager, too quick to believe? Had I confused faith with fact?

These questions were quickly drowned out by another more immediate one: 'Why is the water flowing so freely?'

A low wall of mud and sticks stretched from one bank to the other at the outflow end of the pond. Impressive though the beaver dam was, it was more or less failing in its central purpose: impounding water. After a moment, I saw why. Lodged in its middle, like spears plunged into the gut, were four plastic pipes. A steady stream of water was bleeding through them.

For the beaver that makes its home in a pond or side-stream, stability and depth of water is everything. As cumbersome on land as they are proficient at swimming, they like their water at least 70 centimetres deep, so that they may travel, fully submerged, safe from predators like wolves, lynx and bears (which they evolved alongside and still expect to be present in modern-day Scotland). To add an extra layer of defence, deep water also keeps the entrances to lodges or burrows hidden and prevents them from freezing over in sub-zero temperatures. Stable levels are important for another reason too. As the cold winter months approach, beavers dig sticks into the muddy floor of the pond, close to the entrance to their dwelling. Having set the first branches in place, they weave more around them. This buried treasure, known as a cache, will serve as their winter food supply. The water acts as a fridge, keeping the sticks fresh, stopping them from rotting. Should the pond freeze over, the beavers will be able to swim beneath the surface and access them. Dams slow water flows, preventing the cache from washing away in spates, helping beavers see out a harsh winter and make it through to spring.

Beavers do not always dam, however. Across Europe, damming is virtually unknown on watercourses wider than ten metres and deeper than 85 centimetres. On these bigger bodies the river's flow would be too powerful for any dam to hold back; food caches would be swept off in seconds, and a cache would likely prove surplus to requirements anyway, because the water would seldom freeze. Conversely, when a watercourse is too small and a gradient too shallow for a pond to form behind a dam, beavers tend only to build if doing so will allow them to access desirable trees. In short, they dam only when they have run an appraising eye over their watercourse and decided that impounding the outlet is necessary, that it will succeed either in creating the deep, slow-running pools they desire or in allowing them a decent feed.

In a pond such as this, where the outflow dropped steeply off downhill, a barrier was very much needed to slow the flow. The pipes that punctured it (known in the beaver mitigation game as 'flow devices' or 'pond levellers') were intended to lower water levels and reduce flooding on surrounding land. Their set-up was a delicate business. Angle the pipes too high and insufficient water will drain, tilt them too low and too much will go. If the latter happens the beavers will then either vacate the territory or build a completely new dam and undo all your hard work. The aim is thus to lower levels to the point where surrounding land is made usable again, whilst leaving it deep enough for the animals' liking.

Whether the aim of minimising adjacent flooding had been achieved here was highly debatable. Picking our way around the site, taking care to stick to the dry patches of bank, I saw that the beavers had given a boardwalk which once circled the pond a watery burial. Now anyone wishing to traverse this place would have to do as we were doing: move with the utmost care between islands.

'The trouble is that the water level is so variable here,' explained James. 'The first two pipes, which the Scottish Wild Beaver Group installed, were doing their job well. But when it got like this ' – he raised his eyes to the now pouring skies – 'there was too much water coming down. Two more were installed by Roisin through the NatureScot mitigation scheme, and most of the time the flooding is reduced now ... *Most of the time*,' he repeated, reading my thoughts in my expression.

I turned my attention from the dam to the trees.

Of all our native broadleaves, aspens are believed to have suffered the most deforestation, making them incredibly rare in Scotland today. Those that remain generally occur in small, isolated populations. Larger communities like this were the exception rather than the norm. As a short-lived tree, highly palatable to grazers, which flowers and sets seed only after a hot summer, several external factors impact the aspen's chances of survival. Combined, these problems mean that once they disappear from a landscape, they are unlikely to return without human intervention.

From the number that had been nibbled or felled here, it seemed the beaver family was well settled. Little wonder, for this was surely one of the finest aspen groves in Scotland. In the 1980s the site's former owner had planted it for his Scandinavian wife, who loved and missed the trees that were so common in her homeland. The animals must have been in seventh heaven when they discovered this place.

They had not felled every tree, however. Some had been wrapped in wire, some painted with a mix of game paint and sand, two simple measures that discourage beavers from browsing. Many others had neither been protected nor, for any reason that I could see, gnawed. The forest floor was regenerating, too. Young trees less than a metre high surrounded the pond – clone shoots sent up from the root systems of the parent trees. An aspen population can heal itself, provided that it is sufficiently large to withstand a few losses. Indeed, in parts of Norway aspen and beaver populations have recovered in tandem, with scientific studies suggesting that beaver gnawing stresses trees, encouraging seed production.[17]

No matter how healthy the habitat, one day the beavers' impact here would likely prove too great. They would, for a short time at least, exhaust this resource, eat themselves out of house and home and have to leave. Provided that deer did not nibble any new shoots, the grove would regrow. In time it would welcome beavers back. But for now, we were on a journey which would take many years to complete, a journey towards exhaustion, and the results were far from pretty. Through winter, when plants die back and trees bear neither leaves nor tasty new shoots, beavers survive on cambium, the soft sugar-rich layer which lies between bark and wood. Stripped of that outer skin the felled aspen in its various shades of whites and yellows looked like piles of bones.

One moment of excitement did await me as we reached the heart of the wetlands. A domed-roof structure resembling a mud and stick igloo lay at the water's edge. The sight of it made my pulse race. That was the first sensation to penetrate the numbness, the dumb incomprehension, that the rest of this place had induced in me.

'Is that their lodge?' I whispered.

James nodded in reply.

Like their dams, the beavers' lodge was a remarkable feat of construction. Countless armfuls of mud had gone into the building. It acted as a sealant, insulating the structure from the elements. Even if outside temperatures dropped below zero, inside it would remain above freezing. Hundreds of sticks had then been piled in a bonfire-like mound on top. The whole thing had been built against the root plate of a leaning birch tree which stuck out like a chimney at the mud hut's gable end.

Hard to believe that beneath this metre-high roof lay a two-storey home. Even harder to believe that, so close to where we stood, a beaver family was sleeping peacefully, curled up together, enjoying one another's warmth. That thought made for a pleasant end to an otherwise disconcerting tour. Having completed our lap of the site, I bid James and Andrew a hasty farewell and fled to the safety of my car.

Evening swept down to surround me as I began the drive back to Argaty. I needed this time. Time alone. Time to think. What I'd seen today had shaken me, I couldn't deny that. For the first time I fully understood what scared others about these animals. To let beavers in, to truly accept them back into our world, we must be willing to loosen our grip on the one thing that all previous generations strived for: control. This was not something to toss aside lightly. For so much of human history, control equalled survival. We hunted, slashed, burned, drained, ploughed and battled this countryside because our lives depended on it, because wild animals, climate, disease and famine were ever-present threats, because we knew this land and its creatures could either sustain us or kill us. All our efforts have been to gain the upper hand lest the world get the better of us. Now though, we had gone too far, had beaten our old foe too thoroughly. Now we had to relinquish some control or risk losing it all. But letting go was the one thing that a child from a farm was taught not to do.

Two people live inside my head. One is an enthusiastic environmentalist. He believes in words like 'rewilding' and is full of hope for the world. The other is a cynical old farmer. He's seen those people and their fads come and go. Certain that they have nothing to teach him, he's done his level best to ignore them. Both characters would rather the other was not his neighbour. When they are forced to face one another, they fight like cats. On most occasions the environmentalist wins the argument easily. Not today.

'Once control is lost, can it ever be regained again?' the farmer asked.

The rewilder had no answer. He simply didn't know.

All night long the two continued their fight. Farmer said that the wetland had been a mess, that a lot of trees had fallen, a lot of land had been flooded. Environmentalist countered that 'mess' was a human construct and the countryside was not supposed to be tidy. He said that this grove had been thinned, not clear-felled – one death will never hurt a city as much as it does a village, and a few trees killed amongst hundreds still standing is no real loss at all. Only when habitats are broken, and the tree felled is the only one left on the bank, might we mourn its death. Even then we shouldn't grieve for that tree but for the many we can't see, that have already gone, the habitat lost long ago. Today's woodland had been healthy: it could withstand a bit of browsing. And on days and in seasons less grey than this, in the gaps where trees had fallen, more sunlight would hit the ground, more plants would grow. Environmentalist said that their seed lay below our feet, waiting for warmer times. Environmentalist, warming to his subject, said that insects would be lured to the plants and water. He said that amphibians, birds and bats would be lured by the insects. He reminded anyone still listening that a tree did not have to be alive to be of value to wildlife, that 40 per cent of UK woodland wildlife relied upon dead wood.[18]

'Wait till summer,' he said. 'Then you'll see.'

'Once control is lost, can it ever be regained again?' asked the farmer a second time.

At the end of that long night's deliberation, I sided with beavers. I chose to believe that that night in Knapdale had been no illusion. Because others, whose opinions I respected, did so too; because if we were all wrong, then there was little hope.

The following day James phoned, as I knew he would.

'So, Tom, do you still want them?' he asked, as I knew he would.

'Yes,' I said.

'I'm glad.'

We talked a short while longer, discussing next steps, and he was about to end the call when I cut in.

'Thank you, James.'

'What for?'

'For preparing me.'

'Tom,' he said. 'You're very welcome.'

During the drive back from Comrie, and the long night of mental deliberations that had followed, I had taken stock, and as the witching hour had approached a realisation had come to me. I knew why he had invited me that day. It was not to show me how to prepare our site for the arrival of beavers, how to plant trees and protect them, all of which could easily have been explained through a phone call. He took me there to prepare me for the shock of what beavers might do on our farm, to show me what change truly looked like and to offer me a way out, should I wish to take it. He was not the type to care more for a cause than for a friend. And I thought all the more of him for that.

6

Time to Buckle Up

By November, Roisin was a month into a gruelling canoe tour, surveying the Tay and Forth catchments for signs of beaver presence. Each one spotted, be it gnawed wood, a lodge, dam or scent mound (piles of mud around 10cm tall that beavers build then spray with castoreum in order to mark their territories) was recorded and mapped to give an overview of beaver activity and population dynamics. Somehow still standing after another long morning's canoeing, she joined me at Argaty in the final week of the month. Denise Reed and Jenny Bryce of NatureScot were visiting to walk the ponds and talk through the finer details of our proposal.

How impressive Roisin was in these situations. She explained, clearly and concisely, exactly why certain ponds were ecologically suitable for beavers. Nobody interrupted or disputed any of her points. She was in charge.

'We have to remember that they might not stay here,' she stressed as we reached the last of the proposed release ponds. 'You're doing your best to make the habitat perfect for them, aren't you, Tom?'

'Yes,' I said, truthfully.

Thanks to some incredibly generous donations from several wonderful friends, we'd begun the planting of more than 500 aspen trees around our ponds, preparing for the animals' arrival.

'But if they do disappear off downstream,' Roisin continued, 'it's not a reflection on the quality of the habitat. We have to think of these ponds as release points, not forever homes.'

In a muttered aside, for her ears only, I said, 'Do you actually think they will leave?'

'Bloody hope not,' she whispered back. 'But prepare for the fact that they might. There'll be people out to shoot this project down. We need everyone to stay strong and hold the line. They're wild animals. We can't control what they do. If beavers turn up on your neighbour's land, we don't want anyone saying: "Translocations don't work. You might as well shoot them. Look what *his* beavers did."'

'*My* beavers?' I asked, a flutter of panic creeping into my voice.

'If you get a licence, any beavers in this area will always be *your* beavers . . . even if they actually swim up to your neighbours from the river rather than down to them from here.'

Lingering under the pretence of pulling up a sock that had migrated over my heel towards the toe of my wellington, I allowed Roisin to catch Denise and Jenny up. When all were out of earshot, I let out several expletives.

I appreciated Roisin's honesty, her 'hope for the best, prepare for the worst' pragmatism. I knew it was her way of protecting me. But this was a lot to take in.

Stay strong. Hold the line.

In that moment, those words of warning applied just as much to me as they did anyone else.

*

In December 2020, Alan McDonnell's life took a bizarre twist. On behalf of his current employers, he took his former ones to court.

Until 2015, when he joined Trees for Life, he had worked as an area officer for Scottish Natural Heritage (as NatureScot were then known). For a time he'd loved the job, but since the

Scottish National Party had come to power in 2007, the agency had been placed under ever-closer scrutiny. Where once their staff had been at arm's length and able to freely advise the politicians, now SNH bosses began to openly talk about being 'aligned with government'. Soon nature came to feel like a secondary concern; economic development and political priorities seemed to take precedence.

'You had to show you were doing right by the politicians,' Alan told me recently. 'That manifested itself in not rocking the boat, not upsetting people or constituencies that might vote for Scottish independence.'

'What happened if you failed?' I asked.

'There was a constant fear of being defunded.'

This drew a grimace of recognition from me. According to analysis by Scottish Environment LINK, SNH's overall budget allocation fell from £80.5 million in 2010–11 to £46.5 million in 2019–20, a 42 per cent reduction in real terms. In the same period the budgets of the government's other environment advisory agencies were also slashed, SEPA's by 34.4 per cent and RESAS's (Rural & Environment Science & Analytical Services) by 41 per cent. In the severity of these cuts, we saw the divide between rhetoric and reality, between the government's stated commitment to the environment and their true financial investment.

Feeling the noose tightening, struggling to see the purpose in his role now that government had swept the legs and removed the teeth from the agency, Alan made the leap, escaped SNH and joined Trees for Life as conservation manager. Through the new role he'd become involved in the Scottish Rewilding Alliance and come to meet James Nairne. One fateful chat between the two was to change the future for beavers in Scotland.

It was the summer of 2020. The 2019 cull numbers had recently been published, the #MoveDontKill petition was underway and James was explaining NatureScot's approach to licensing.

Alan recalled: 'I felt I knew enough about the Habitats Regulations to write a shitty letter to their CEO asking, "How are you going to explain this?" Of four hundred and fifty, as the population was then, eighty-seven had been shot! As far as we can see, no other species gets treated with the kind of optionality that beavers do in terms of what NatureScot licenses. Look at bats...'

As any builder or roofer will tell you, bat roosts cannot simply be removed from a domestic property. If they are causing significant damage a licence to exclude them must be sought from NatureScot. An area officer will assess the situation, going through a step-by-step computer process, always aiming to license the least-damaging option.

'... the system is entirely designed so you *do not kill the bats*,' Alan concluded, placing heavy emphasis on the final five words.

'So, what was the rationale when it came to beavers?' I asked.

He exhaled sharply. 'Their rationale was: "A licence is a licence. And once you get to the point of having to issue one, it makes no difference whether it is for the notching of a dam or the shooting of a beaver. This was the same legislation that every NatureScot officer *was* using every day ... Internally there would have been people looking at the beaver situation and knowing that the approach wasn't consistent with their strategy for other species.'

Following his discussion with James, Alan had gone home to write the letter of complaint to NatureScot. It was a letter that he would never send.

At a conservation event he ended up in conversation with Adam Eagle (a trained solicitor and CEO of The Lifescape Project). Adam asked to read the letter and, having spoken to senior partners at the law firm, Clifford Chance, reported back: 'You've got a case here. And more than that, we think you can win!'

So began the next phase of the #MoveDontKill campaign. In October 2020, Trees for Life wrote to NatureScot making three requests:

- that the agency assess each lethal control licence and withdraw any which lacked objective, robust, site-specific evidence that beaver presence posed a risk of serious damage to property.
- that translocation to any suitable site in the UK be permitted in preference to lethal control, where the aforementioned evidence suggested that serious damage to crops or property would indeed occur.
- that lethal control be used only as a last resort, when evidence suggested that damage to property would otherwise occur if beavers weren't removed, when translocation at that site was demonstrably impossible and when the issuing of licences would not cause a detrimental impact upon the return to favourable conservation status of beavers in the UK, Scotland or Tayside.

Come early November the Trees for Life team of Alan, Steve Micklewright and Adam Eagle met online with NatureScot representatives to talk through the proposals. They gave the agency until the end of the month to respond.

At the eleventh hour, just as the deadline looked set to expire, the reply came.

'They said a load of things that we felt weren't true about how they avoid unnecessary lethal control,' Alan said. 'We then had another meeting and asked if they'd make the requested changes. They said no. The head of the Scottish Government's wildlife and flood management unit was on the call. He was urging us to bear with them. They seemed to have this long game in mind that they were going to nudge the Tayside farmers and NFUS along and they were going to be okay with beavers and with translocations in a few years. The phrase they used was: "We're bringing people with us." And I remember thinking: "Yes, you've got to bring people with you, but in order to do that you've got to go somewhere."'

At the close of the meeting, Trees for Life made it clear that if NatureScot agreed to move beavers ahead of killing them, then Trees for Life would bow out.

The demands would not be met. NatureScot refused to back down.

'And suddenly' – Alan laughed – 'I find myself filing a petition with the Court of Session and swearing an affidavit on Zoom!'

Trees for Life and NatureScot were destined for a day in court.

In some respects, NatureScot could consider themselves slightly unlucky to be the target of this legal action. As Steve Micklewright acknowledged: 'It was good for us to try to negotiate, but it wasn't NatureScot that was the cause of the problem, it was the government. Do you remember when Roseanna got an award from the RSPB for her beaver policy?'

'I was there,' I said. At RSPB Scotland's 2019 Nature of Scotland Awards, Roseanna Cunningham was awarded Political Advocate of the Year in recognition of her work to help reintroduce and eventually protect beavers.

'I always think the RSPB should strip her of that award because her policy caused the death of 20 per cent of the beaver population for two years running,' Steve finished.

Although their quarrel may have been with the politicians, the legal advice Trees for Life received was that NatureScot had to carry the can for the culling policy.

'That gives you an idea of where they're at,' Alan said. 'They're an arm's-length agency that has to take the flak, even if the decision was made by the politicians.'

As Trees for Life geared up for legal battle, one issue presented itself: How was a small rewilding charity to afford the expense of taking an organisation of NatureScot's size to court? There was only one answer: launch a crowdfunding campaign and appeal to the same people who had backed #MoveDontKill. The call went out via print and social media, and thousands of people rallied to it. By the end of January 2021 nearly £51,000 had been raised. It was more than enough to take on the challenge.

Even with that problem solved, another much greater issue remained. As anyone who has ever been involved in legal proceedings knows, costs can swiftly escalate beyond a party's means. Trees for Life's legal team, led by The Lifescape Project, prevented this threat from ever becoming a reality by obtaining a Protection of Expenses Order under the Aarhus Convention. This was a significant step, with huge ramifications.

As Lifescape's managing lawyer Elsie Blackshaw-Crosby later told me: 'Typically, the loser in a legal case pays the winner's costs, and that's a huge barrier to justice, particularly in environmental cases. If Trees for Life lost and didn't have cost protection in place, they might have been ordered to pay close to £100,000 of the winner's costs, but, as it was, we got them capped at a few thousand pounds.'

The case set an important precedent as to how the Aarhus Convention should be interpreted in Scotland. In the future, should any party of limited finances wish to take on a case similar to that of Trees for Life's, their jeopardy should be limited by this ruling. They should not be denied, as Adam Eagle termed it, 'access to justice'.

'Fifty-one grand raised and expenses protected!!!' I wrote in a text message to Alan.

The reply came instantly: 'Time to buckle up.'

7

Flood on the Tracks

February began with the most wonderful news. Sarah was pregnant. For fear of jinxing things at that early stage, when so much lay in the balance, we kept the news from Rowan for a time, but lockdown had made us an inseparable trio and secrecy now felt strange and wrong. When we told her, we thought she might explode – both through excitement and from the pressure of keeping the news a secret from the outside world. The next day she came home in tears. She had made it as far as morning break, and then told the whole class. The following weeks were spent in quiet confab, discussing baby names, trying, with increasing desperation, to find one we all liked.

Later in February NatureScot published a report, *Anticipating and Mitigating Projected Climate-driven Increases in Extreme Drought in Scotland, 2021–2040.* Extreme drought events, the writers warned, could increase from an average of one every 20 years to one every three, and could also last two to three months longer than they have in the past. Water scarcity could impact crop yields, drinking water supplies, peat bogs and other wetland ecosystems.

'Imagine if there was a free abundance of an animal that could help us tackle this,' wrote the Scottish Wild Beaver Group in response to the findings. 'Beavers get a lot of praise for helping to lessen the impact of flooding, but they are also massively important in times of drought. A beaver pool can hold back millions of litres of water, which can provide a trickle of constant filtered water through its leaky dam all summer. We need to use these cheap and effective nature-based solutions if we want a brighter, greener future.'

The timing of the report's publication felt somewhat ironic. At that precise moment, droughts were far from anyone's mind. That winter we were seeing the other face of climate change. Rain flogged the land until it bled. Fields turned to rivers, rivers to oceans. On Argaty ponds filled then overspilled, the stream above our yard burst its banks, washed away the farm track and raged through two sheds. The following morning we inspected the damage. The track had been so deeply gouged that it resembled the Grand Canyon. Brought inside for the winter, the calving cows now stood huddled on an island of dry straw, watching as the moat around them grew higher. Taking to the digger, Gordon Bradley (the jack of all trades who works on our farm and prevents everything from falling apart) began the tiresome job of rebuilding the track. Then he stood back, watched the grey clouds gathering in angry mobs and wondered how long it would be before it all happened again. That winter alone the stream would breach four times. Every year was the same.

Flooding hadn't always been so common here. Events like this seldom happened in my childhood. Only as the years passed and the climate grew less and less predictable had the problems started. Hoping to ameliorate the damage, we had dug a pond and planted trees upstream. All efforts were in vain.

While inspecting the latest wreckage, my thoughts returned to beavers. That angry, destructive stream flowed out from one of the proposed release ponds. If my visit to James had taught me anything, it was that beavers would attempt to dam that pond. Fed by a hill burn that ran at a trickle in hot summers and a torrent in wet winters, it rose and fell with remarkable fluidity. The beavers' only means of maintaining stability would be to wall that outflow. And what would happen if they did? Would it save us from the floods?

Sadly, I felt we were barely any closer to gaining answers. Over the festive period I'd been labouring over the Scottish Code for Conservation Translocations application form. 'A document which strikes me as having the primary purpose of making translocations extremely difficult, if not impossible,' was how James had described it.

His warnings had been well-founded. Having wrestled with it for several weeks, trying and failing to decipher it, I accepted defeat, called Roisin and begged for her help.

The application was just one small part of the process. Stood towering over it was a giant of a task: the stakeholder engagement. Reading through NatureScot's list of suggested consultees, my heart sank. On it were neighbouring landowners between us and the River Teith; so were SEPA, Stirling Council, Forestry and Land Scotland, Kilmadock Community Council and local representatives of both NFUS and Scottish Land & Estates (SLE). I'd been invited to address the Scottish Beaver Forum as well. All of this was to be presented in a report for which there was no template, which I would have to invent from scratch.

'I can't do this,' I thought, reading, then re-reading the email. 'It's a full-time job in itself.'

My first instinct was to argue. Any other native species can be released in the UK without need for a licence. Approximately 50 million non-native pheasants and partridges are also released in the UK every year, again without any licences. Who in power was questioning what *their* environmental impact was? Who of them cared whether those birds artificially swelled predator numbers, outcompeted native species for food, predated insects, lizards or even snakes? Why were beavers, with all of their biodiversity-boosting credentials, being treated differently? An unpalatable thought came to me: 'Is it easier to wreck a landscape than to restore it?'

In my heart, however, I knew why NatureScot were pushing me to such lengths. As the regulator in charge of approving or rejecting this application, all eyes would be upon them. One slip-up and they'd wake up to another unwanted headline. As a result, they would gravitate towards caution, dotting every i and crossing every t, and checking their work ten times over before any beaver was relocated in Scotland. Overly cautious this may have been, unfair to beavers it certainly was, but what would I gain from arguing? Although the email had been couched in terms of *coulds* rather than *shoulds* – 'We would suggest that it *could* be worth speaking to …' – the truth was plain. Fail to do this properly, and our application would fail.

On the face of it, we appeared to have two options: give up or do as they'd asked. But the more I considered it, the more I came to feel that a third way existed. Conjuring up a mental list of hypotheticals, I tried each on for size.

What if we not only did as they'd requested but went above and beyond? What if we spoke to all the people on that list *and* many other relevant parties as well? What if we carried out a more thorough consultation than they expected, the most comprehensive one we could possibly manage?

All questions led to the same conclusion. If we did this, if we gained enough support, we would succeed.

*

To add weight to our proposal and demonstrate just how badly people wanted beavers to be moved rather than killed, I decided to ask Scotland's largest environmental organisations for supporting letters. Thanks to Duncan Orr-Ewing, head of species and land management for RSPB Scotland, and to Bob Elliot, director at the animal campaigns charity OneKind, my first statements arrived. Both men offered valuable advice too.

'Get the community on side,' Duncan said. 'With their support opponents will struggle to block you.'

'Wherever possible, hold your consultations,' Bob warned. 'Avoid town hall gatherings. You just get shouted at.'

Take note, aspiring rewilders . . . As we shall soon see, these may be the two most crucial lessons you will ever learn.

*

I had one last call to make. There is one person living in Britain today who knows more about reintroductions and their associated politics than anyone else. He knows more for a simple reason: he has reintroduced so many species back across these isles. In the final stop on my advice-gathering mission, I placed a call to Roy Dennis.

Roy led one of the first sea-eagle reintroduction attempts in Scotland, devising methods that would prove crucial when the birds were successfully restored in the 1970s. In 1989 he brought red kites back to Britain, and since then he has been a key figure in the restoration of other species, including ospreys and red squirrels, to places they'd long been absent from.

I hoped to obtain a statement from him, but I also hoped to learn what had made him successful and understand what I must do to see my own project through.

'What I'd do is identify the key people in the community,' he said in his soft Hampshire burr. 'Shopkeepers, community councillors, the school headmaster. Speak to them, tell them about beavers, find out if there's ways that your tourism business can help them.

'Just as important, though,' he continued, 'is how you approach this whenever you speak to NatureScot. You want to be very clear with them on why you're doing this. Give them a clear reason why you want beavers. I'd say something like: "To have them carry out ecological restoration of wetlands on our farm and compliment the visitor experience of watching red kites at Argaty."'

'Great,' I said, frantically scribbling notes.

'But remember,' he said, a note of caution entering his voice. 'You have to be firm with them, and if they try to stall you, which they almost certainly will, you tell them, "Come on. I want to get this done!"'

I heard these words, and thought I heard the subtext too: 'The authorities are not your friends. If they get between you and your goal, don't play the nice guy.'

Roy taught me how to be a bit of a bastard. I hope he'll smile when he learns that.

'You know, Tom,' he said towards the end of our conversation, 'if they've entertained the idea this far, I think you'll get your beavers.'

How my spirits soared to hear those words. Roy, who'd run this course more than anyone else, thought we could do it.

His statement arrived by email the following morning. 'I fully support the proposal,' it read, 'and believe that the ecological restoration of the Bowsers' property will be very important, for they are demonstrating an ethos of wise multiple use of land. The opportunity for people, already visiting the farm to watch red kites, to see and learn about beavers in Scotland is very important.'

I'll never forget the kindness and support that he, and others, showed me. I'll always remember the strength that they gave me. Whether your rewilding venture succeeds or fails is, to a large extent, down to you – who you are, how skilfully you navigate the obstacles that land in your path. But success is also dependent upon those good people who guide you. Without their help, none of us would make it through.

8

Two Sides of the Story

What can I say of the whirlwind two months, from February to March 2021, when I consulted the community on bringing beavers to our farm? Should someone ask, how would I describe what happened?

'It was a thrilling time,' I might say. 'I was living on my wits, battling opponents, trying to work out how to outflank them and get this done. It was a time of great optimism. I made hundreds of friends, saw the very best of people. So many supported us in so many ways, and whenever I stumbled their goodwill carried me on.'

I might say that.

'It was one of the hardest times of my life. I was drained from the fighting and running on fumes, absent as a father and a husband, and I'm so sorry for that. In those months I lost hope. I saw the worst sides of people, and I've seldom felt so alone.'

I might say that too. I could tell either story. Neither would be a lie.

That period passed in a blur. I worked tens, if not hundreds of hours, and in a series of online meetings – face-to-face indoor gatherings still being prohibited due to coronavirus restrictions – put our proposal before hundreds of people. And hundreds of people gave us their backing.

The wildlife community united behind the proposal and by the end of February we'd received supporting letters from the Royal Zoological Society of Scotland, Wild Justice and from Scottish Environment LINK (the forum for Scotland's environment community). The latter was countersigned by a formidable line-up of the Scottish Wildlife Trust, Froglife, the Bumblebee Conservation Trust, Scottish Badgers, Butterfly Conservation, the British Dragonfly Society, the Scottish Wild Beaver Group, the National Trust for Scotland, the Woodland Trust Scotland, Trees for Life, Badenoch and Strathspey Conservation Group and Amphibian and Reptile Conservation. With OneKind, RSPB Scotland and Roy Dennis having already pledged their support, we had now amassed a strong portfolio. To NatureScot and to the Scottish Government, I hoped that the letters would send a clear message: Too many beavers have been shot and the wildlife community has had enough. Argaty is offering a solution. Take it.

We held more meetings, gained further backers. At times I felt like a travelling musician, running through his back catalogue, a different audience every night. Supporting letters came from wildlife and heritage groups, Stirling Council, Doune Primary School, the University of Stirling's Biological and Environmental Sciences Department and Mark Ruskell, the Scottish Greens' MSP for Mid-Scotland and Fife, who would go on to become an amazing ally.

To be a part of the community into which you are trying to reintroduce a missing species is a great help. Not for a second do I believe that everyone who backed us did so because they desperately wanted beavers to come to Argaty. Many of them knew little about the animals and their engineering abilities. Some had no idea that they were even back in Scotland, far less that they desperately needed our help. Would they have put pen to paper on beavers' behalf in other circumstances? Perhaps I'm flattering myself, but I doubt it. Because they knew me, they gave me a fair hearing and granted me a favour when I asked for one.

Being a local boy was useful in another sense too. James Nairne was the only other rewilding supporter I knew who still lived in the same place he had grown up. As individuals and as a collective, rewilders often fall victim to unhelpful tribal stereotypes. If you weren't born here, if your accent isn't the same, you can easily be cast as just another outsider trying to impose your ideas upon a community that you don't truly belong to and will never fully understand. Such accusations can swiftly derail a proposal, but thankfully they never really came our way.

Hoping to capture the voices of individual people who supported beavers but had no affiliation to an organisation, Roisin and I co-hosted an invitation-only webinar at the start of March. The audience listened to the presentation, quizzed Roisin on beaver biology, behaviour and mitigation, and at our request went on to complete a survey that Sarah (hero that she is) had created for us. Their answers delivered more clear messages to include in our report. Each of the 246 respondents said that they would support beavers being relocated rather than killed when they came into conflict with people. Most importantly, 100 per cent said that they would support them being relocated to Argaty.

Twenty-six supporting organisations and 246 supportive surveys. To my ears, those sounded like big numbers. Privately, I was proud of what we had achieved. Exhausted, talked-out, but proud.

When I look back on that time, I'll remember an intense and exhilarating period when people came together in support of nature and of beavers.

How I wish I could end there. How I wish there wasn't that other story to tell.

*

There's an uncomfortable truth about rewilding that most of its advocates don't talk about. Should we, who wish to see missing species and broken habitats restored, accomplish our goal, our victory will leave some feeling disenfranchised. Put more simply, when you are firmly for this, and you come up against people and organisations who are firmly against, one side will have to lose. For us that realisation cut especially deeply because those who opposed us, who felt they stood to lose, were our friends, our neighbours, our people. In that same period I met with them, put our plans before them and learned, quickly and painfully, that this would be a fight.

Of the stakeholders that NatureScot had suggested I consult, there were two I most dreaded meeting. Scottish Land & Estates and the National Farmers Union Scotland were reputed to make a tough double act in all beaver-related negotiations. That lethal control licences had been so freely distributed and translocations so long embargoed was, many believed, due to the political influencing of these two organisations. My meeting with SLE was pain-free, however. Their staff were pleasant and polite, and we got on well.

Their policy advisor outlined the organisation's position, which was little different from that of Martin Kennedy of NFUS, and seemed to revolve around mitigation budgets and the need for adaptive management. I told her that I agreed, and I was heartened when she acknowledged that it was hard to oppose this specific proposal, given the proximity of existing beaver populations to Argaty. At the close of the meeting, I sent her a list of our neighbouring landowners, so they might contact any who were SLE members and discuss our plans. All had been cordial, all seemed well. I ticked another name off the list and looked ahead to the discussion with the local NFUS representative.

The fear of a fight with the Union, of being cast out from the herd, had not left me for a moment, but this consultation, too, passed almost without incident. Almost. The rep reiterated Martin Kennedy's points and, again, I accepted them without challenge.

'While we're speaking, is there anything else you need to ask me?' he said as the conversation was drawing to an end.

The question surprised me into momentary silence, until I remembered that my parents and I were still Union members – a fact that had somehow escaped me to that point – and he therefore was still our representative.

'No . . . no, there's not,' I said, gathering my wits. 'Anything else *you* need to ask *me*?'

'Aye,' he said, quick as a flash. 'Not to do this.'

Hoping that he was joking, suspecting that he wasn't, I gave an uneasy laugh and ended the call.

The next names on my consultee list were our neighbouring landowners. One by one I began to work through them. Two instantly pledged their support, one stated their neutrality, and five opposed our plans. I can only describe the conversations with the latter group as excruciatingly civil. Had we all lost our tempers, had we screamed and shouted, it would perhaps have been more honest.

These were not conversations so much as exchanges of unshakeable opinions. Neither party made the slightest dent in the other's thinking and nothing much was achieved except that at the end of it all I could tick a box to say that these people had been consulted.

As I write this, I can almost hear the voice of my cousin, Jock, a farmer who always takes a balanced view of such things.

'People always complain when they aren't consulted about rewilding projects,' I remarked at the time. 'But you are literally consulting them so that they can say "No."'

'Yes,' he replied evenly. 'But if you don't bother, they'll always be able to say that they weren't consulted, and they'll always be right.'

Hard to quibble with that analysis.

I've often been asked why those neighbours opposed us, what it was that caused such concern. The issues raised were many and varied. Some were worried that beavers would block field drains, rendering farmland unusable. Others thought they would bring more red tape, restricting their freedom to farm as they saw fit. One person believed that felled trees would make watercourses look unnatural. Several said they would 'remove' any beavers that came. ('That's your prerogative,' I said, wondering what they meant by 'remove'.) Another was more open, stating that the beavers already living wild on nearby rivers would never make it all the way upstream to our farms.

'Trust me, they will,' I said.

'They won't. Someone'll shoot them.'

I learned too that I was known locally as 'the Beaver Man'.

Like soup spilling off a plate, my stomach gave a watery sideways lurch – not, it must be said, because of the nickname (I've been called worse) but because of the idea that people (plural) were using it.

Each concern seemed to stem from the following issue, expressed by my final landowner consultee: 'Most people don't have to live with the consequences of reintroductions.'

This was a perfectly valid point. Over half of Scotland is owned by less than 1 per cent of the population. If rewilding is to happen, it may affect private landowners' property, it could affect their income, and that of course is unfair. To this point, I could have put the equally valid counter that a system where nature's future lies in the hands of so few people is even more unfair. Instead, I asked if they would be concerned for their children's future, should people fail to address the environmental crisis.

'You're going to solve that with a few beavers, are you?' they replied.

What could one say to that? On a fundamental level the point was inarguable. When China contributed nearly a third of all global greenhouse gas emissions and 70,000 acres of Amazon rainforest were being cleared every day, what difference would saving a few beavers in Scotland make? But what choice do we have? Do we give up, tell our children that we didn't try because we saw no point? Or do we do what we can, attempt to influence what happens in our own country and hope that others do the same in theirs?

Had I been afforded the opportunity, I might have voiced this thought, but the conversation stopped there. The line had gone dead.

What pains me, both to remember these moments and to write about them, is the very business-like way in which they played out. It's knowing that only a couple of those people really engaged with us, while the rest barely gave us the time of day, ignoring messages and phone calls, closing off any possibility of meaningful discussion. What pains me is knowing that the idea that they might accommodate beavers never seemed to enter most of their heads, and the matter-of-fact way that people told me they would 'remove' them ... the matter-of-fact way that I just accepted that, when inside I wanted to scream, because the creature I wanted so badly to save they would remove without a care, without a moment's thought. What *really* hurts is the suspicion that none of this was unusual or unprecedented, that every single day people decide what lives and what dies based not on research, discussion or recourse to science, but in defiance of those things.

Those interactions knocked the wind out of me, and it took some time before I felt quite right again. And the disappointing truth is that it only got worse. In the early days of March, I made a terrible mistake. For the first and only time, I went against Bob Elliot's so-sound advice. I held a town hall-style gathering, and it backfired horribly.

*

That date – 4 March 2021 – will live long in my mind. That was the night that I presented our beaver plans to the Kilmadock Climate Action (KCA) group, the night that relations with some of those neighbours and their representatives really turned sour.

Founded in 2019 by two local residents, Anna Clark and Jayne Whitehead, KCA is a forum for people to discuss their concerns about climate change and consider ways to improve the environment around Kilmadock, the parish area that includes the villages of Doune and Deanston. Hoping to add the group to our list of supporters, I suggested we arrange a webinar. I would present our plans, a short survey would be distributed to members, and if the overall mood was favourable, they would write us a supportive statement. To my delight, Anna and Jayne agreed.

As had become my habit, I entered the meeting early in order to run through my slides before the attendees arrived. One other person was already logged in, though their camera was turned off. Their name box merely read: *Owner*.

Co-presenting was Professor Nigel Willby, the freshwater scientist from Stirling University who had worked at both Knapdale and Bamff, demonstrating the biodiversity benefits of beavers in a Scottish context. Once I had delivered my presentation, he would be on hand to answer questions. As well as being a beaver expert, Nigel was a Kilmadock resident and trusted voice in the community. I could think of no one better to have alongside me for the evening.

As 8 p.m. arrived, Anna and Jayne welcomed the attendees, and the meeting began.

Summing up 15 minutes later, I clicked a tab on the screen to check who was online. Most were people I knew. *Owner* was still in attendance. One of our neighbouring landowners had tuned in as well and was watching with their camera turned off. My heart gave a brief spasm to see their name listed, but I quickly composed myself. Let them watch. I had nothing to hide. There was someone called Adrian there too, and another whose name read *Karen's iPad*. I couldn't remember an Adrian or a Karen being members of KCA.

Questions came thick and fast. Nigel handled them with

aplomb, dispelling fears that beavers would flood Doune or fell all of its woodland.

Everything was going swimmingly well until someone asked what could be done to mitigate against unwanted beaver impacts. I launched into what by now felt like a well-rehearsed spiel, detailing the various methods available through the NatureScot mitigation scheme.

'There is no fund,' said the attendee who'd named herself *Karen's iPad*, turning her microphone but not her camera on.

The heat rising to my cheeks, I paused. Fatally. For the first time in the whole consultation process, I'd been caught off-guard, without a pre-prepared answer. Concerned faces stared out from the screen before me.

Don't just sit there gaping like a fish, an inner voice hissed. *Do something . . . reassure them.*

As I tripped and fell over my words, I listened with growing despair as Karen addressed the audience. She had been involved with beavers for some time. NatureScot had even installed a pipe through a dam on her farm. 'There is no fund,' she said again.

Trying to regain some level of composure, I asked where her farm was located.

'I don't want to disclose that, for obvious reasons,' she replied. 'But not far.'

A comment appeared onscreen from the neighbouring farmer. 'Are you worried about beavers contaminating water supplies?'

My face was burning now. Bob Elliot's warning came back so loudly it was though he was standing beside me, yelling in my ear. 'Avoid town hall gatherings!'

'Could you tell us where your spring is located?' I asked. 'There's a good chance that it won't even be suitable beaver habitat.'

No response came, and now my embarrassment gave way to frustration. This particular neighbour and I had discussed this topic at length already. In Tayside a story had spread that a man attempting to remove a dam had contracted giardiasis (an intestinal parasitic disease) by ingesting untreated water contaminated by beaver faeces. Known in North America as 'beaver fever', giardiasis' colloquial name derives from a case where hikers in Banff National Park drank water said to have been fouled by beavers. Any wild or domestic animal can carry the parasite however, and symptoms usually only appear one to two weeks after infection. (In the case of the man in Tayside, a sewage outflow was located near where he was removing the dam. Incidents like this stretch the credibility of conclusively linking the beaver to the fever beyond breaking point.) Hoping to assuage my neighbour's fears, I'd sent a report which explained giardia transmission in finer detail. They had my number and knew they could call me at any stage to discuss these concerns, but since sending the report I'd heard nothing. Why had they chosen to raise the issue in this way?

Too late I understood what was playing out. A group of opponents had joined forces. They were here to sabotage the meeting and discredit us.

In Tayside I had a farmer friend, quietly supportive of beavers, who knew many of the animals' opponents. Reaching for my phone, I hurriedly typed out a message: 'Can we talk?'

*

By the time I left the house, night had set in, but a late winter moon bathed the land in light. My collie Jill at my heel, I followed the track that led down the edge of our wildflower meadow, making for the pond beyond. The meadow was still just a carpet of leaves, a secret waiting to be told. Only in later months would the flowers appear, the colours explode, and the world see it for what it truly was. The moon's spotlight shone over the pond, turning everything yellowy-white. The wind ran its fingers across the surface, playing it like strings on a harp. The light reverberated away in ripples.

'I'm sorry to call so late,' I said into the phone.

'I'm only just back home myself. What's up?'

In a few words I relayed the story of the night.

'And she said that NatureScot had installed a pipe in dams on their farm,' I concluded. 'Know any farmers who've had that kind of mitigation done?'

'You know who you had in your meeting tonight?'

They proceeded to tell me the name.

'NFUS's beaver representative? Are you sure?' I said, knowing already that they were. 'Why would she come to a meeting like that and not say who she was?'

The answering silence spoke a thousand words. 'Welcome to the real world,' it said.

The wind came surging across the water, passing through me as though I wasn't there. The reality of my situation hit me afresh. I could never prove it, but I suspected I knew who the attendee called *Adrian* was now too. And what about the one called *Owner*? I'd have laid bets that they were either Union, Tayside farmer or one of our neighbours. A chill that had nothing to do with the wind was climbing the rungs of my spine. It was a feeling born on nights such as this, when we stare into the shadows, to the places that moonlight doesn't reach, and wonder if we are being watched. The feeling was made more intense because tonight, for the first time in my life, I knew that I was.

*

The days that followed were taken up with endless phone calls and a great deal of ruminating. Sarah, always fiercely protective, was aghast on my behalf and cursed the cowardice of those people.

'All of them crowding in, keeping their cameras off. It's pathetic,' she raged. Everyone needs a Sarah in their team.

I reported the incident to NatureScot. Though sympathetic, they said there was little they could do. As a NFUS member, it was for me to pursue, if I so wished.

'What would happen if I wasn't a member?' I wondered aloud. 'What protection would I have then?'

Perhaps they thought the question rhetorical. In any case, no answer was forthcoming. Attempts to escalate the complaint to a higher level bore just as little fruit.

'Sometimes our role is to hold the jackets,' they told me.

Nothing would be gained by pursuing this further. That much was clear. My only option was to let the matter drop.[*]

I spoke to a friend who knew NFUS well and always struck a pragmatic line between farming and conservation. 'For a Union representative to be there, saying those things, not declaring who she was . . . It doesn't feel right,' I said.

'I'm bloody sure it wasn't right,' they replied. 'Leave it with me.'

The following evening, I received a call from the NFUS CEO. I explained that I wasn't seeking a fight and merely wished them to tell the neighbouring farmers that there *was*, in fact, a government-funded mitigation scheme. (Since the meeting I'd established that.)

I thought that that would be the end of it. With the NFUS recognising that we hoped to resolve this through quiet diplomacy rather than wage a war, I thought that they would quietly back off. I was wrong.

An email from Karen landed in my inbox later that month. Surprise and indignation colliding, I read the NFUS's response to the translocation proposal.

Most of it was fairly childish and amounted to little more than a mud-slinging exercise. Much of her anger was directed at NatureScot and the Scottish Government, for considering translocations before a robust mitigation scheme with guaranteed

---

[*] At least NatureScot's Tayside area manager, Denise Reed, made an impressive stand, telling Karen that her behaviour had been inappropriate and that an apology was warranted. I was grateful for that.

funding was in place, and for failing to produce clear procedures for applicants to adhere to. I wasn't to be spared from scrutiny either, though. She doubled down on her claim that there were no mitigation measures available for land managers from NatureScot. The proposal process we had followed had, she said, led to frustration and anxiety on the ground. She also noted NFUS's extreme disappointment that we had not undertaken an extensive consultation process by speaking with all interested parties, but had instead hand-picked individuals who would speak in favour of beavers. Of everything that she wrote, the suggestion that *we* had been the dishonest actors in all of this is what I remember the most.

The following morning another response arrived, this time from Sarah-Jane Laing, Scottish Land & Estates' CEO. Though slightly less vitriolic, its wording was so similar to NFUS's that one might have copied the other's homework.

Perhaps I should have expected this – we know what they say about birds of a feather – but all the same the behaviour was massively disappointing. We had tried to be decent and open with both organisations. We had tried to resolve the Karen issue quietly. We had tried. Everyone knew where to find me if they wanted to discuss concerns – and amid the bile, I still recognised that the proposal did elicit some understandable fears. By working together, we could have addressed these issues. Instead, they had waited until the last minute and then tossed grenades. They hadn't the slightest interest in making translocations a fair and inclusive process; their sole aim was to prevent them from happening.

'Did you ever see that First World War army recruitment poster?' James Nairne asked when I phoned to update him. 'You know the one with the little girl sitting on her father's knee, asking, "Daddy, what did you do in the Great War?"'

I mumbled an affirmation.

'Sometimes I imagine the modern-day version of that poster,' he continued. '"Daddy, what did you do in the Great Environmental Crisis?" And I try to imagine what some beaver opponents might say to their children, because the only honest answer would be: "I did everything I could to slow the spread of biodiversity-boosting beavers."'

For the first time in what seemed like forever, I found myself laughing. Sometimes a little gallows humour is just what the situation demands.

But just as incoming clouds can quickly smother the sun, that moment of light was quickly extinguished by another phone call. RSPB Scotland hoped to translocate beavers to their Loch Lomond reserve. Since the news of our consultations had gone public, I had been in constant dialogue with their senior species and habitats officer, James Silvey.

'How are you getting on?' he asked me.

I shared our news before asking him the same question in return.

'Man, it's not looking good,' he replied, with a tired sigh.

Though the RSPB were still keen, NatureScot and Loch Lomond & the Trossachs National Park, who co-managed the site, seemed reluctant to proceed without a clear steer from government.

The last glint of sun disappeared. Black clouds smothered the sky. If the RSPB weren't applying, then we really were flying solo.

'Couldn't you look at another site where you don't have partners to consult?' I asked.

'That's the luxury of your position, Tom,' he replied. 'The RSPB always has someone they have to consult.'

I saw his logic. I agreed with it, too. Many in conservation would probably kill to be in my shoes, enjoying my level of autonomy. But at that precise moment I could see no luxury in it. Everything that I had once considered a positive – being a local, being known instead of some faceless organisation run by 'outsiders', being the first person to apply ... all of it now felt like a negative. I'd have given anything not to be any of the things that I was.

9

Fighting Back

Derek Gow would help dispel the gloom that had settled in my soul in those weeks. Described by journalist Patrick Barkham as 'Britain's most notorious and successful introductionist', Derek is a bearded behemoth of a man and one of rewilding's great characters. Equal parts philosopher and barrelling prop-forward, he shoots from the hip in newspaper articles and across social media, denouncing with humour and scorn anyone who opposes his straightforward, 'just-fucking-do-it' approach to returning lost species. Amongst his many projects he has led the charge to restore water voles, breeding them from his Devon farm and supplying them to projects around the country; he has played a key role in returning white storks and wild cats too. He is best known, however, for reintroducing beavers, bringing the first animals back to English and Scottish enclosures, and advocating tirelessly for their nationwide reintroduction ever since.

Put in contact by Roisin, with whom he'd worked since the Scottish Beaver Trial, Derek had visited Argaty the previous summer. Never had I met someone so absolute. He had no time for shades of grey; his was a shirts versus skins mentality. If you weren't on his team, then you emphatically weren't; but if he was on your side and you on his, then you knew it, felt it and were stronger for it.

'Give Derek a call. He wants to help,' Roisin repeatedly urged, noting how the fights with neighbours and unions had sapped my energy.

What anyone could do to help, I didn't know, but I trusted her judgement and did as she suggested.

There is a side to Derek Gow that many people don't know. Many see only the punchy persona and hear only the searing wit, the scornful tirades and the barrage of expletives that punctuate the sentences with bullet-hole brusqueness. (Where most of us breathe between words, Derek swears.) Many do not see the other side, which is very warm, very understanding, very human.

Like a drunk bending the barman's ear I poured out my woes, telling of the troubles with NatureScot, of the neighbour convinced that beavers would contaminate his water, and the others who'd 'remove' any that came. What we hoped to achieve with this project was no longer clear to me. Were we really saving beavers, or simply moving them from one place so that they could be killed in another? We'd gathered so much support, but those people couldn't be there for those difficult discussions. Some roads must be walked alone. In those moments you haven't a friend in the world.

'Tom, it's bloody depressing,' he agreed. 'But you're not alone. The majority are with you on this. And maybe landowners will shoot your beavers, but you know what? The more they do it, the more beavers will come, and eventually they'll stop shooting them because they'll realise there's no fucking point and they're better living with the ones they've got.'

I could deny neither the brutality nor the accuracy of this assessment. It crystallised a thought which, until then, had been slipping with maddening fluidity through my mind, which had squirmed and slid from me like a fish from the hands any time I'd tried to grasp it. The realisation was this: the fight for Scotland's beavers, at the point at which I'd joined it, was no longer about whether the animals would be successfully restored to our country. That question had already been settled. They were not only back, but back for good. The real questions now were how quickly we could re-establish them nationwide, and how many would die along the way. There was some comfort to be drawn from this. Whatever happened, however this played out, those of us who were on their side had already won.

Whether or not they realised it, there was a message in this for those still shooting them too. Once numbers in a catchment grow to the point that all available territories are filled, beavers self-regulate their populations. Litter sizes decrease, sub-adults delay their dispersals, sometimes for several years, and animals fight (often to the death) for control of a territory. Shooting delayed the point of self-regulation, creating a vacant territory for another beaver to fill. When new animals arrived, they'd create their own dams and lodges. Their impact would likely be greater than the previous inhabitants'. Whenever possible it is always better to tolerate the beavers that you have, knowing that they are keeping others out.

'What's the story with NFUS?' Derek asked.

My story was greeted with the most unexpected of responses. Down the line came a joyous belly laugh. 'Oh, that's good. That's very good,' he said. 'Are you going to write it up?'

'*If* we ever get beavers, I suppose I might.'

'Do it,' he replied instantly. 'The more examples of this idiocy the better. Why the fuck are we asking NFUS's permission anyway?'

'For fuck all,' he added, answering his own question. 'Because traditional conservation has just become a load of pathetic people sitting in pathetic rooms being pathetic together . . .'

This superb tirade continued for some time. When talk returned to our beaver plans, he made it quite clear that we would not achieve our goal because politics, bureaucracy and lobbying by vested groups would foil us.

'We're very close,' I assured him.

'I shall eat humble pie,' he replied knowingly. 'You can serve it on the surface of your farmyard.'

I made a mental note to remind him of this if we ever did succeed. 'Any thoughts on what I can say to the neighbour that's worried about giardia?'

'Yeah,' he said, mirth already in his voice. 'Tell them that the only way they're going to get giardia is if they pick up a beaver, give it a squeeze and drink from its fucking arse.'

Tears of laughter were still streaming from my eyes later that night when a message arrived.

'Tell your beaver story. Clear and true.'

'If we ever get them,' I thought. 'That's precisely what I'll do.'

Though I've never quite found the words to tell him so, that conversation lifted me. Knowing that others had been through this, that they understood the isolation of the lone furrow, was a strange sort of solace. The call was instructive too. Throughout my life I have always strived to avoid angry confrontations, viewing them as a failure of wit and of reason. In almost every situation this tactic has served me well, but when dealing with those of limited wit and no desire to be reasonable, it was of no use. In Derek I saw someone who would never bend, never cave. And while I knew I would never be exactly like him (this world is not big enough for two Derek Gows), his was the attitude I had to adopt now.

I would never pick a fight, never start a war. My old principles meant too much and those people too little for me to abandon the former for the sake of the latter. But from that moment onwards things would change. I would not be leant on. I might not seek a battle, but if one came my way I would fight it.

*

Assisted by James Nairne, who helped to sculpt an angrily drafted diatribe into something much more cohesive and pointed, we sent responses to NFUS and SLE, refuting their allegations.

At Karen and NFUS, we fired a few additional shots, telling her that we were at a loss to understand her assertion that there was no official government mitigation scheme. We stressed that our consultations had been neither limited nor selective – their success was merely a reflection of public support for rehoming beavers rather than killing them. We finished by saying that her conduct at the Kilmadock Climate Action meeting had been a serious breach of trust, a clear attempt to turn people against the proposal. Such behaviour was unworthy of a Union representative.

On the same day that I sent these replies, I made an official complaint about her to NFUS. Their CEO responded a week later acknowledging the points made. He wrote: 'I have explained that I expect all NFUS staff who are taking part in any discussion to identify themselves at any meeting ... She has learned from the experience and will in future always identify who she is and that she holds a position in NFU Scotland when taking part in a meeting on behalf of NFUS.

'In relation to your second point regarding mitigation support measures, I do not dispute the fact that NatureScot do provide some mitigation support measures. Therefore, the line "This is not the case" [written by Karen in her consultation response] is incorrect ... I have spoken to her to clarify the position on the mitigation support that is provided by NatureScot so that she is clear on the position that should be put across.'

'What does it say?' asked Sarah. 'Is it bad?'

'No,' I said, sliding the laptop across the table. 'I don't think so. Have a look.'

As she read, her face relaxed. The tension left her body.

'It's great,' she said.

In the coming days I would begin to write up my report and had already resolved to put all of this on record. NatureScot would read an account of the Kilmadock Climate Action meeting and receive copies of all correspondence between us and NFUS;

they would see that even Karen's own CEO had upheld our complaints.

'You won,' Roisin told me via text message that night. 'Be happy.'

I supposed I had. I supposed I ought to be, though how much joy anyone can derive from winning a battle they would sooner never have fought I really can't say. In the end I supposed it didn't matter. The sorry episode was over and we were free of NFUS. Several large drinks were enjoyed in the Bowser house that night.

10

Holding Back the Beaver

'Probably landed on the desk of some licensing team intern who soiled themselves and deleted it!' laughed Andrew O'Donnell, the filmmaker friend who'd visited James with me the previous year.

'Mmm,' I grumbled, failing to see the funny side.

On the beaver front all had gone deathly quiet. Having at last completed the consultation report, I'd submitted our application to NatureScot in the second week of June and received not so much as an acknowledgement.

The writing of the report had been an arduous task, another example of bureaucratic overkill, and I sorely wished there'd been some form of template to follow. I was never more grateful to Sarah than when she took over the formatting of the document. From the sort of amateurish eyesore that your computer-illiterate grandparent might produce she transformed it into something very professional-looking.

When writing, I had done my best to record our neighbours' concerns, recommending that NatureScot visit each farm to investigate whether the fears were likely to come to pass and consider how they might be mitigated against if they did. In my heart I still wished this to be an inclusive process. Some of those people might never speak to us again, but if curiosity should move them to read this book, I hope they'll recognise that we tried not to leave them behind.

Having spent so long working on the document, I could not help but feel disappointed at the lack of response from NatureScot, even if the reason for their silence was clear enough. One week earlier, their legal team and those of Trees for Life, National Farmers Union Scotland and Scottish Land & Estates[*] had put their respective arguments on the legality (or otherwise) of the beaver licensing policy to Lady Carmichael in the Court of Session. Now all sides were waiting for the verdict. The long wait had begun.

A mid-July phone call to the agency brought frustrating news. They had indeed received the application but were unlikely to process it for some time yet. They hoped to bring their people together to discuss the matter. Perhaps by September. Nothing was certain.

Despair washed through me when I considered the ramifications of such a delay. A month from now, the kit dependency season would come to a close; licensed shooting could then legally resume and animals that could be moved to Argaty might instead be culled. For us and for the beavers of Tayside, September was too long a wait. Conversely, for an overstretched agency that seldom moved swiftly, the deadline seemed almost too near. Even *if* the licence was eventually granted, so much remained to be settled before beavers could be brought here. We still didn't know what health screenings the agency would insist upon, how much the tests would cost, who would foot the bill. NatureScot still had to visit our neighbours in order to discuss and assess their concerns too.

Channelling the spirit of my inner Roy Dennis, I wrote the first of many sharp emails, banging the table, demanding a workable timetable.

---

[*] NFUS and SLE took legal advice and were represented in the judicial review hearings.

Through Paul Roberts, NatureScot's local operations manager (who, to his great credit, did his very best to keep lines of communication open), I received an answer to one question: NatureScot would provide no financial assistance for the translocations. As happened whenever beavers were moved from Tayside to enclosures in England, the cost of trapping time, carriage, captive zoo care and health screenings would fall upon the applicant.

'We can't sign up to that,' my father said, his tone apologetic as he saw the disappointment upon my face. 'I know how badly you want this, but we've no idea how much it could cost, and this isn't an enclosed project. If the beavers don't stay, we'd have lost all that money.'

'Stick to your guns,' Mum said. 'What you do sets a precedent for whoever follows you. Translocation can't become a rich person's game and you can't set a standard that prices others out of being able to help.'

Taking to the laptop, I hammered out another angry email.

'We simply can't afford to pay to provide everyone – NatureScot, the Scottish Government, Tayside landowners – with a solution to the current human–beaver conflicts, only to risk seeing beavers swim off downstream, never to return,' it read.

Paul replied to explain that, while he understood the arguments I'd laid out, this had been discussed up to director level, and there was strong consensus on the decision.

'You knew they wouldn't budge, surely?' Sarah asked.

But the truth was that I didn't. Their position seemed so unreasonable, so detrimental to the health of the wildlife that they were constituted to protect, that I thought we'd at least reach a compromise.

'Tom, chum, it's a broken system,' said Derek Gow when I told him the news.

I was beginning to see that.

*

While all of this was playing out, like infuriating elevator music in the background, at home our lives were in turmoil. During a routine pregnancy scan we learned some terrifying news. Sarah's placenta wasn't functioning as expected, insufficient blood was reaching our baby girl. She had stopped growing.

In the weeks that followed we made many hospital visits, spent long hours in waiting rooms, met consultants who spoke gently but matter-of-factly of 'early caesareans', 'complications' and 'survival chances'.

Each day and week that passed without Sarah being rushed into theatre felt like a blessing, but as the next appointment loomed we found ourselves on edge, lying awake at night, unable to sleep.

Anguish still bubbles to the surface whenever we think of those times, but the situation improved. Our baby began to grow; she started turning constant cartwheels in her mother's stomach. Even as a foetus she was all mischief and mayhem. We got lucky.

*

'Conservation success as beaver numbers double in Scotland', read the NatureScot press release.

It was August and the results of the National Beaver Survey were out. Ranging from Glen Isla to Dundee and Stirling, from Forfar to Crianlarich, there were now 251 territories, more than twice the number recorded in the 2017–18 survey.

Twenty-one years after their return to Tayside, the population had finally reached the phase of rapid expansion. Slow starts are not unusual when a small handful of beavers arrive in a new catchment. Dispersing sub-adults travel far and wide, seeking the best available habitats; in those early years a scattered patchwork population is the norm. But as further youngsters disperse, meet and breed, numbers will take a sharp upward turn.

'An increasing beaver population is great news for nature in Scotland,' said a proud NatureScot spokesperson.

One person less than thrilled by their press release was Trees for Life's Alan McDonnell. On the same day that the survey was published, the agency had, with rather less fanfare, slid their latest Beaver Management Report out of the door. It revealed that a further 115 beavers had been shot under licence in 2020. Added to the 87 from the previous year, 202 had now been killed under licence since protection came into place. Their population was estimated then at 954 animals.

How many were *actually* being shot remained a mystery to everyone but the shooters. As Elsie Blackshaw-Crosby, managing lawyer at The Lifescape Project, explained to me, 'One hundred and fifteen was the figure quoted in the report, but these licences weren't restricted in terms of how many beavers could be shot. With one licence a landowner could potentially shoot tens of them – it was up to them whether they reported the true number or not. NatureScot issued a licence, but they had no control or oversight over what was actually happening. They could only go on the basis of what the shooters reported.'

Through Freedom of Information requests, Lifescape had unearthed troubling evidence on the agency's licensing process.

Elsie recalled: 'There were call logs, where applications were being made over the phone. Someone rang up and said, "We've got beavers on Prime Agricultural Land," and the licence was sent out the very next day without any further investigation. There was evidence that some lethal control licences had been issued to PAL where there weren't even any beavers present. We wanted to know how you could claim there was serious damage being caused when there aren't even beavers there? Sometimes Roisin was contracted to go and look at the damage caused, but in other cases NatureScot hadn't been out, hadn't considered what could be done rather than issue lethal control licences.'

Little wonder that Alan McDonnell was unimpressed by the agency's good news story. Speaking to *The Herald*, he said, 'NatureScot has sat on this grim tally since December, refusing to confirm it until today's bid to hide the figures behind a welcome turn of events for the overall beaver population. This is such a waste of life and opportunity when Nature is in crisis.'

'Still no word on the judicial review?' I asked him via text message.

'Could come any day,' he replied. 'Or even in a few weeks. One morning it'll just drop into the lawyers' emails and everything will kick off.'

While they waited for their verdict, we continued to wait for ours.

In August, Paul Roberts visited Argaty with colleagues from NatureScot, looking at the connectivity of our watercourses. Having seen what they came to see, they went to meet some of our neighbours to discuss their concerns. Of the five who'd originally opposed our proposal, only three had responded to their offer of a site visit. As my father had said at the beginning of all of this, 'Some of them will do the sensible thing. When they find out that beavers are coming, they'll learn what impacts they might have and prepare for that. The others will complain like hell, do nothing to prepare, and then complain like hell when they arrive.'

Credit to Dad, he'd seen the lie of the land all along.

On the final day of August, a monumental change occurred at political level: the Scottish Green Party entered government in a power-sharing agreement with the Scottish National Party. Back in May, the SNP had won the Scottish Parliament election, taking 64 of the 129 contested seats, and formed a minority government. Since June they had been in negotiations with the Greens (who had won eight seats) on a deal that would eventually see pro-independence parties hold a majority at Holyrood. As part of the deal, dubbed the Bute House Agreement, Green co-leaders Patrick Harvie and Lorna Slater were appointed as junior government ministers. Slater became Minister for Green Skills, Circular Economy and Biodiversity. For Scotland's beavers, the appointment was to prove crucial.

The penultimate page of the agreement contained a small but significant paragraph – a hint of things to come: 'We support the continued expansion of the beaver population. Where practicable, more use will be made of translocation of beavers, including considering other locations in Scotland. Financial and practical support will be made available to facilitate translocation.'

As the Greens' spokesperson for the environment, our MSP, Mark Ruskell, had been at the heart of the Bute House negotiations.

'I'd get back to NatureScot quoting that paragraph. Ask if you're now eligible for support,' he told me on the day that the news broke.

I did just as he suggested. Though Paul replied to say that colleagues were considering my email and would be in touch, I never heard another word on the matter. The question was quietly swept under the rug.

Autumn began to creep closer, its footsteps felt in the weeping of leaves from trees, the beech nuts that showered the ground in hailstorms, the gradual dulling of the days as roadside wildflowers died back, nights drew in and the last blush of youth left the world. August drifted into September. The hazy deadline mentioned in June by NatureScot came and it went. We were no closer to a decision.

*

On 21 September 2021 Ellie Rose Bowser arrived into the world. A red-faced screaming little ball of energy, she howled and howled in my arms, only settling once Sarah came out of theatre and fed her. The doctors, who were superb throughout, had Sarah so full of morphine she could barely keep her eyes open as the new arrival nestled into her. After all the complications of the pregnancy, and of entering hospital while Covid still lingered, my relief at seeing both her and Ellie come through unharmed was overwhelming.

'Little girl, you don't know what you put us through,' I whispered, cradling our sleeping baby, squeezing her tiny hand.

I returned late to my parents' house that night. Rowan lay awake, awaiting news. 'You're a big sister now,' I said.

She smiled a gigantic gap-toothed grin – a first baby incisor had fallen out two days earlier – and we curled up together to scroll through pictures of the new arrival.

The weeks that followed were a maelstrom of emotions, of which my sleep-deprived brain recorded only snapshots. I remember Rowan visiting the maternity ward, meeting her sister and devouring the hospital cake and custard that had been intended for her recuperating mother; the joy we all felt as Sarah and baby made it home, Ellie meeting her grandparents, Rowan reading her a first bedtime story. Then there were the broken sleeps, the dirty nappies, the struggle to juggle two children rather than one, the feeling that we would never have a spare minute again in our lives. But Ellie slept, she fed, and life soon slipped into its own pleasant rhythm. She was a wild spirit, but a happy one. She remains so to this day. She doesn't know what she put us through before she arrived into this world, but I hope she'll always know how glad we are to have her in it.

*

> I have spoken to the only individual so far who has applied to translocate free-living beavers onto his estate in Scotland. No light touch was applied. Nine months on, he is getting nowhere... He has been told that he will

have to bear all the costs of moving the beavers if a licence is granted, consult with the organisations that harbour the species' most bitterly determined foes, and fall out with his neighbours as a result. He has been informed on innumerable occasions that his application to move individuals, which would otherwise be shot, to his near-ideal location of well-wooded pools is contentious, even though the nearest wild-living beavers requiring no licence are only 8km away, more "serious time and consideration will be required". When you contrast this with the simplicity of process for licences to kill beavers, which can be issued in a single day, the system is quite clearly designed to ensure killing over conservation.

While I appreciate for those not involved in species restoration this might sound like an insane statement.

It's not. It's an appalling truth.

So corrupted by this trend of thought have the official bodies become that this lunacy is their reality.

Derek Gow was on the attack. The article, entitled 'Holding Back the Beaver', appeared on wildlife campaigner Mark Avery's website in early October. By that point my patience with NatureScot had been exhausted. I had had enough. Nobody would tell me what was happening with our application, when we might get a decision, who would make it, on what basis it would be arrived at. It had begun to feel as though we would never get one. Others around me clearly felt the same and were tiptoeing delicately around the issue. The phrases 'You've done all you can' and 'You mustn't be disappointed if . . .' became the soundtrack to my days.

Things got worse. A day before Derek wrote his blog, I received a sincerely apologetic message from a good guy at the agency. One of our neighbours had requested to see our consultation report, and NatureScot, believing it to be their intellectual property rather than mine, had granted the request. It had since been forwarded to Scottish Land & Estates and to Karen at NFUS. Once I had calmed down, I recognised this for the honest error it had been. The person in question had always tried to be open and transparent. These traits made them approachable and human. I couldn't remain angry for long. But the truth remained that NFUS and SLE had seen the report, and if they could find anything within it that they could twist to their advantage, I was sure that they would. Not for the first time NatureScot had left me hopelessly exposed.

'Daddy, we're talking to you,' Rowan would say, for what felt like the umpteenth time each day. 'Mummy, he's not listening. He's thinking about the B word again.'

I'd look up just in time to see my wife and daughter share a disappointed look.

'You weren't there,' Sarah told me recently. 'You'd begin conversations mid-sentence, and nobody knew what you were talking about. You'd make us explore the arguments with NFUS, SLE and NatureScot from every angle ... It got to the point where I just couldn't hear any more of it.'

A rawness spread across my throat. 'I had to be that way,' I said in meek self-defence. 'If I hadn't been that obsessive, I'd never have stuck it out.'

And when she made no reply, I asked: 'Did you think I'd manage it?'

'Get the beavers?' she replied, her eyes wet now. 'I almost hoped you wouldn't. I believed in what you were doing, but you had all these farmers angry at you and folk were in my ear saying things like, "What if someone comes and burns your house down?"'

'You weren't seriously worried about that, were you?' I cut in with an incredulous laugh.

'How was I to know how seriously to take it?' she shot back, the restrained but audible anger shaming me into silence. 'Honestly, a big part of me just wished this had never come our way and would now just go away.'

To my family, all I can say is that I am truly sorry.

Sarah was right. I was lost, consumed by rage. In the face of that mountain of bureaucracy I felt as small and inconsequential as a speck of dust or a grain of sand. All of my requests for clarity and timescales had been ignored. The NFUS issues had gone unaddressed. I had no voice; I didn't matter.

I thought of the neighbours I'd angered, the friendships lost, of my wife and daughters, whom I was failing with every turn. I imagined the jokes made in farming circles.

'Did you hear about Niall Bowser's son?' (In farming I never felt like a person in my own right. I was always my father's son.)

'Daft wee laddie thought he was going to reintroduce beavers. Ended up falling flat on his face.'

I'd earned myself this unwanted reputation. It would follow me for life. No matter how my journey ended, I would always be remembered as the guy who tried to force beavers upon his neighbours. I'd made my peace with that because I'd believed in the democratic process. I'd been sure that we would get beavers quickly and without complication, provided that our proposal had been well-received by the community. But now everything was in doubt. In this endless silence I saw endless possibilities, one of which was the devastating thought that we might fail, that forces much bigger than us would stymie a perfectly good bid. And still that reputation would linger. I would always be 'the beaver man'.

By now everyone knew of our application. Every self-anointed expert in the world was keen to tell me that I ought never to have bothered with the official routes, that I ought instead to have quietly released beavers here, kept my head down and claimed they'd arrived naturally.

rom his holding pen at Five Sisters Zoo, Mull, the father from our first beaver family, says hello to the amera. (Roisin Campbell-Palmer)

lanning our first beaver release with Roisin Campbell-Palmer. (Lynn Bowser)

And they're off: the beaver kits take to the water, watched by (left to right) journalist Richard Baynes, Dad, Mum, Roisin, Gary Curran, Emma Howe and me. (Mark Hamblin www.scotlandbigpicture.com)

Dancing on ice: Mull surveys his new home. (Mark Hamblin www.scotlandbigpicture.com)

Dad steadies the crate as the final kit goes free. (Mark Hamblin www.scotlandbigpicture.com)

Storm Arwen provided a dramatic backdrop on the day of the beavers' arrival. (Mark Hamblin www.scotlandbigpicture.com)

Rowan helps to release the mother beaver. With beavers back in our landscapes our children may come to know more wildlife than their parents or grandparents did. (Mark Hamblin www.scotlandbigpicture.com)

James Nairne is one of the heroes of this story. Were it not for him, none of these events would have happened. (Lynn Bowser)

My girls: Walking to the beaver wetlands with Sarah and Rowan.

Our first beaver lodge: The beavers piled heaps of mud and sticks around square bales we'd left them, creating their home. (Lynn Bowser)

Dam right: This curving wall of mud, sticks and stones increased the volume of water in the pond by an additional million litres. (Lynn Bowser)

Dealing with drought: During the heatwave of 2022, our second beaver family dredged their pond, creating deep channels and mud islands. Their efforts kept water in the pond all summer. (Roger Stewart)

What a difference a year makes. Notice how the water level changes between the beavers' arrival in February 2022, and the summer (middle) and winter (lower). By the end of that year the beavers had built a cascading series of dams downstream from the pond, helping store water on the land and mitigate flood damage. (Roger Stewart)

Floating like a crocodile: In their early months on Argaty, the beavers were less than pleased to see people – as this picture shows. (Lynn Bowser)

It's a baby. The first beaver kits to be born on Argaty for over 400 years arrived in 2022. (Lynn Bowser)

Soon the kits went to work, eating whatever vegetation they could find. (Lynn Bowser)

Another baby (of the human variety) arrived in our lives in 2021. Ellie Rose Bowser was a livewire from birth and showed much more interest in stealing other people's possessions than posing for photos.

Rowan stops for a snack by a beaver-felled tree. Landscapes like this will be as familiar to future generations of Scots as they are foreign to present ones.

Derek Gow, one of Britain's greatest rewilders and a trusted friend during difficult times.
(Gerhard Schwab)

Alan McDonnell and his Trees for Life colleagues showed incredible courage, taking NatureScot to judicial review and making change happen.
(Trees for Life)

Did you know that beavers help to clean water? When they dredged their pond's floor, aquatic plants flourished and oxygenated the water. Four years after the first photo was taken, the water is as clear as glass. (Nigel Willby)

When *Springwatch* visited Argaty, presenter Megan McCubbin described beavers as having 'one of the best bottoms in the animal kingdom'. We very much agree. (Lynn Bowser)

A beaver-dug canal links a pond to a nearby rainwater pool. Our wetlands are expanding and diversifying. Water flows in places that have been dry for centuries. (Roger Stewart)

Felled trees are a regular sight at Argaty now. As they break down, they give life back to the soil that birthed them. (Lynn Bowser)

Paul and Louise Ramsay and their daughter Sophie are beaver heroes, having fought tirelessly to restore them to this country. (Dave Maric)

David Sexton stands on the banks of Loch Na Keal, Mull. David has been a superb ambassador for white-tailed eagles, helping to increase public appreciation of these incredible birds.

Ruth Tingay addresses the audience at Hen Harrier Day. Often to her own detriment, Ruth has been a true champion for the natural world. (Stewart Abbott)

For people of my age, Roy Dennis is like the founding father of Britain's rewilding movement. His work to restore missing species surpasses anyone else's.

Mother beaver carries a freshly severed branch back to her lodge. With a second set of lips located behind their teeth, beavers can dive with food and avoid swallowing water. (Lynn Bowser)

The beaver family show little wariness around us now. We have been accepted as a benign part of their landscape. (Lynn Bowser)

Land of the dammed: Beaver dams appear in unexpected places around Argaty. Finding a new one is always a thrill. (Lynn Bowser)

Big the beaver breathes the fresh air of freedom. He was lucky to be alive. (Elliot McCandless, Beaver Trust)

Scotland's beaver advocates gather at Argaty to visit our wetlands. Pictured (left to right) are: Pete Creech (Heart of Argyll Wildlife), Charlotte Maddix (Scottish Rewilding Alliance), Sally Mackenzie (Cairngorms National Park (CNP)), Tobias Leask (Trees for Life), James Nairne, Jonathan Willet (CNP), Nigel Willby (University of Stirling), Alan McDonnell, Kirsten Brewster (SCOTLAND: The Big Picture), James Silvey (RSPB Scotland), Alana Skilbeck, Sheelagh McAllister and Elliot McCandless (all Beaver Trust), Lewis Pate. (CNP)

Gordon Buchanan visits Argaty to discuss human–wildlife coexistence for Jamma International's *Beneath the Baobab* podcast.

Spending a glorious evening watching the beaver family with Megan McCubbin and the BBC *Springwatch* team. (Matt Andrews)

'Someone has to get this over the line by legal means,' I said again and again. 'We've moved beyond white van releases...'

Privately, I wondered if that was true.

I don't think that NatureScot ever appreciated what that long period of not-knowing did to me. They, enjoying the anonymity of working in a team, buried in the belly of a large organisation, could never understand what it was like to stray from the pack, to burn bridges and have no way back, to be alone with no way of knowing if it had all been for nothing.

For months Derek had been offering to help us. Should we wish to go public and tell the world in explosive detail quite how hard this process was, I knew where to turn. But I had resisted. Tagging him in felt like setting the Rottweiler on the Poodle. Derek was the red button. Would a licence come our way if he nuked NatureScot? I doubted it. Diplomacy dies the moment you drop the bomb.

But when he messaged, a day after our consultation document had been handed to beavers' opponents, to say that he'd written about us as an example of technocrats 'controlling all', 'contributing nothing' and ruining beaver reintroduction, I shrugged and thought: 'Well, what have we left to lose?'

'What's your next move?' wrote SCOTLAND: The Big Picture's Pete Cairns, having read the article. 'It seems to me that you either sit tight, continue to be subjected to poor treatment in the hope that you might get some very expensive beavers, or you call out NatureScot in a respectful but very public way. They're hoping to wear you down so that you'll crawl away.'

'I know. But if we walk away, we junk all our hard work, and I'm not sure if I can do that,' I texted back. 'The concern is how long it takes and how much more it takes from me along the way. This isn't good for me, mentally. I know that.'

Derek was more direct. 'Go to the press and give them all the paperwork,' he advised. 'You're not giving up. You're responding in a different way. Left to their own devices these idiots will do nothing. Situations like yours show just how useless the system is.'

I understood where they were coming from. I knew that they were correct. If you were a farmer on Prime Agricultural Land and wished to shoot a beaver, all it took was one phone call. If you wished to save some, you had to wade through bureaucratic treacle for months, anger friends, alienate family, have your head repeatedly served to your enemies. And *if* they eventually granted you a licence, they'd force you to pay every penny of the translocation costs. Why on earth would anyone wish to go through this?

Throwing in the towel was the only sensible option. I knew it. But I couldn't do it. We'd been through too much, had given too much and, sentimental as it might sound, I couldn't turn my back, knowing that beavers were still destined to be culled. We were tied together, our fates intertwined. I no longer knew if their future depended upon us or ours upon them.

11

Trees for Life, Take a Bow

There are moments when life takes on a momentum of its own, when one event leads to a series of others, when a raindrop becomes a stream, and a stream a river. When all of that pressure comes to bear, dams break, and old worlds are swept away.

For beavers in Scotland that first drop had fallen decades earlier when animals escaped to the River Earn. In those moments, the stream was born. It grew in strength when campaigns for eradication were drowned out by the calls for protection, when beavers were brought to Knapdale, when studies proved the environmental gains they could bring to the countryside. And as protection came but still more animals were killed, as authorities refused to change and a legal challenge was mounted, as a beaver-supportive party entered government, that small stream became something else – a river in spate that would not be stopped.

In October 2021, the pressure told. One by one, the barriers that had stood in our way were taken by the flood.

Roisin set this chain reaction in motion. In March she had taken on the job of restoration manager for the charity Beaver Trust. Through that happy connection she solved the first of our problems.

'Funding sorted!' she wrote. 'Beaver Trust will cover us!'

'Everything??' I wrote back, disbelieving.

'Everything. Zoo stay, health screening, translocations, the lot. Cost needn't be an issue now. If we get the licence, let's just get this done!'

Days later Jenny Bryce from NatureScot called to let me know that they had sent their recommendations to the Scottish Government. Their response, she hoped, would soon be forthcoming. What the politicians would say was anyone's guess. So much seemed to hang on the result of Trees for Life's legal challenge.

As if the gods of fate had heard my prayer, on 21 October Alan McDonnell texted. 'Verdict just in . . .'

'And??' I replied instantly.

'Need to get lawyers' take . . .'

Fearing the worst, I searched online until I found the court's document. As I read, my heart plummeted, landing somewhere in the pit of my stomach, where it would sit wallowing for hours. Only one of the five complaints raised by Trees for Life's legal team had been deemed 'well founded'.

'It is a requirement of EU law that reasons be given when licences of this sort are granted,' wrote Judge Lady Carmichael. 'In approaching matters on the basis that it has no duty to give reasons for granting a licence, the first respondent [NatureScot] had erred in law.'

The remainder of the verdict seemed very much to support NatureScot's approach.[19] To my (admittedly uneducated) eye, this looked like a 4–1 defeat.

The remainder of that grey October's day trundled slowly, miserably by. I spoke to the Jameses (Nairne and Silvey); both were glum. No further word came from Alan. Then, as I was finishing up for the day, the phone vibrated in my pocket. Withdrawing it, glancing at the first line of the newly arrived message, my free-falling heart rebounded.

'Rewind . . . QC says we won!'

'My initial reaction was the same as yours,' he explained later that night. 'But this isn't a football match. The lawyers were clear on that. Succeeding on one count is enough.'

'JRs are usually won on technical points,' Elsie Blackshaw-Crosby of The Lifescape Project would explain to me. 'It's sensible to take multiple different approaches in building a case. A big part of strategic litigation is the narrative that's built around it – the PR, press reaction and the pressure that's put on policy makers as a result.'

If those were indeed the real measures of success, then there could be little doubt as to the outcome. Trees for Life may have lost some battles, but they won the war.

'Trees for Life wins court battle over NatureScot culling policy', wrote *The Herald* the following morning. *The Scotsman*, *Times* and BBC News took the same line, each declaring Trees for Life victorious.

'Top work for wildlife by @treesforlifeuk, not such top work by @naturescot and never any expectation of top work by @ScotLandEstates,' tweeted naturalist and television presenter Chris Packham.

I allowed myself a quiet chuckle at that one.

Later, NatureScot published a statement. 'We want to clarify a range of inaccuracies in media reporting,' it read. 'Of the five complaints under consideration by the Court, four were rejected entirely ... We welcome the Court's broad vindication of our licensing process.'

But it was too little too late. By the time they shared their rendition of events, news outlets had already gone with a Trees for Life victory.

Whatever NatureScot's claims, the fallout of the verdict amounted to no vindication of their approach. Thereafter, they would be required to explain why they had deviated from the Habitats Regulations (in allowing beavers to be captured, disturbed or killed) every time they issued a licence. The moment they issued reasons was the moment they could be challenged again, in both the Court of Session and the Court of Public Opinion. As Steve Micklewright wrote, in an opinion piece for *The Scotsman*, henceforth there would be no more 'rubber stamping of official killings'.

For him, the main moral of the Trees for Life beaver story could be encapsulated in a simple two-word instruction: Be bold.

As he later told me, 'The thing people keep telling me about Trees for Life is, "You're such a *brave* organisation. Who else would have done that?" And I think it's about being bold actually, not brave. If we're not bold about the things we're trying to do, then nothing will change and nature will stay in peril. We can really make things happen – little organisations can make a massive difference.'

Meanwhile, when walking the streets around his home in Inverness (the city where NatureScot also has its headquarters), Alan McDonnell was amused to note how former colleagues at the agency reacted to seeing him. Some gave him such a wide berth that an onlooker might reasonably have concluded that he carried a fatal infectious disease. Others checked their surroundings furtively, then rushed up to shake his hand.

Of all the column inches dedicated to the result, the most gratifying (from a Trees for Life perspective) and most devastating (from NatureScot's) were written by Jim Crumley in *The Courier*.

'Wildlife in Scotland is under siege and it looks like the Scottish Government's own advisers cannot be depended upon to fight nature's corner,' he wrote. 'If there is anyone in the Scottish Government looking at the events in the Court of Session with a critical eye and a thoughtful mind, they might conclude that NatureScot is a meaningless name for a meaningless organisation and that the time for a new nature-first agency is at hand.

'Pouring resources into nature is the biggest single investment we can make right now ... Everything on Earth, including the human race, is dependent on the health of the planet itself. The truth we must swallow is that we are nature too, and we must learn to fit back in. While we come to terms with that, a round of applause please while Trees for Life take a bow.'[20]

*

What tipped the balance? Was it the arrival of the Greens to government, the judge's verdict, neither of these things or both? Would we have succeeded regardless, or was our result a consequence of this wider chain reaction? I'll never know and nobody at NatureScot will ever tell me, but a week after the court ruling I received word. Our application had been approved. Beavers were coming to Argaty.

'You must be delighted, aren't you?' asked Sarah when I returned home that night. It was gone eight o'clock. The sky had long since turned dark.

'Yeah,' I said, considering this for a moment. 'I guess ... It feels like a lot to take in.'

'Tom,' she said, fixing me with a stare. 'Be proud of yourself ... She's still awake if you want to say goodnight. I'll pour you a drink for when you're back down.'

I tiptoed quietly upstairs, keen not to wake Rowan if she'd slipped into sleep.

Her already pale skin had taken an even lighter shade, as it always did when she was overtired. Blue bags hung like rainclouds beneath her eyes. Perching on the end of her bed, I swept a tangled strand of blonde hair from her face.

'I'm sorry I missed your story,' I said.

'That's ... OK,' she replied, her words separated by a yawn. 'Where've you been?'

'On the phone all day, sharing some good news. We're going to have beavers living on the farm.'

'What do you mean?' she asked, her tired eyes regaining some of their focus.

'I've probably never told you what I've been doing, and why I've been so busy this year, have I?'

She shook her head.

'... Roisin will bring them here,' I concluded five minutes later. 'Soon. I hope. And it's good news, because people didn't want them, and they might have been killed if we hadn't been allowed to give them a new home.'

She was lying back now. Sleep was coming soon.

'Daddy,' she said dreamily. 'You're a hero.'

Of all the kind words that would come our way in subsequent weeks, none would top those four. I ruffled her hair, pulled the covers up to her chin and left her to sleep.

12

Beavers!

'Threatened Beavers Given Sanctuary at Argaty Red Kites' read the greatest headline ever written, published in *The Times* on 10 November 2021.

The brilliant Richard Bunting, who'd managed all the press relations around the Trees for Life verdict, had again played his hand to perfection. Together with Beaver Trust, we had contracted him to publicise our licence decision. How the media lapped up his press release. The story featured on Graham Norton's Virgin Radio show and Radio Scotland's *Out of Doors* programme; it appeared in *The Sun*, *Daily Record*, BBC *Wildlife* magazine and *Countryfile* magazine. News broadcasters clamoured to film the release. What a thrill to watch our little family-run project which, for all that we loved it, had never attracted anything like this amount of attention, suddenly garner so much of it. I felt like the songwriter who, after years spent playing to half-empty bars, writing songs in his bedroom, finally writes the hit that sees his band make the big time.

Not everyone was as delighted as we were with the news. *The Telegraph* produced a fantastic tale of 'serious' problem-causing beavers, 'fierce opposition of neighbouring farmers' and fears of 'major' flooding and destruction of crops. (In an area of next to no arable farming, this latter point came as a surprise.) The story ran under the headline: 'Refugee Beavers to be Rehomed rather than Shot'.

'Good old *Torygraph*,' I said to Roisin. 'Given their politics, I'm surprised the title didn't read: "Refugees (and Beavers) should be Shot rather than Rehomed".'

We laughed it off. One can't please everyone in this world. Indeed, there are some whom one would never wish to please.

Through the grapevine I heard that NatureScot staff were also less than delighted with the press release, which touched (albeit lightly) on the history of lethal control, stated (with a certainty we didn't really feel) that the licence marked a landmark change of government position, and implied that translocation would henceforth always be prioritised over lethal control.

Days earlier I'd declined the agency's request to issue a joint release announcing the good news. The guilt had been haunting me ever since. There were decent people there who had always treated me well; ultimately, they had supported our application too, I had to remember that. I was waving two fingers at them and I knew it. However, I simply couldn't bring myself to smile politely, shut my mouth and pretend that the process had been a partnership. Nor could I be a poster boy for NatureScot's policy. A handful of animals saved did not make up for the many that weren't. Their own press release landed a day after ours and sank without a ripple.

The terms of the licence would allow us to translocate two families and an adult pair. The families would go to the two ponds Roisin had deemed most suitable for long-term occupation, the pair onto a less wooded one. The release sites were sufficiently far apart that the chances of animals roaming and fighting appeared slim. With luck they would remain on these ponds for many years to come. With even more luck, their dispersing offspring might one day meet in the middle and pair up.

'That's a lot of beavers!' said Roisin, when she read the licence conditions. 'We'll make sure the first release is a family unit. People will love seeing the kits on camera...' She broke off, and it was clear from her expression that something was on her mind.

'What is it?' I asked.

'Nothing,' she replied. 'Just ... Well, we've gone and bloody done it!'

By mid-November, she'd trapped a male and his three kits. Days later she caught the mother too. The family unit was now reunited at Five Sisters Zoo in West Lothian, awaiting release. For so long we'd been running this gruelling marathon. Now we were sprinting towards the finish. Minutes sped by in seconds, days fell away, time had no meaning. Our beavers failed a health screening, had to be retested, and this time passed. The release date was set for Monday, 29 November. Richard Bunting juggled requests to film the release from journalists and TV crews. He drafted a new press release, embargoed until the day of the translocation, entitled: 'Family Farm Saves Death-Sentence Beavers in Historic Relocation'. This one would *really* anger NatureScot. I felt no guilt now. It was a political move, not a personal attack. We had this one moment to turn the screw and ensure that translocations really were prioritised over lethal control going forward. We would use it. Mum and I visited the fabulous beaver holding facilities, managed by Gary Curran and his family, at Five Sisters Zoo. For the briefest of moments, we glimpsed one of the beavers. It scuttled across its enclosure and plunged into the safety of a cattle trough filled to the brim with water. There it remained, floating like a furry crocodile, eyeing us angrily, waiting for us to leave.

In the midst of all this mayhem, on 24 November, 16 months to the day since Trees for Life had first launched the #MoveDontKill petition, the Biodiversity Minister, Lorna Slater, made a major announcement. The Scottish Government would actively support the expansion of the beaver population, promoting translocation and helping to establish the animals' presence in new catchments. The ban on out-of-range translocations was over. Seldom in wildlife conservation does so much happen so quickly, but something special was happening in that moment in Scotland; a raindrop had grown into a flood.

Delighted at this latest piece of good news, I sent a text to Mark Ruskell thanking him and his political colleagues for their work, then resumed my planning for the release day. Dad and I set to work building lodges for the beavers, ably assisted by our volunteer, Sandra McDerment. Three square bales were placed in a U-shape at the water's edge, roofing sheets and cut branches piled on top. The squat structure bore closer resemblance to a collapsed hay barn than a beaver lodge, but should they need it for the first few nights, shelter would be there.

'How do *you* feel about the beavers coming?' Sandra asked Dad as we headed for home. (While my views on rewilding matters are usually taken as read, people often seem interested to know where my livestock farmer father stands on it all.)

'Personally, I wouldn't have voted for them . . .' he replied. After a beat he smiled and added: 'But it's quite exciting.'

That night events took another unexpected turn. A cyclone known as Storm Arwen hit the UK. Armies of trees dropped as though mowed down by machine gun. Electricity pylons were variously crushed, scythed or yanked down, their wires falling like tape from unspooled cassettes. Argaty, like much of the country, would lose power for days. Camping out in our living room, Sarah and I fed the fire every hour, keeping the room warm while Rowan and baby Ellie slept.

Experts would later estimate that the equivalent of 16 million trees had been damaged across Scotland by the storm. Oddly, however, Arwen was greeted with very little frustration from the land managers that I knew. Most shrugged their shoulders, because these things happen, and stoically set about clearing the damage. Passing our own scenes of devastation, my mind could not help but remark on the irony of that. How strange it was that the beaver that felled a few riparian trees was reviled, while the storm that took an entire wood was accepted. Our concepts of what does and does not constitute an act of nature are fascinatingly illogical.

In the days that followed, Arwen tightened her hold. Freezing conditions swept the country. By the morning of the beaver release a thick layer of ice lay smothering the pond. With an air of sad resignation, Sarah and I concluded that she and the girls could not join us in these temperatures.

An odd crunching sound greeted my ears as I neared the release pond. Some strange creature was lumbering across the pond, smashing trails through the ice. 'For somebody who wouldn't have voted for beavers, you have a funny way of showing it,' I shouted.

My father turned, placed hands on wader-clad hips and smiled.

'Thought I'd better break the ice. It won't be much of a release if there's no water to release them into,' he said.

By lunchtime a small crowd had gathered at the farm. In the centre of it all were James Nairne and Elliot McCandless. Seeing the old friends together, deep in conversation, my imagination drifted. I pictured them nearly two years ago, huddled over a map, searching for a site within existing beaver range and a landowner who might be willing to rehome animals in need. How long ago that seemed. A different time, a different life. Those had been different times for them, too. Though both now worked full-time in conservation, Elliot for Beaver Trust, James for SCOTLAND: The Big Picture, neither had done so then. This whole journey had only begun because of the efforts of two volunteers, one an accountant, the other an unemployed lawyer. There was something wonderfully empowering about that.

Still unable to venture indoors due to Covid, our crowd stood outside, shuffling their feet in the cold. I made small talk with the news team from Channel 4, cracked a few jokes with Nigel Willby. Soon a procession of vehicles arrived. First came the wildlife veterinarian Romain Pizzi, then Gary Curran and his colleagues from Five Sisters Zoo, then Roisin, and finally the film team from SCOTLAND: The Big Picture.

'How're you feeling?' I asked Roisin as she opened her van's back door to check in on her passengers. A line of shining steel boxes, three-parts covered by large towels, stood in a row before us.

'OK,' she muttered, looking anything but. 'The female wasn't happy being put into her crate.' Her eyes moved to the furthest metal box, then back to me. 'Let's keep her here. We'll take her down and release her quietly once the crowd's away.'

Unable to resist temptation I lifted the corner of the nearest towel. In those stolen seconds I studied the animal, squaring everything I'd read in books with his reality. He met my gaze with dark, shining eyes. They sat to the side of his head, allowing him a wider field of vision than that of front-facing predators. They were small, however; as a night dweller that spent much of its time underwater, this made perfect sense. Beavers have evolved to rely upon smell and hearing more than eyesight. He turned and waddled away from me. I saw that his back legs were long, their feet webbed – adaptations that would help him to swim – while the front legs were shorter, the feet minimally webbed. Like people, the beaver uses it dextrous hands for skilled tasks such as building and holding food items. Black and lined with tiny diamond-shaped scales, the tail lay flat on the straw bedding that lined the crate's floor. Perhaps because it lay beside the beaver like a casually discarded item, perhaps because it was one of only two body parts not to be totally covered in fur (the other being the paws), it seemed not to belong to the animal at all. In my peripheral vision I noted people moving. I waited a moment longer, hoping to catch a glimpse of the beavers' iron-mineralised orange teeth, but to no avail. Letting the towel drop, I returned him to the comfort of darkness. It was time to go.

I've no clear memory of the walk to the ponds. My sense of euphoria was so great I was blackout-drunk upon it. All I can recall is the sound of our all-terrain buggy echoing through the surrounding woodland, the sight of it emerging through the trees, Dad at the wheel, beaver crates in the back, the feeling of joy that seemed to radiate from everyone in attendance. Smiles, high fives, handshakes and hugs were exchanged. We looked like the world's least athletic sports team, celebrating victory.

As soon as I'd offered to help lift the crates from the buggy down to the water I regretted it. For those reading who have never lifted a beaver, count yourselves lucky; they are burly beasts, about the size of a fat Labrador. The dad, who the Five Sisters staff had named Mull, weighed a full 25kg. Full of curiosity, he paced up and down continually, pressing his nose to the mesh doors and gazing out at the world. Each movement sent the steel box pitching as though a cannonball was rolling within it.

Arms popping from sockets we heaved his crate and the others containing his three kits to one bank. (Mercifully, the youngsters made for a much easier carry. At less than a year old, they weighed in at around 6kg each.) The watchers were ushered to the opposite side. If the beavers swam towards the outflow, looking to make a hasty escape, the presence of people there would be enough to turn them back.

Everything and everyone was in place. We were ready.

'Go on then,' said Roisin.

'What?' I said, flummoxed. 'You're doing it, aren't you?'

'Go on,' she said in a whisper that no others could hear.

Heart hammering in time to my footsteps, I moved towards the crate. I slid the bolt that held its door in place.

Mull bellyflopped gracelessly through the rushes and slipped into the pond. Midway across, he mounted the ice and reared on hind legs. In the slow seconds that he stood there, back arched, surveying the canvas that was now his to paint, he was poised and powerful, feral and free.

One by one, the three kits bum-shuffled across the bank and followed after him. I stood with James and Roisin, my friends, my teammates, watching them navigate precarious paths, sometimes slipping, sometimes slamming down into the dark depths below.

Beaver kits tire more easily than adults and can stand the cold only so long. As the warmth left its body, one youngster soon began to slow. Whimpering like a beaten dog, it toiled towards Mull, who stalled in the water. With much kicking and splashing, the youngster clambered onto him. Tiny paws fastened like leather gloved hands around his neck and they swam off, the baby riding piggy-back, safe from the water's chill.

Time sped by. Soon I found myself shaking hands and saying goodbyes. While Roisin went to fetch the female from her van, Dad sped off down the road. Alone for the first time, I allowed myself a tired but contented sigh.

A distant burr soon announced the buggy's return. Dad was not alone. Sat alongside him, wrapped in a thick jacket and dazzling snow-white scarf was Rowan. A picture of her as she was in that moment still hangs framed in my mind. Whenever I stop to stare at it, it's her massive gappy grin that always draws my eye. Both upper incisors had by then fallen out; the adult ones had yet to grow in. That gap tied her to a particular stage, a special time when life began to change. Opening the door, I pulled her in for a hug. Tears long held at bay stormed my eyes. Holding her tightly, I buried my head and sobbed silently onto her shoulder.

Hand in hand we retraced our steps to the pond, where the zoo staff were setting the crate in place on the bank.

'Want to open it?' I asked.

Eyes darting from me to the small group of remaining watchers, she shook her head.

'Both of us?' I whispered.

Another swift glance was followed by a small smile, a barely perceptible nod. Together we pulled the door and watched in silent delight as the mother crashed off through the ice, glassy shards spiralling in her orbit, heading in the direction of our makeshift lodge, where her husband and babies sat waiting.

And so it was that two generations of one family reunited two generations of another. The beavers were returned to the waters, the waters were returned their beavers, and life for both began anew.

Part Two
Living with Beavers

13

Thinking Like a Beaver

A week passed before we saw the beavers again. Blackbirds shucked and peeped from the adjacent woodland as I approached the pond at the end of a day's work. Their song provided a welcome soundtrack to my walk; with the release completed and the crowds gone, a strange sort of hush had fallen on the farm again. The hardest thing for any obsessive person to do is live with themselves during life's quiet moments.

The blackbirds were not the only ones intent on interrupting the silence that day. In the pond ahead of me two shadows were burling in a slow pirouette. They came together and rose as one, paws interlinked, groaning and whining. One soon fell back, overpowered, hitting the water with much flapping and splashing. I had just witnessed my first bout of beaver wrestling – a form of play where youngsters develop their motor skills, preparing for the future. Battles then will be matters of life and death.

Sightings thereafter were sporadic. One afternoon Sarah and I caught a glimpse of an adult sitting nonchalantly on the pond's island grooming its fur. Another evening, our ranger at that time, Nicky, heard them on the bank as she approached with carrots and was forced into a hasty retreat. Otherwise, they proved highly adept at eluding us, appearing only after darkness had descended.

True to their *busy* reputation, they made their presence known in other ways. Childlike pudgy handprints appeared in the mud. Flattened pond-side rushes told of a heavy animal's coming and going. Piles of bark-stripped sticks grew nightly on the island. Remains of the food we left them were discarded there too. (They'd gnaw a corn on the cob to the husk, eat every last inch of a carrot, but wouldn't thank you for pears.) Bark ripped from trunks left blood-orange wood exposed as they taste-tested trees. Some they bypassed after just that bite, but they waged war on others. Like convicts marking each day of their sentence with a tally on the walls, the beavers recorded the length of their stay on the trunks. As each night passed, more marks appeared. From their slant one could tell which way the animals had craned their necks before biting. By their third week, a first tree had fallen. More would follow.

There was a rationale to their work that we understood only after the event. One night they dug a trench so perfectly straight you'd have sworn it had been created by navvies' spades rather than the stubby forelegs of semi-aquatic rodents. The pond connected to a pool some ten metres away; water began to travel from one to the other, the trench became a canal. By its midpoint stood a willow. On trail cameras we watched the beavers swim their new highway, stop to gnaw off branches then float them over to the island.

'So *that's* why they dug there,' I thought. 'Why heave wood across land when you can travel by water and avoid predators to boot?'

Such things made sense when one thought like a beaver.

Scanning the ground between the pond and other distant willows we saw that more canals would be dug, that our wetlands would expand and diversify, that water would flow in places that had been dry for centuries.

Progress was slow, however. As with so many things, change

does not happen overnight. Beavers' worlds are not created with one big bang. The explosion of biodiversity these animals trigger was not, upon closer inspection, one explosion at all, but hundreds of small charges, detonating all the time throughout their wetlands. Some were so tiny you'd be forgiven for missing them. The fly basking on the warm centre of a beaver-gnawed tree trunk. The harvestman seeking prey in the woodchip pile below. The woodchips beginning their process of decomposition, their death giving life back to the soil that birthed them. The cobweb in the crack of the felled tree which slumped, top half at right angles to the bottom, held on by the slenderest thread of bark. Green shoots no bigger than your thumbnail beginning their slow skywards climb as the tree coppiced and began a second life as a thicket.

These explosions were so small as to seem insignificant. To witness one, you might shrug your shoulders and say, 'So what? You've got a few more flies or a few more spiders. What's the big deal?' And you'd be correct. *Individually* they did not amount to much. But multiply them across a pond, a tributary, a whole catchment, and you begin to see the cumulative benefit of beavers.

From the ponds and bogs we've drained to the rivers we've straightened and the riparian margins we've farmed to the bone, the UK's watercourses are suffering death from a thousand cuts. In the last century alone, the UK has lost 90 per cent of its wetlands. Today they cover just 3 per cent of our land mass, and over 10 per cent of our freshwater and wetland species are threatened with extinction.[21] But beavers could just be the thousand sticking plasters we need to seal shut so many wounds. These animals are restoring the very thing we have removed: diversity. Throughout their territories, beavers create niches, and nature loves a niche.

Night after night these small changes exploded around our pond. Injuries inflicted over the centuries began to heal.

*

Two days after Christmas, there came an unexpected invitation. NatureScot were seeking stakeholders to help develop a new national beaver strategy, a 23-year roadmap detailing how Lorna Slater's policy of actively expanding the population could become a reality. Roisin, the Jameses (Nairne and Silvey), Steve, Nigel Willby, Roy Dennis, John Lister-Kaye and Pete Creech (of Heart of Argyll Wildlife) were also on the lengthy invitee list. My initial reaction was one of such unbridled joy that I surprised even myself. Once the beavers had arrived here, I'd feared that our involvement in the wider cause to restore them across Scotland would come to an end. Difficult though the past year had been, working with friends towards this common goal had been a true pleasure. The thought that we would now be afforded a second chance to collaborate therefore came as a delightful surprise. One thought tempered my high spirits, however. If so many beaver supporters had been invited, NatureScot would have asked an equal number of opponents. A quick scroll down the invitee list confirmed as much. Various NFUS representatives were there; on the seven-person steering group was Karen. With waning enthusiasm, I accepted the invitation. The strategy meetings would begin in February and beavers needed as many supporters around that table as possible.

Hogmanay came and went, and in early January 2022 Gemma Varley, a keeper from Five Sisters Zoo, visited with treats for the beavers. Great mountains of carrots were piled in her boot. When she opened the door, she began a landslide.

'Where on earth did you get so many?' I asked, bending to scoop bundles up.

'There's a depot where a major supermarket sends its waste food,' she said. 'We go along and fill up crates to feed the zoo animals. It's pretty much an endless supply. Twice a day any unsold veg is sent for incineration.'

Twirling several in my hands, I sought signs of rot but found none.

'But there's nothing wrong with them,' I said.

She shrugged. 'One Christmas the supermarket asked if we could use 700 turkeys they hadn't managed to sell. They were just going to burn them.'

If ever you hear the argument, frequently espoused by the National Farmers Union, that beavers are a threat to food security, I'd like you to remember this story.

The theory goes that beavers will damage farmland, reducing our ability to feed our people with our own produce, making us more reliant upon foreign imports. Food prices will rise and the poorest in society will suffer. Let us explore this argument for a moment.

People in this country go hungry for a variety of tragic reasons, but beavers are most certainly not one of them. In fact, it may surprise you to learn that in the UK we produce significantly more than we actually eat. According to WWF-UK, 12.8 million tonnes of food is lost or wasted in the UK annually. From the same source we know that 9,600km^2, an area almost half the size of Wales, is used to produce food that, for a combination of factors, never even makes it off-farm. An unintended and disastrous consequence of food becoming so affordable for the affluent in our society is that those people no longer value it as they should. Of the food that does get into shops, 9.5 million tonnes is wasted each year; 70 per cent of that occurs in people's homes.[22]

So much is being produced, yet demand for food banks has never been higher. How can that be? A variety of issues, including global conflicts and attempts to recover from the coronavirus pandemic, have caused a sharp rise in food and energy prices. As the average wage has not increased at the same rate, many from less affluent backgrounds are struggling to afford to eat. According to the Trussell Trust, over 3.12 million emergency food parcels were distributed to people facing hardship in the UK in 2023–24, a 94 per cent increase over the past five years.[23]

The implications for people of this broken system are clear. At a time when millions of Brits are struggling to afford food, millions of tonnes of perfectly edible produce are going uneaten. From these wasted surpluses alone, The Food Foundation estimates that seven billion meals could be made.

The impact upon nature of this culture of waste should be clear too. The more land that we put into agricultural production, the less space there is for wildlife. The less space there is, the more conflicts ensue when wildlife encroaches upon productive farmland/productive farmland encroaches upon wildlife (delete as applicable).

When beavers' activities impact Prime Agricultural Land, farmers cry 'food security' and the authorities leap to attention and sanction lethal control, but how real is this threat that beavers are said to pose? Setting aside the fact that much of farmers' produce may never be eaten, many of the affected fields are either not growing crops that directly feed people, or growing ones for use in non-essential foods. Almost 80 per cent of Scotland's cereal harvest is used for production of alcohol or animal feed.[24] A quick scan of the Rural & Environment Science & Analytical Services (RESAS) Scottish Crop Map reveals just how many of those fields of spring barley are located in the very heart of East Tayside beaver conflict zones. A great deal of winter wheat is grown there too. From NFUS themselves, we learn that 'milling wheats grown in Scotland are mainly used for biscuit making'.[25] In this situation, one must wonder what the true threat to food security is: the beaver that floods productive land, the farmer that uses that land to grow non-essential crops, or the system that encourages them to do so.

To further complicate matters, according to the Scottish Government, 'Many of the calories produced in Scotland will be consumed elsewhere and many of the calories consumed in Scotland will have been produced elsewhere.' For example, 66 per cent of Scotch beef, 58 per cent of Scotch sheep meat and 86–8 per cent of potatoes are sold to England and Wales, while 21 per cent of our mutton and lamb is sold to the EU. However, 29.2 per cent of the beef and 33 per cent of the potatoes that the UK consumes are imported from the EU, and 22 per cent of the sheep meat comes from non-EU countries.[26]

When so much food is wasted each year ... When so much land is dedicated to growing crops that either don't directly feed us or that will be turned into luxury items like biscuits ... When the wider public have no real means of influencing what is produced where and in what quantity, how much remains in the country and how much is exported... how can anyone know how food secure Scotland is, or has the potential to be? I don't and I'd bet my last penny that those who've championed lethal control of beavers don't either.

Land use choices, labour shortages, supply issues, cheap food culture and food waste may all present a threat to food security; beavers do not. What they may (and do) sometimes impact is the income of certain farmers. If we are to work towards a solution that allows people and beavers to coexist, we must drop the hyperbole and admit that farmers' loss of earnings is the real issue we need to address.

So, what might a solution look like? How might 5.6 million Scots learn to live alongside our small but growing beaver population? To answer this question, we might look to the 12 million Bavarians living alongside 23,000 beavers.

In a Scottish Wild Beaver Group blog entitled 'Beaver in Bavaria: Lessons for Scotland', James Nairne identified the key measures behind the Bavarian model's success.

Active land use on 10 per cent of all state-owned land was relinquished, net gain legislation required developers to buy farmland and return it to nature whenever a development was planned elsewhere, and farming within five metres of a watercourse was prohibited. With beavers mostly active near the water's edge, this final rule was crucial.

No system is perfect and there are still occasional unwanted impacts, but compensation schemes are available, and a 1,000-strong team of beaver consultants is on hand to advise on mitigation.

Could such schemes work in Scotland? Could we – through government funding, private, or both – incentivise farmers to pull back from the water's edge, set their flood banks further back, restore riparian woodlands or even to allow their land to flood if it meant that land downstream did not? The benefits would be huge. Less soil, nitrates, pesticides and animal pathogens would contaminate waters. Trees would store carbon; their roots would stabilise riverbanks and soak up water, further mitigating against downstream flooding. Wildlife would thrive in these restored habitats. And by making space for water, Scotland would make space for beavers and unleash their many benefits.

In an environmental crisis that is outpacing us all, Scotland needs an honest, measured conversation on land use. Food production and wildlife are vital and we must seek ways to accommodate both. To do this, we must ignore the scare stories and focus on the real barriers that prevent us from reaching the goal.

While we seek a way forward, there's a question we must ask ourselves: Did beavers *really* deserve to die in such numbers for the crime of threatening food security, or might their lives have been worth more than some packets of biscuits, bottles of whisky, or the carrots that we throw away uneaten?

14

The Common Cause

The tiny outlet burn wended its way through a wet woodland of alder and willow carr. Those scrubby half-grown trees rose at every angle except 90 degrees to the ground. No human hand had planted them. They were Nature's work. Once upon a time this was a moss, a peat bog. Decades earlier, in an era when few knew or cared about the importance of preserving bogs, this one had been dug out and turned into the pond which fed this stream.

To be releasing beavers here, of all places on Argaty, had a special significance. On the pond's northern edge lay a collapsed heap of roofing tin and rotten timber, the corpse of a wildlife hide. It was here, back in the late 1990s, that the Argaty Red Kite project began. In the wake of the birds' arrival on the farm my parents began trailing enthusiastic birdwatching groups across field and hill, past stream and pond, to this quiet corner, where they stood waiting, sometimes for hours, for kites to dive for food on the distant hills. As time passed and the birds grew more accustomed to people's presence, we began to attract them to fields closer to the farm; a new hide was built, the old one forgotten. Nobody came here after that. It too had slipped from memory. Until today, the second week in February 2022. This afternoon our second beaver family was coming. Our latest step into the world of rewilding would be taken in the very place where our journey had begun.

More than once I'd come to reflect on the similarities between the arrival of the beavers and the coming of the kites. I remember when word escaped that those majestic raptors were back and hordes of birdwatchers descended on Argaty. There was an electricity in the air in those days. Something big was happening, change was afoot, and somehow our farm had ended up at the centre of it. I'd never had that feeling since. In truth I thought such moments came only once. But I was wrong, and glad to be so.

A thrill ran through me again as I gazed at the pond, imagining what would happen here in the days and years to come, as the beavers set about their work. I was thinking like them now. I had my eye in. To maintain a stable depth of water, they would dam. I knew it. I knew too that the main pond, well-wooded though it was, could hold them only so long. In time the wet woodland that overlooked its outflow would tempt them downstream. They would engineer their way through it, canalling, damming and harvesting willow as they went. My eyes followed that mud-black stream, watched it curl easily through the scrublands and off towards the farm below. Its life was set to change. Soon it would be made to sidestep fallen trees and vault dams in order to escape this place. Its lazy days were almost over.

Half a mile south of here our first beaver family had been busy on the home-improvement front. Much to our delight they'd moved permanently into our man-made lodge, plastering the entrance over with mud, loading the roof with sticks. In the process of building, they'd lopped the arms from several trees. Since Christmas they'd been hard at work on a particularly large one whose plentiful branches would only be reached when they brought the whole thing down. The kits provided free child labour, assisting their parents' slow assault on the trunk. They worked as a family, a cohesive unit. They could think their way around a problem too. When a new canal, dug along the base of an old dry-stone dyke, failed to hold water, those clever animals identified the source of the leak. We arrived one morning to find the wall caked in mud, preventing water from leaching out between the stones. Beavers are not easily defeated. Now watertight, this latest canal served as a further logging route. Within days they'd dismembered the trees that flanked it and floated the severed limbs home.

Other nocturnal creatures were now visiting the pond too. All around, on rocks and tree stumps, sat squiggled otter spraints. The tiny white bones within told of the death of many a small creature. In the times when beavers were sought after for their fur, hunters baited their trap lines with castoreum, the yellowy-brown substance that concentrates when urine passes through the animals' castor sacs. The sweet vanilla scent attracted the attention of the ever-territorial beavers, who believed another was in their space; it also drew other creatures in too, and trappers enjoyed huge amounts of bycatch. Clearly the perfume was no less attractive today than it had been then. In the dead of night, the otters came to roll and writhe in woodchips and beaver scent piles; from the sett on the hill, badgers appeared too, wandering past the piles then doubling back, entranced by the smell. All of this was caught on our trail cameras. The beavers were frequently filmed too. They passed, dragging branches three times their length. They stood on hind legs (tails functioning as a third prop) to gnaw bark from trees. They waterproofed their fur, sitting back to expose their cloaca (the orifice in which their anus, urethra and genital openings are found) and spreading anal gland secretions over their bodies with their hind feet. They also groomed one another, using their incisors and specially designed split nails (located on the second hind-foot toe) to comb parasites and debris from those hard-to-reach places on the coats of their kin. In every action their close familial bonds – so unusual in the rodent kingdom – were in evidence.

To have beavers on that pond was, and would always be, a delight, but if today's animals stuck, if they liked this spot and chose to stay, I knew that this would be the family we would follow more closely and come to know best. The first pond's banks were so flat that the only means of seeing what was happening in the water was to stand right beside it and risk spooking any wildlife swimming at our feet. Today's release pond was different. Here the steep banks rose in an amphitheatre. From our seats in the back row, we could watch the action below. The beavers would hardly know we were there.

The new arrivals would provide a welcome distraction from the wider world of beaver politics. Earlier that month, the national beaver strategy webinars had begun, and they'd resembled a family wedding gone wrong. One half of the room had been drunk and shouting, the other half staring at the floor pretending it wasn't happening. Much of the anger had come from the east Tayside farmers. Their feelings were understandable enough, and the near-total silence from the Scottish Government when asked how Holyrood planned to incentivise land managers to accommodate beavers had been infuriating. Aware that these people represented a small (if vocal) minority, and that beavers were not high on the public's list of concerns, it seemed the government had made few plans to help. Could anyone blame the farmers for being angry? Allowing conflicts to play out and one beaver in ten to be shot was clearly a more affordable option than actually dealing with the issues.

Over 50 stakeholders attended the meetings, many of them land managers and conservationists. Between those two disparate-seeming groups there was clear common ground to strive for: push for the aforementioned incentive scheme; enact a hierarchy of mitigation where culling remained on the table, but only as a last resort when non-lethal mitigation failed and translocation was deemed impossible. Most would have accepted that. Somehow this obvious-seeming solution became lost in all the anger and mistrust, obscured by spurious claims that beavers were reducing farm productivity to zero, by refusal to accept that so many animals living in the wild could not be excluded from the whole Tayside region, by fisheries managers' unsubstantiated accusations of beaver threats to salmon, and lichenologists' sinister insistence that 'exit strategies' would be required should beavers have unacceptable impacts upon existing biodiversity (which I took to mean that, even if they increased overall biodiversity, beavers should be moved or killed if they gnawed a tree upon which rare lichens grew. So much for bio-*diversity*).

Beneath everyone's fury lay an emotion that was much more human. Most in those meetings were surely afraid of something – the conservationists of imminent environmental collapse, lichenologists and anglers of the loss of their favoured species, farmers of enforced changes to a way of farming they'd known all their lives. Fear has a way of bringing tempers to the boil, of obscuring our vision so that we can no longer see the common ground. The International Union for Conservation of Nature (IUCN), who coordinated the meetings, would deserve huge credit for keeping sight of the goal and eventually producing a strategy coherent enough for everyone to sign up to.

Ultimately, as James Silvey (who represented RSPB Scotland at the meetings) would wisely conclude: 'Ten years ago who would have thought there would be a government-backed strategy saying we need *significant* expansion of the beaver range and population? My younger self would be calling that a win.'

He was quite right. That even NFUS and SLE had been added as signatories meant a great deal too. As with all things beaver-related, the pity was that progress only came after so much shouting.

Thank goodness for today's release, I thought. With beavers en route, who could be miserable?

That morning passed quickly. The BBC had come to film the action for the opening episode of the new *Landward* series.

Touring the first release pond, I showed presenter Arlene Stuart the canals, felled trees and the lodge, and discussed our reasons for bringing beavers here.

As with the first release, we had invited a small group of friends and supporters to join us. Present among them was the owner of the farm from which the animals had been translocated. Her experiences were sobering. When their beavers first arrived she had been excited, but when they bred and took up new territories they made life rather difficult. A newly planted woodland was heavily browsed, an essential livestock grazing field badly flooded. As a final coup de grâce, the beavers gnawed through an electricity pylon. Never let it be said that living with these animals is without its challenges. Stories like this showed how vital a measure translocation was as part of the mitigation toolkit.

Come one o'clock most of the day's guests had arrived, but two were still missing. Just as I began to worry that they'd got lost, a spaceship whir announced an electric car's approach.

'Here come the Trees for Life heroes,' called my mother.

Smiling bashfully, Steve Micklewright and Alan McDonnell crossed the car park and joined the waiting group.

Roisin arrived soon after and we made our way to the pond. Although nothing compared to the stormy conditions that preceded the first release, the previous day had brought sub-zero temperatures and an icy glaze lay on the water. The field beside the pond was also treacherously wet. (One day earlier, while manoeuvring an old pig arc which would serve as a makeshift lodge, the wheels of Dad's tractor had begun to spin. He'd come within a foot of plunging into the water and had had to be towed to safety.) Feet slipping on the slick surface, we heaved the beaver crates to the semi-frozen outflow stream, but when we drew back the doors some of the inmates were less than keen to re-enter society. One kit stole a glance at the frozen water and doubled back inside. Another took two steps across the bank then made a swift 180, heading directly towards those of us who stood behind the crates. Using the mesh door, veterinarian Romain Pizzi deftly ushered it back towards the pond. One animal refused to even leave its crate and had to be tipped into the water. One way or another, soon all were freed, but while the female and her three kits splashed and smashed delightedly through water and ice, the male seemed less than thrilled at our presence. Hovering in the shallows like an angry hippo, eyes, nose and ears exposed, everything else hidden below the surface, he glared and growled for several minutes before at last swimming off to join the others. This protectiveness would always be a part of his nature. With him for a father, the young would be safe.

After several minutes' swimming one kit took a dive and disappeared beneath the ice. When, minutes later, it had still not risen to the surface, my heart began to pick up pace. Clare, one of our volunteers, would later compare it to 'watching a film when someone is under water for so long that you realise you're also holding your breath'.

Adult beavers can remain submerged for a full 15 minutes, and the lung power of this youngster was impressive too. Eventually it crashed up through the ice and, neither panicked nor out of puff, resumed its tour of the pond.

Casting my gaze from right to left, from the beavers splashing happily around their new home to the delighted onlookers, a sense of sweet serenity washed over me. The feeling was shared by Steve, who was watching the scene unfold from the adjacent bank.

'When the cage door was lifted I thought, "Oh my God,"' he told me later. 'These goosebumps came up on my arm, and when I was watching the beavers swimming around, one of them came up really close and it really made me shed a tear, properly cry, because that was a moment when we could say: "Look at what we've done. We've managed to get beavers to a place where they weren't allowed before and we all did that . . . If it hadn't been for the Scottish Rewilding Alliance, most of us wouldn't have known each other. All these connections helped you to do it and will hopefully help to make the next proposals happen . . . It's just like dominoes, isn't it?"'

Already we'd heard rumours that other organisations were considering their options. James Silvey and his RSPB Scotland colleagues had reopened internal discussions on a translocation to their Loch Lomond reserve, Trees for Life hoped to move beavers to Glen Affric and an even bigger announcement lay just over the horizon. Just like dominoes? One could only hope.

'Have you seen beavers often before today?' I asked Steve as we walked back to the car park.

'Actually . . .' He gave an embarrassed laugh. 'This was my first time.'

'What?' I spluttered, disbelieving. 'But . . . you've done so much for them.'

'Ridiculous, isn't it?'

Though my first instinct was to agree with this assessment, I supposed that my own journey had been just as unusual. He'd taken a leap of faith, making a stand for an animal he'd never set eyes upon; I'd done so for an animal I'd seen just once. Looked at dispassionately, it was hard to see why either of us had acted as we had. Maybe we were both ridiculous. And yet, somehow it didn't feel that way.

Later that night Alan McDonnell would help me to understand why.

'It's not ridiculous because this isn't about beavers,' he wrote in reply to my message.

'What isn't?' I responded dumbly.

'This fight. Yes, on a superficial level this particular fight was about them, but aren't we really pushing for something bigger?'

Still the identity of this *something* would not reveal itself.

When I failed to reply he continued: 'We believe that rewilding is the answer. People and nature can work together at scale. That's powerful and it brings people together. I think that those involved with beavers believe that there's a way to make this happen. And if we have it conceptually, we can find ways to make it work practically.'

And just like that, in a few short sentences, he had identified the exact thing that linked me to him, and him to me, and both of us to the other protagonists in this story. People and nature working together at scale. This was the common cause, the tie that bound.

15

Shifting Baselines Back

At the head of the outflow stream a low muddy ridge had *appeared*. I can think of no better word to use than *appeared*. One day it wasn't there, the next it was, and somehow it blended into these surroundings so naturally that it seemed always to have been a part of them. As it grew taller, so the pond rose higher. The new beaver family had taken to their pond. Argaty had its first dam.

When viewed from upstream little about the construction arrested one's attention. It looked like nothing more than a lip of mud, lying an inch proud of the water. Seen from below, however, one realised the true majesty of the beavers' engineering. They had built against the trunk of a fallen tree and followed the natural curves of the pond. A ribcage of branches had been dug into the soil, angled to point from downstream to up. Stones of all sizes weighed the sticks down. As with all beaver building works, mud was the glue that held everything together. The result was a wall that wiggled a snakelike path around the pond's perimeter.*

Hard though I tried to think like a beaver, one element of their dam-building proved beyond my comprehension: why did they

---

*Each of the dams they'd go on to build would zigzag in this manner. The curves increased their surface area, which in turn increased their strength.

add recycled materials into the mix? Across the world all sorts of weird and wonderful objects had been found in dams, including beer bottles, cattle bones and a wooden leg. The additions here were more prosaic than prosthetic. Plastic tree tubes had been packed in at regular intervals, and on the dam's eastern edge a giant, tangled ball of old fencing wire (rotting strainer post still attached) had been heaped. What these objects added to the architecture was anyone's guess.

While most dams last less than a decade, by which point the beavers have often exhausted their food supplies and left the territory to regenerate and the dam to fall into disrepair, some remain in place for much longer. Typically ranging from 20 centimetres to three metres high, dams can be as tall as five metres. (The longest Eurasian beaver dam recorded, incidentally, was 265 metres.[27]) Gazing the length of this miraculous curving wall, I wondered how long it would last, how high it would grow, and what changes would occur while it continued to hold water.

The dam was not the only new addition to the surroundings. At the water's edge a mud and stick mound had been sculpted. To have built their lodge barely five metres from the artificial one we'd constructed was bad enough; to have also stripped most of the materials from ours was a real slap in the face. We forgave them their ingratitude. Theirs looked rather more homely than our straw-bale efforts.

As February turned to March our first beaver family finally succeeded in their mission. Two months after they'd begun gnawing at it, they brought the big tree down. Snow fell overnight and lay like a hospital bed sheet, pulled hurriedly over the tree's corpse. In the days that followed, the beavers raided what limbs they could reach from it.

The snows disappeared as quickly as they'd come, to be replaced by brilliant sunshine. Spring was upon us. Come the month's end, the air had begun to echo with the sound of croaking; water pulsed in the beaver-dug canals. A closer look revealed the source of both sound and movement. Below the surface an orgy was playing out. Legs and bodies twisted and tangled at impossible angles; lovers were locked in deadly strangleholds. The frogs had come to breed and this year they found rather more water in which to conduct their contortions. Soon herons began loitering, hoping to spear food. As lusty amphibians hurried to the party, and sex-spent ones departed it, kites and buzzards picked them off. Another guest had begun to frequent the area, too. One morning I saw a shadow bank sharply away through the woods. From its movement, the way it turned, so swift and low to the ground, I knew that creature even before I heard its voice. The previous summer, in a dark conifer plantation in Argaty's northern reaches, I had discovered the nest of Britain's most secretive raptor. As I'd walked that wood, another shadow had slipped away, a full-bodied shriek had filled the air. The memory of that movement and that sound had been seared in my mind ever since; from that moment on I would always know that creature.

Confirmation came as this bird put distance between itself and me and let out that now familiar scream. I had flushed a goshawk as it prowled the waters. Seeing both kite and hawk hunting over beaver ponds brought a lump to my throat. Such scenes would have been unimaginable only a few decades earlier, when all were extinct in Scotland. But here they were again today, sharing in each other's worlds, and to bear witness to that was like gazing through a window onto both the past and the future. For those brief seconds I thought I knew what this landscape used to be, and what it could be again if we can only continue to restore some wildness to it.

Sometimes my daughters accompanied me on my visits to the ponds. Rowan sat on the felled trees, gazing out over the water. We took Ellie's tiny hands and ran them over the contours of chewed stumps, feeling the places where beavers had set their teeth just a few hours earlier. To have those animals here will be as normal for my children as it is unfamiliar for my parents, Sarah and me. The term 'shifting-baseline syndrome', that 'gradual change in the accepted norms of the natural environment due to a lack of experience, memory and/or knowledge of its past condition' is seldom if ever used in a positive sense.[28] How could it be? In most places, in most of our lifetimes, the natural world has experienced nothing but death and decline. But when I explored the beaver wetlands with my girls, when we moved between the standing trees and the felled, when a shadow passed over the water and we looked up to see a kite soaring above, I thought that beavers could change our understanding of the term. With them back in our lives we might rewild our children and shift their baselines back, so they grow up knowing more nature than previous generations did. In such thoughts, the mind finds peace.

*

Peace of mind was something I sorely craved at that stage. For all that the beavers' works delighted me, in other respects I was less than settled.

There was a time when I believed that those of us who crave change do so because the world is broken and change is what it needs. However, I came to question this assumption at the same time as I realised an uncomfortable truth about myself: that I was happier when striving for a change than having achieved it. Today I wonder if the urge to shake things up might have less to do with the world being broken and rather more to do with something inside of us being so. Whatever the truth of it, the sense of restlessness which, for me, always followed the completion of a task seemed so much greater in this instance because the scale of the task had been greater than any I'd previously attempted and might prove greater than any I would attempt again.

Compounding this were other feelings that were as confused

as they were contradictory. On the one hand, I was struggling to make peace with the idea that our time in the limelight would soon come to an end. Others were bound to complete translocations and we would slip from view, becoming little more than a sentence in the beavers' story. On the other hand (as I reminded myself again and again) my ego was not what mattered here. This was about beavers. Rehoming as many as possible. Growing their population. The *whole point* of what we'd done was that others *should* follow. And here lay the real frustration, because when I looked around I did not see a queue of people waiting in the wings to take the stage.

Since the first release, perhaps in lieu of other translocation stories to tell, media interest in our project had remained steady. We had featured in newspapers and on radio, on domestic and foreign television. While the interviews differed in many respects, sooner or later the same question always reared its head:

'Why did you move beavers to your farm?'

Each time, I recycled the same three answers:

'Because we are in an environmental crisis.'

'Because they massively boost biodiversity.'

'Because they might have been shot otherwise.'

Each of these (somewhat predictable) replies was true. Each seemed to satisfy the interviewer. But when I took time to reflect I realised that none of them quite satisfied me.

The problem was not the question, which was a reasonable one to pose, but that it had to be asked at all. What that told me was that translocation was still light years away from becoming a normalised process that offered a viable alternative to killing.

James Nairne used to say that he'd retire from beaver advocacy once animals that might have been culled were rehomed instead. Having achieved that ambition he did not in fact put himself out to grass, but instead set his sights higher, swearing that he'd go once more were relocated than culled each year. Privately, I suspected he might be with us for some time yet; however, I fully understood why he'd changed the plan.

For all the progress we had made, beavers were far from safe. At that time an average of one in ten was still culled annually, and to make matters worse, nobody knew if they were being shot well and dying swiftly, or the very opposite. When issuing licences, NatureScot asked that cadavers be recovered for post-mortem examination, but, as an article by investigative journalism platform The Ferret would later reveal, since protection came into force the shooters had not handed in a single body. The reason given: that the animal was shot in deep, fast-flowing water and the body was unsafe to recover. With many beavers living in drainage ditches or slow-flowing side streams, this scarcely seemed credible, but nobody in power had challenged it. Were I in James's shoes, I couldn't have retired then either. So much remained to be done.

Establishing translocation as the go-to method for irresolvable conflicts was the key. But the issue we kept returning to was 'How to do it?' Although RSPB Scotland and Trees for Life hoped to relocate some, many more sites would be needed for the cull numbers to be significantly lowered. Everyone knew that suitable sites existed. An estimated 12 per cent of Scotland is publicly owned, managed on behalf of the Scottish people by the likes of Forestry and Land Scotland and NatureScot; 2.5 per cent is owned by charities and other third sector organisations.[29] The trouble was that those organisations were not coming forward to help.

The Scottish Rewilding Alliance went back to work. We wrote pointed letters to public land managers, asking what they intended to do to help relocate beavers; primed friendly politicians and journalists, asking them to dig into the matter; Steve and I penned editorials on the subject. But it was to no avail. Those organisations refused to be drawn.

Often, during those frustrating times, I would revisit that frequently asked question: 'Why did you move beavers to your farm?'

How tired I was of answering it. How I wished that, just once, an interviewer would delve deeper and ask the more pertinent question: 'Why are beavers killed in Scotland?'

I would avoid giving the obvious answer – 'They are killed when they cause unmanageable impacts on Prime Agricultural Land' – for this explanation only told part of the story. Beneath the surface lay the more unsettling truth. Beavers were killed because, over and over again, the Scottish Government and the organisations we trusted to protect Scotland's nature were letting them down.

In an environmental crisis, the question was not why we had re-homed beavers. It never had been. The question was why others hadn't.

And here I found a final reason for disquiet. Those who had fought for beavers had done so because they saw no option, because nobody else would. It should not have been this way. Beavers' future ought not to have been reliant upon so tiny a handful of determined individuals. The line that divided survival from death was terrifyingly thin. If these people had not drawn it, there would be no line at all.

*

Weeks passed, spring sped towards summer and a change came over the mother of our second family. Each afternoon, in broad daylight, she left the lodge, lumbered onto the bank and gobbled every single carrot we had laid out. By early evening, when the rest of the family emerged, all the food was gone.

'It's odd,' I told Roisin. 'She's out at 4 p.m. every single day.'

'Set your trail camera low to the ground,' she advised.

'Why?'

'Do it,' she said cryptically. 'You'll see.'

I did it; I saw. Mother beaver heaved her bulk from the pond and moved with purpose towards the carrots. Passing the camera, four teats shaped like swollen thumbs came into view. Mother beaver was heavily pregnant.

Beavers living in northern latitudes can mate between December and May, but sexual activity tends to peak between January and late February.[30] Doing the maths, I realised that she may have been in the early stages when she arrived here. In the weeks that followed, she continued to appear early for dinner. As their reproductive organs are hidden inside the cloaca, for most of the year male and female beavers are indistinguishable, but during pregnancy and lactation the swollen teats and the insatiable appetite always reveal the mother's gender.

Summer arrived. Snowy speckles appeared in the water as the trees cast their catkins. They built up like lint in the coat of the beaver mother as she swam, long branches grasped in her mouth, and plunged into the lodge with them. A series of special adaptations allow beavers to make these dives without swallowing water. They have a second layer of lips behind their incisors which they can close even while the outer set is open. By holding the back of their tongues against the palate, they create a seal across their mouths too. Like humans they also have a flap of tissue known as an epiglottis, which forms a further barrier preventing the things they swallow from entering their lungs. Unlike in humans, the beavers' epiglottis is located at the back of the nose.

Following a gestation period of three and a half months, beavers tend to give birth between May and June. The young weigh between 500g and 550g on average, and they are quick developers, being born thickly furred and becoming mobile within a few hours. As they grow, they make early attempts at swimming, but their coats are not yet water-repellent and they cannot yet close off their nostrils or ears to prevent them from ingesting water. These limitations mean that an adult or sub-adult must be on hand to babysit and usher the adventurous youngsters back to land.

Watching the mother dive towards the lodge, we wondered what was happening within the walls of her home. Were the babies in there, being watched over by their father or older siblings as all awaited her return? And if so, how many were there? The average litter size is between two and four, but six-child families are not unknown. Although kits depend on their mothers' milk for the first three months of life, they can eat vegetation from a few days old. Was the mother gathering wood for herself or for her hungry young? The wait for answers was agonising.

In June there came two exciting pieces of news. First, the Cairngorms National Park Authority committed to lead on translocating beavers to the Scottish Highlands. Then, days later, RSPB Scotland announced their desire to relocate animals to their Loch Lomond reserve. The first dominos were lined up. How I hoped they would fall.

*

That month we released a sub-adult beaver pair onto the last of our licensed ponds. The young female went out first; the male arrived a fortnight later. Of all the translocations, these were perhaps my favourites for the simple reason that, with Ellie in nursery, Sarah was at long last able to join us for them. Thanks to a school in-service day, Rowan was there when we released the male too. What a joy it was to drive to the pond, open the crates and, with no crowds and no television cameras, just my girls, parents and a couple of friends, simply turn the beavers loose. Much as I'd loved the sense of occasion that surrounded the first two releases, the lack of ceremony added a suitable air of finality to these last ones. For us at least, translocation had become normalised; when a beaver was in trouble and had to be moved to a new home, this was just what you did.

With that translocation completed we had fulfilled the terms of our licence. Our job was done, our chapter in their reintroduction story seemed complete. We closed that book for what we imagined would be the last time.

16

Drought

The summer of 2022 brought Europe's worst drought for 500 years. Temperatures soared, the sky refused to rain. On the continent, yields of crops such as soybean, sunflower and maize fell to 9 per cent below average due to water and heat stress. Satellite studies warned that Europe had been experiencing drought since 2018 and its water situation had become precarious. Energy shortages worsened due to a lack of cooling water for nuclear power plants and insufficient flows for hydroelectric plants. There were 25,000 grass and wildfires in England alone, while in Scotland firefighters were called to over 1,400 blazes involving grass, woodland and crops. East Tayside farmers, known for their desire to remove beavers from their land, complained of reduced potato yields due to a lack of irrigation. ('With no apparent irony,' wrote James Nairne, sending me a screengrab of one farmer's tweet. 'If only they had a semi-aquatic rodent known for impounding water,' I replied.) The climate was breaking down before our eyes.

On Argaty the impact of the heatwave, which experts claimed had been made ten times more likely by climate change, was plain to see. A fever had struck the land. Streams that had raged in the winter slowed to a trickle, ponds ran dry, the grass turned a jaundiced shade of yellow.

While the first and third beaver ponds were deep enough to

withstand some evaporation, we had no such confidence in the second one. Its level continued to drop, the water turned a rank shade of stale hot-chocolate brown; the pond was fast becoming a puddle. Several burrows became visible on the banks. Now we knew where the beavers disappeared to for lengthy spells each night. Around their territories, beavers maintain a number of these bolt holes where they'll hide when they suspect danger. They were neither hidden nor safe now. For the time being, the entrance tunnels to their lodge remained submerged. When they too came into view, I was sure that the beaver family would go. They would travel south over parched fields, along the rocky beds that marked the death places of former streams until they met the river, the only water that still flowed in the area. After all of the effort of getting them here, we would lose them. My stomach twisted horribly when I considered the prospect.

But the beavers had other ideas. Their bond with these fast-vanishing waters was strong and they had no intention of leaving them.

'What on earth are they doing?' we wondered aloud, watching them dive headfirst, bums and tails shaking in some ungainly approximation of a handstand.

As always, their rationale became clear only in hindsight. Pushing with their powerful forearms, they dredged the floor of the pond, piling up heaps of mud, which protruded from the surface like hilltops seen above a layer of clouds. Around the base of these mounds ran a network of canals. Some passed right through the pond's middle, but most of those Venetian highways followed its perimeter. Again, we saw their logic: should they sense danger while on land, one small step would take them to the safety of deep water. Just as glaciers once shaped Scotland's landscape, beavers had created mountain ranges and hanging valleys, corries and glens. In their own way they were every bit as much a force of nature as those sheets of ice had once been.

Further rainless weeks passed, ponds without beavers evaporated to nothing, but this one held water. The beaver-sculpted landscape became an oasis in the desert, the sole green place in a landscape of deathly yellow. Mushroom clouds of midges exploded from the waters. Vegetation took hold, the mud piles began to green up, grey wagtails hopped between them, grubbing for insects. Love-locked dragon and damselflies drifted towards them too. Stuck together in post-coital ecstasy, the male grasping the female by the neck, they landed on the beaver islands and laid hundreds of eggs upon them.

The benefits were felt below the dam too. We learned as much from Stirling University's Alan Law and Nigel Willby, who had installed temperature loggers in various streams around the farm. In beaver-free areas their readings resembled a cardiogram of a heart attack. Huge spikes in the heat of the day were followed by crashing dips at night. The logger placed below the beaver dam told a different story. As we all know, a full pan of water will take longer to reach a boil than one that is half-empty. Because the beavers had created a deep reservoir when they'd first blocked the outflow, because they'd further deepened the pond through their dredging, the sun could do little to warm it. A cool, steady flow seeped downstream. The temperature did not spike and it did not crash. Crucially, it remained below twenty degrees Celsius, the critical limit for various wildlife species.

All summer long the beavers regulated those water supplies. They created a refuge and nature flocked to it. Through that harshest of periods, that premonition of the harder times that will come, they were the difference between survival and death.

*

When, in 1998, a pair of red kites nested on Argaty, a moment of history was made. Their two chicks were the first young kites to fly a nest in Central Scotland for over a century. A century... To my then 15-year-old self, such a timeframe had seemed unimaginably vast. But my sense of scale would change shortly after midnight on 3 July 2022.

My trail camera was well positioned. It caught the exact moment that two perfect little beaver kits emerged from their lodge and clambered onto the bank to join their parents and older siblings.

How long had it been since a baby beaver was born to these waters? Four hundred years? Perhaps longer. The significance of what is playing out in twenty-first century Scotland, as beavers return across this country, recolonising these lost lands, is so great that we may never be able to step back far enough to appreciate its enormity.

'I could cry,' wrote Roisin when I sent her further videos of the kits firing off through the water with all the speed and coordination of an untied balloon.

How many people saw this tender side to her? In her work she prided herself on never being hysterical, in always giving rational, evidence-based advice. When all around her were shouting the odds, Roisin could be relied upon to remain calm. Inside I knew that she felt the strain more than anyone. Most people could not do what she did – wading waist-deep in ditches to unblock dams and prevent fields from flooding, trapping animals and driving through the night to move them to the safety of English enclosures, recovering the bodies of shot beavers. Most could not face what she faced.

For many months I'd been holding tight to a question, waiting for the moment to ask it. Roisin had a good heart, but her external toughness meant that probing, personal questions could only be asked at certain times, when conversation drifted naturally in that direction.

'Wanted to ask you something,' I wrote, having sent her another baby beaver video to soften her up. 'What is it about these animals that makes you do this?'

'You're going to crack my hard exterior ...' she answered, by way of forewarning. And then in a moment of utterly unguarded sincerity she added: 'They endlessly fascinate me and when I look them in the eyes I can't do anything other than try.'

From that moment, I felt I understood her better than I ever had before.

Since the first beaver family had arrived we had been overwhelmed by requests from people wishing to visit them. They had to be allowed time to settle, though. What fools we'd have felt had we opened our doors too soon and scared them off. With this in mind we'd politely declined every request. Now that the kits were safely out of the lodge and enjoying their first taste of the wild, we took the plunge and began running tours. They sold out within minutes.

On each evening tour an arrow shape, moving across the water as a skein of geese moves across the sky, would announce the arrival of the adults or sub-adults. We watched that arrow, waiting for a slick-furred head to appear. With their impressive lung capacity and their nictitating membranes (third, translucent eyelids), beavers are designed to spend long spells under water. In our early tours they avoided us studiously, diving and disappearing, only surfacing for air once they'd swum far beyond the place where we sat. Beavers use their tails as an aid when swimming, for balance when they rear on their hind feet and as a fat storage depot (by the end of winter, when food supplies have been scarce for months, the tail will be noticeably thinner than in spring and summer). But by far the most dramatic of the tail's functions is to fire a warning shot when an intruder enters a beaver's territory. In a swift motion the animals kick their legs back, creating a vacuum in the water. Then they bring their tails crashing down to fill it. The action sent a warning to us: 'I'm a big powerful animal, I've sniffed you out and I'm ready to defend myself.' It sent a message to family members too: 'Dive for cover. Wait for danger to pass.' This behaviour is known as tail slapping, though the word 'slap' did not do it justice. When the adults slapped, it was as though a boulder had been thrown into the water. During those first tours we grew quite used to the sound.

Soon they overcame their wariness. The slapping ceased, they spent less time submerged, more time swimming on the surface. We appeared to have been accepted as a benign part of their environment. I confess to feeling very moved by that. That these animals – trapped and removed from their home, relocated to this foreign place – could allow people back into their lives, when so many people refused to accept them in return, seemed incredibly poignant.

The kits shook me from my sorrows. Never once did they evince any wariness of us, or of anything else, for that matter. They whizzed past in full sight, pushed on not just by their webbed hind feet but also their tails, which they used as a propeller. They lost their footing and fell into the pond constantly, thrashing about like cats struggling to escape a hot bath. They harried their poor mother for milk, chasing her across water and land. By now she was heartily fed up of breastfeeding. The young had inflicted many injuries as they fed from her and she had had enough. When a few throaty growls failed to deter them from begging she raised a branch in her teeth, swung it and pitched them into the cold depths.

'You could get arrested for parenting like that,' one visitor remarked.

'Doesn't necessarily make it wrong!' another replied.

How those kits delighted us on those mild midsummer nights.

Soon after their arrival, another wild and hairy beast descended upon Argaty. Derek Gow was back in Scotland, promoting his new book, *Birds, Beasts & Bedlam*. To a sold-out audience he delivered a wonderfully punchy, humorous, expletive-ridden presentation in our visitor centre.

Later that night we sat down at my kitchen table with a bottle of gin and not enough tonic and traded stories. We spoke again of the loneliness of the rewilder's life, of the difficulties of fighting organisations much larger than you will ever be, of the fear that any small victory one achieved would not be enough, that the environment would continue to collapse and all of our efforts might be in vain.

'At least you know you've tried,' I said. 'That counts for something.'

As the night wore on and the drink took hold, a question that had been circling my thoughts, half-formed, found its way onto my tongue.

'Derek,' I said. 'When you look at the things you've done, the life you've led, how do you weigh it up? Would you say it's given more than it's taken from you?'

He furrowed his brow, then just as quickly unfurrowed it, his expression suggesting that the question had never occurred to him, and now that it had, he considered it to be of little consequence.

'I don't know.' He shrugged. 'I guess it just becomes something that you do.'

I nodded, mentally filing the answer away for future reference. Soon Ellie began crying for her bottle of milk. I bade him goodnight and made my way upstairs.

When I woke the next morning my first thought was of that question. Should anyone ever put it to me, I had no idea what I might say in reply.

17

Bamff

Questions of give and take, credit and debit, would come to dominate my thoughts in the days and weeks that followed. In those times I was a combustible combination of hope and arrogance, hurt and dismay; proud to have done as we had, appalled at what it had taken to do it. Was I up or down? I couldn't say and there seemed little hope of finding an answer simply by ruminating alone. I had to discover how others, who'd faced much greater adversity, had come to terms with their journeys.

Identifying those people was easier than you might imagine. I was seeking prominent individuals, known advocates of species or causes. While they could work for an organisation, they had also to stand apart from the crowd somehow. If we are honest, most of us are drawn to the mavericks in this world, and perhaps this influenced my selection. However, it struck me too that the more solitary someone seemed, the less of a team they had around them, the more likely they were to have felt the true extremes of life's highs and lows. As my tale was about the reintroduction of a polarising species, I decided (initially, at least) that my interviewees would have to have experience in that line of work. (This proved too limiting a stipulation, however, because Scotland had seen so few reintroductions of this sort. So, I broadened my search to include people who worked in contentious areas of ecological restoration.) This being a story about rewilding in Scotland, I chose to discount anyone not working in this country. To avoid repetition, I also ruled out those I'd interviewed elsewhere in this or my previous book...

On I went, sifting through prospective interviewees, whittling my shortlist down until only a handful of candidates remained. Not all of them were associated with beavers, but in a book about these animals, it made sense to begin with the one family who categorically were.

And so I headed north, to Alyth on the edge of the Scottish Highlands, where I would meet the people most synonymous with beaver reintroduction. In that corner of Perthshire, I hoped to find answers.

*

To drive the roads that lead towards Bamff estate was to enter a different Scotland to the one I knew. Though familiarity might have been found in the surrounding hills, which do not look so different to those that circle Argaty, arable production dominates much of the low ground. Somehow it seemed impossible to believe that in the midst of this agricultural intensity, beavers were to be found.

Keen to see what a farm might look like when the animals had been present for two decades, my mother had joined me for the trip. Having passed through the town of Alyth, we met our first Bamff road sign, a charming hand-drawn logo in which the estate name was surrounded by a ring of trees, beavers and wild boar.

Birch scrub, broom and some impressive standing deadwood lined the roadside as we made our way up the drive.

According to local legend, in 1232 a doctor by the name of Neish Ramsay removed a hairball from the stomach of King Alexander II, brewing a potion made from a white snake and saving his life; in thanks, the doctor was given Bamff. Today, nearly eight centuries on, the estate remains home to his descendants.

Louise Ramsay and her daughter Sophie were waiting at the door of an imposing tower house as we pulled up. While we stood making introductions and I tried, without success, to count the building's many windows, Louise's husband Paul also appeared at the door.

'I'm afraid I won't be joining you,' he said, gesturing to a heavily bandaged toe on his sandalled foot. 'Just an infection,' he added, noting our concerned expressions. 'Although at first I feared it might be gout . . . I was terribly worried I'd have to stop drinking wine.'

Led by Louise and Sophie, we headed away from the house, into the former-fields which lay opposite. With all its modern agricultural connotations, the word 'field' was, I realised, no longer an appropriate descriptor. Fields they may once have been; now they were wild land. The previous year the Ramsays had launched a crowdfunding campaign, hoping to raise enough through donations to rewild over 450 of Bamff's 1,300 acres. In the end they raised more than £42,000 pounds, enough to tear down internal fences and to repair and reinstate perimeter ones, to sow wildflowers and plant trees, to install osprey platforms and erect barn owl nest boxes. Into this area cows, pigs and ponies would roam. The land would be free to march to its own beat, to become whatsoever it wished. The Bamff Wildland project began.

Bamff was now in the first stages of change. The ground was clumped with thistles. Chicory ragwort was emerging. The occasional snuffle mark showed that pigs had passed through, though today the animals were nowhere in sight.

An old drainage ditch cut across the middle of the former-field and here we caught our first clue as to the presence of the estate's most famous residents. Midway along the stream, half hidden amongst grass and cow parsley, lay a felled tree. Age had darkened it, vegetation had long since covered the woodchips that must once have gathered around its roots, but the pencil-point shapes of the stump and trunk left no doubt as to the lumberjack's identity.

Further downstream, lesser spearwort was growing through a rusty cage in which a plastic pipe was housed. This was, I realised after several seconds' deliberation, an early incarnation of a flow device, designed to drain a dammed pool.

'Why the device?' I asked. 'Were they flooding the fields?'

'No,' Louise said. 'We were just trialling new mitigation measures to establish what did and didn't work.'

The word 'new' gave me pause for thought. Flow devices had long since become standard tools in the mitigation arsenal. The prototype that sat redundant before us was a powerful reminder that the Ramsays had been true pioneers when they first brought beavers to Bamff.

While Mum and Louise stopped to examine some wildflowers, Sophie and I fell into step and conversation turned to the animals.

'How did your parents become involved in this?' I asked.

It began, she explained, with a group of leading conservationists, among them Roy Dennis, John Lister-Kaye and Paul, who wished to establish a project to demonstrate beaver benefits in a Scottish context. For his part, Paul had been obsessed with the animals since attending a lecture on them in 1996; from that time on, he'd been determined to see them back in Scotland.

At the same time as his fascination with beavers was developing, SNH were also studying the possibility of a reintroduction, but lobbying soon slowed their efforts to a near-standstill.

'I think people grew tired of waiting for them,' Sophie said. 'They wished to make progress and, to Dad's delight, Bamff came out as being the most suitable site.'

Sophie was home from university on the fateful day in 2002 when the first animals arrived. Her father had driven through the night to collect them from a site in Kent and bring them back to Bamff. Sophie watched as the two beavers were released into a fenced pond, little knowing how others of this species would go on to impact her life. That first pair did not last long. One perished as a result of a parasite, while the other died having felled a tree onto itself. More were sourced, however, and these stood the test of time. Soon they started to breed and Paul began running evening tours, teaching visitors about their history and ecology.

For some time after the release, all remained calm, but as is nature's way, the young beavers sought to disperse. At some stage, perhaps 2006 – nobody was quite sure – they escaped their enclosure.

'We didn't purposefully let them out – definitely not,' Louise had told the *Daily Mail* in a 2017 article. 'But I think later it became difficult to keep them enclosed because the numbers were going up. We also had three very wet winters, so there will have been escapes.'

Those escapees' direction of travel was to be ours too. Leaving the Wildland former-fields behind, we followed the water as it passed beneath the Bamff driveway and emerged on the far side. A sign marked 'Cateran Trail' directed us down a narrow footpath. Here we entered the world of the beavers.

To our left stretched a series of long pools, each one bookended by a dam. Although the UK was enduring its worst drought period since 1976, you wouldn't have known it to look at Bamff. Thanks to the dams, the water level remained so high that even in this, the driest of summers, Louise could still swim in the pools. A few feet inside the first dam stood a drowned tree, its position giving an indication of just how much the beavers had raised the water table. In the crook between branch and trunk a tiny rowan had sprouted, its seed perhaps deposited there in the droppings of a passing bird. On the other side of the path, scrub was developing at an impressive rate.

'We cleared rhododendrons here with help from volunteers,' Louise said. 'The birch regeneration has been incredible. I'm sure the beavers have helped. That dam' – she pointed to the next beaver-built wall – 'has kept a stable, high water level, helping the mycorrhizae* in the surrounding soil.'

The lush collage of green on green which surrounded us was totally at odds with the wilted yellows currently on display across most of the Scottish countryside. A 2020 study from the western United States showed that beaver wetlands provided an important refuge for plants and animals during wildfires: the ground and surrounding vegetation was too damp to burn. The raised water table kept plants hydrated and the fire chose the path of least resistance, moving around the wetlands entirely.[31] Although Britain has historically been known for its temperate climate, drought summers turn the land to tinder, increasing the chances of fires breaking out. In the not-too-distant future, we may rely on nature's firefighter, the beaver, every bit as much as other parts of the world already do.

Gazing around, revelling in the incredible colour, a sigh of relief escaped my lips. Though I'd told nobody this, in a far corner of my mind I'd been afraid to see Bamff. When I'd first been put in contact with Sophie several years earlier and she had extended an invitation to visit, I had demurred, afraid that I'd see a terrifying vision of what Argaty might become – some treeless waterworld where nature had seized control. Now, I realised that I'd had nothing to fear. This series of pools and dams, of old trees and young, living and dead, was no threat, it was simply very . . .

'Beautiful,' Louise said, concluding my unspoken sentence. 'Isn't it?'

'Definitely,' I agreed. 'Would you say beavers have changed your outlook on life?'

---

* According to the *Encyclopaedia of Microbiology*, 'mycorrhizae are the symbiotic association between plant roots and fungi. Their major role is to enhance nutrient and water uptake by the host plant by exploiting a larger volume of soil than roots alone can do.'

'They forced us to give up control,' Sophie said. 'Their landscape plays with your memory because there's so little time to hold onto it before it changes again. I found myself realising I had to change inside, and that changing was actually a relief. You never are completely in control anyway. When you realise that, you can let go and welcome this new world of possibilities.'

My eyes roamed across our surroundings, taking in the rich greens of grass and plants, the standing deadwood, the coppiced trees which rang with the sound of birdsong. At every turn was evidence of the world of possibilities that she had described. Argaty was not there yet. Only in years to come would our home look as the Ramsays' did. Their today was our tomorrow, their present our future, and the thought of relinquishing control, allowing it to become this, brought only excitement.

A sparrowhawk piped angrily from an adjacent wood as we took a seat on a felled tree beside the last in the series of ponds and discussed a dark chapter in the Ramsays' beaver story.

While keeping those first animals in a secure enclosure did not require a licence, releasing them into the wild without one was considered a criminal act. When a beaver gnawed a gatepost at a house near Alyth, the police turned up at Bamff. Paul was arrested under suspicion of a deliberate and illegal release.

'It must have been awful for you,' I said.

Louise brushed this off with a defiant laugh. 'My brother, who'd often dealt with legal matters through his work as a building surveyor, kept saying it would be fine. They wouldn't press charges. Paul was too old. The worst he'd get was a fine that he wouldn't pay. Besides' – she gave me a grin made of pure mischief – 'if they had put him in prison there'd have been a mass outcry, and we needed a martyr for the cause!'

Paul was ultimately released without charge when he pointed out that nobody could prove that the animals swimming *outside* his fence had come from *within* it. Nonetheless, certain reputations stick. Throughout my consultations and again during the strategy meetings, I'd noticed how land managers and their representatives clung to the idea that beavers had returned to Scotland through planned, illegal releases. Questions about the 2001 Comrie wildlife park escape always seemed to fall upon deaf ears. Even NatureScot seemed not to hear them. For many parties, the Ramsay narrative would always be the chosen truth; Paul and Louise would always be the ones responsible for first reintroducing beavers.

This made little sense to me. True, the Bamff beavers may have *added* to the population and some farmers were bound to feel angry about that. When your land has been impacted by beavers, what difference does it make if someone deliberately released them or failed to keep them in? However, the point remained that, thanks to the earlier escapes, Scotland would have beavers anyway. Why then did the Ramsays get *all* the blame? I remembered putting this very point to James Nairne as we travelled back from that first Scottish Rewilding Alliance meeting all those months ago.

'I put it down to a number of reasons,' he'd replied. 'Apparently the wildlife park denied the first breakouts. Another landowner who had them and also suffered escapes kept his head down and stayed quiet too. And then you had Paul and Louise, who had this well-known demonstration project and really got in the faces of SNH and the Scottish Government as they tried to eradicate the Tay beavers. Because they were brave and stuck their heads above the parapet, I think they became easy scapegoats.'

Making our way back towards Bamff House, Louise detailed some of the troubles they'd experienced as that narrative gained traction. At a friend's funeral, an angry farmer had accosted her. When floods rampaged through Alyth in 2015, wiping out two footbridges, severely affecting shops, the hotel and a hundred homes, some locals were quick to blame beavers. They claimed that dams upstream had breached, releasing wood and debris which collided with and took out the bridges.* But the most painful consequence of bringing beavers to Bamff was how people Louise had once considered friends turned away from her.

'I'm a highly sociable person,' she said. 'We had quite a few friends in the area. And then I started to notice that invitations were dropping off. I'd hear that people had got together and we hadn't been invited ... I found that very hard.'

Though she still wore a smile, it had pulled a little tighter and no longer carried to her eyes. For the first and only time during that visit, I saw a vulnerability in her.

Where you stand on the morality of this history will perhaps be defined by what keeps you awake at night. If you believe that the sixth mass extinction is not something invented by woke scientists intent on spoiling everyone's fun but in fact the greatest threat our planet faces ... If you believe that ecosystems are collapsing and the world as we know it is slipping through our fingers ... If you believe that beavers can help reverse these losses, but the only means of restoring these allies across Britain was via unauthorised releases and escapes ... If you believe each of these things, then you will find it hard to criticise those who, wittingly or otherwise, made beavers' return possible.

Many people now believed exactly this, and in recent times the dial had swung in the other direction for the Ramsays. Where once they were castigated for their part in the reintroduction story, now more and more people applauded them for it. Attitudes towards beavers had also changed as public appreciation of their ecosystem engineering had grown.

'Your article in *The Scotsman* was an example of that,' Louise said, referring to an opinion piece I had written criticising public land managers for failing to offer sites for translocations.

---

*We should note that no evidence was provided to substantiate this, and the dams remained in place throughout the floods.

'There was a time, not long ago,' she continued, 'when the idea of *The Scotsman* publishing anything pro-beaver would have been unthinkable. We did enjoy the article, by the way. Paul and I are growing too old and tired for this fight. You've rather taken the torch.'

'I don't see either of you growing too old for the fight,' I said, deflecting the compliment.

We were nearing the house now; soon we would be surrounded by people and the opportunity to steer conversation in certain directions would vanish. This seemed like the best and last chance to ask the question that was still driving me to distraction.

'When you look back on your life since the beavers came, and weigh up the positives and negatives, would you say that rewilding has given you more than it's taken away?'

'God, yes,' she said without hesitation. 'We've made so many friends through this. The beavers brought so many people into our lives ... but what would your answer be?'

I had none to give. I was too close to events to have any sense of perspective.

Ten minutes later I found myself at the head of a large table, deep in conversation with people I'd never met before, most of whose names I hadn't caught. Not that it appeared to matter. Names seemed like the sort of dull formality that had been dispensed with in this place. I'd heard it said often that Bamff was something of a commune. Sitting there talking so freely on beavers, rewilding and the environment while children flitted through the sunlit room, I understood why. Several seats away Paul was regaling Mum with stories from beaverdom. Sophie's brother, Adam, stood over the stove, ladling portions of curry into bowls.

'When Adam's home, he makes sure everyone is well fed,' said Sophie, dashing through the room in pursuit of her daughter,

Flora (who'd passed this way with a group of other children moments earlier).

Just as a beaver wetland is alive with colour and joy, so too was this table. To glance at this scene was to know, instantly, what Louise had meant when she said that beavers had brought people into their lives.

To my left, Adam's wife Juliet excused herself and I moved seats to join in Paul and Mum's conversation. He was reclining in his chair, reminiscing about a time when a father and his young daughter had visited Bamff. The girl had been obsessed with beavers, but had never seen one in the flesh before.

'One swam right by us,' said Paul. 'The girl squealed with happiness and leapt into her father's arms.'

The emotion of that memory had seeped into his voice. For a second, I thought he might cry. But then an explosion of laughter erupted from the far end of the table, the children came crashing through the room again, and when my eyes returned to Paul, I saw that the moment of unguarded sincerity had passed; he was smiling serenely. From being arrested, to being shunned by society and forever targeted as the sole source of Scotland's beavers, Paul and Louise knew what it meant to suffer for the cause. But it had not broken them. Beavers had brought people into their lives, and those people had brought happiness. Although the Ramsays had seen both sides of rewilding, the light and the dark, they had endured.

18

Different Species, Same Story? Sleepless Nights and Worry on Eagle Island

A glorious late summer sun lit the waters of Loch Lubnaig. Glen Ogle's disused railway viaducts and the peaks of Ben More and Ben Lui gazed benevolently down on me. Throughout the journey to the Oban ferry terminal a grin remained fixed upon my face. Soon I would be on Mull, the home of one of Scotland's greatest rewilding success stories. After this brief drive and even briefer Caledonian MacBrayne journey I would be there, immersed in it all.

The realisation that most of my friends and family considered this trip to be something of a skive rather than a serious work trip tickled me.

'Why Mull?' they'd demanded to know. 'Are there beavers there?'

'No,' I'd said simply.

No evidence of historical beaver presence has ever been uncovered from the Scottish islands.

'What then?'

'Eagles,' I'd replied, chuckling at their looks of confusion. 'Eagles and David Sexton.'

The truth was that, for the first time in many, many months, beavers were not at the forefront of my thinking. Yes, those two words, give and take, were still lingering. However now, like commuters running for a last train, other questions had also forced their way into my head.

Why was it so hard to move beavers a few miles?

Why was there such opposition?

But as I boarded the ferry, it was a bigger question that dominated my thoughts: Had the conflict I'd unwittingly stepped into been specific to beavers, or was it something that every rewilding project, and every rewilder, had to face? That final unknown was what took me to Mull.

Sitting on the ferry's outdoor deck, I was struck by both the range of accents and the array of Gore-Tex hiking gear on display. According to RSPB Scotland between £4.9 million and £8 million of annual tourist spending on the Inner Hebridean island was inspired by white-tailed sea eagles. Had I been a betting man, I'd have laid money on most of my fellow passengers being eagle tourists.

White-tailed sea eagles were once present across Britain, from coastal areas to inland rivers and marshlands, but habitat loss and human persecution had pushed them into extinction south of the border by 1800. As sheep numbers in Scotland increased, attitudes towards these predators hardened and bounties were paid for their destruction. In 1918 the last known surviving bird was shot on the cliffs of Shetland.

Early unsuccessful reintroduction attempts were made in the 1950s and again in 1968. Of the many invaluable lessons learned, the most important was that a large number of young eagles would have to be released over a lengthy timespan in order to create a sustainable founder population. Between 1975 and 1985, 82 birds were brought from nests in Norway, flown to Scotland and eventually released from aviaries on the Isle of Rum. Further reintroductions in Wester Ross and Fife helped to bolster the population and in recent years numbers have grown remarkably. As of 2022 there were approximately 150 breeding pairs in Scotland. At the current rate of growth, by 2040 we may have 700 pairs established.

These numbers are highly encouraging. White-tailed eagles, or *iolaire súil na gréine* (the eagle with the sunlit eye), as they are known in Gaelic, are apex predators which bring balance to the food chain. They control numbers and influence behaviours of prey species, often suppressing the amount of mid-level predators in turn. By carrying food gathered at sea and sometimes travelling several hundred kilometres to nest sites, they can also play an invaluable role cycling nutrients between aquatic and terrestrial landscapes. These are but a few examples of the ecological roles they fulfil. How much damage did their removal do to our countryside? How many vital services were lost? One shudders to think.

The ferry pushed determinedly on towards Mull. Salt breeze clawing my face, I stood gripping the rail, gazing out as the island loomed larger. Its hills rose up to meet us. Houses nestled in their crooks and corries. Young and old woodland stretched down to seaweed and pebble beaches. By Hebridean standards Mull, with its 300 miles of coastline, is big. Big hills, big sea lochs. And, of course, big birds. Tomorrow I would see the biggest of them and meet one of their greatest champions.

*

David Sexton stood on the northern shore of Loch Na Keal, his back to the water. On the far bank, the broad shelf of the Ben More mountain range reared up as if ready for a fight, but then had second thoughts and sloped away until it disappeared from sight. A curlew blew a tremulous whistle from the rocky beach beside us. In the distance a tone-deaf chorus of ravens, Canada geese and hooded crows cronked and honked in monotones, their calls frequently interrupted by the many cars and campervans that passed on the nearby B-road. In this whole scene only one figure remained impassive. Perched in an anonymous spruce tree high in the hills above was a white-tailed eagle.

'So, what brings you to Mull, Tom?' David asked, lowering his binoculars and turning to me.

I explained that I was writing a book on beavers and the human side of rewilding, and if he thought it strange that I had come to him and this markedly beaver-free island, he hid it better than my friends or family had.

By way of further clarification, I listed some of the questions that had been troubling me, and in conclusion said, '... and I wondered if it's the same for everyone, regardless of what species they're trying to restore.'

'A case of different species, same story?' he asked.

'Exactly! So, I'm travelling around meeting people – people like you – to learn about their work and experiences.'

He nodded and in the minutes that followed we discussed his background. Born in London in 1960, David first encountered sea eagles during a holiday to Mull in 1980. One of the birds had flown overhead and he'd been instantly and forever captivated. On a short-term contract for the RSPB, he'd started monitoring the birds in 1984. Working in 12-hour shifts, he and colleagues camped out and watched Mull's nests through a telescope, helping to keep them safe from egg collectors. Although those nests failed, he was there the following year, watching with colleagues Keith Morton and Mike Madders, when a moment of conservation history took place.

'We started to see the mother shifting, getting up and down on the nest, and at last this fluffy head emerged,' he recalled.

The first sea eagle chick of the reintroduction project had hatched in Scotland. Twelve weeks later it successfully fledged.

When that contract came to an end, David left Mull for several years, working in the BBC's Natural History Unit in Bristol, then as a ranger at Aigas Field Centre, before re-joining the RSPB in 1988, moving up the ranks to become head of reserves in Scotland. At that point he took a tangent that surprised many around him. Although he was close to the charity's upper echelons, he'd grown tired of meetings and stress and found that he didn't want to climb any higher. When the Mull officer job came up, he applied.

'My boss thought I was mad,' he said with a smile. 'I was basically going back to taking on an entry-level contract job and salary.'

For Mull's growing sea eagle population, which stood then at only nine pairs, the timing would prove fortunate. Farmers had begun voicing concerns about lamb predation. Furious headlines were appearing with greater regularity in the *Oban Times* and farming press. To counter the negativity and deter those politicians susceptible to lobbying from calling for culls, positive sea eagle news stories were sorely needed. It was time to tell the world about the birds as individuals, to share tales about their family life and celebrate the benefits they brought to ecosystems and to people.

'And it was really you, more than anyone, who provided those stories, wasn't it?' I asked.

'Well . . .' David began, staring at his shoes in what I knew to be embarrassment. 'I don't think I'm overstepping to say that those stories probably wouldn't have seen the light of day had I not pushed them.'

In 2005 the much-loved BBC series *Springwatch* first aired. Featuring in its opening episode were Skye and Frisa, a pair of eagles nesting by Loch Frisa in the heart of Mull.* The following

---

*The pair have gone on to become the UK's oldest white-tailed eagles. At the time of writing, Skye is 30 and Frisa 32. Frisa also has some remarkable lineage. Her mother was Blondie, the female who (watched by David) reared Scotland's first eagle chick back in 1985.

year, wildlife cameraman Gordon Buchanan returned to his home, filming the BBC Natural World documentary *Eagle Island*. More television appearances would follow. On the back of this publicity, ever-increasing numbers of tourists and politicians flocked to Mull. The island and its eagles were on the map and David had become their most prominent spokesperson.

Eagle numbers were increasing and public interest was growing, but in those blue skies one dark cloud still lingered. And here, sooner than I'd expected, David touched upon the less-than-happy side of his work.

'Most people get a thrill from seeing the first lambs in the fields,' he said. 'For me, it's the start of sleepless nights and worry . . . especially when it's a wet spring.'

Wet springs are the bane of a lambing shepherd's life. Like all plants, grass requires water and light to grow. But if the balance is wrong, if it receives too much of one and too little of the other, an unwelcome chain reaction begins. Ewes will have insufficient food, produce insufficient amounts of milk, their lambs will struggle and many may perish. In these years, David explained, reports of lamb predation by eagles always seemed to be at their highest.

'How bad did it get?' I asked.

'I could've been called out to two to three farms a day. Farmers would storm out of the house waving dead lambs in my face, saying: "Look what your f-ing birds have done!" I'd run into those people again at the school gates, in the bar or at restaurants . . . They didn't know what else to talk to me about – I don't suppose I did either. It was all very stressful for everyone . . . I don't go out very often now,' he concluded with a sad smile.

We were, by this point, barely ten minutes into the interview, and I saw that this would be unlike any other I would conduct in the course of this project. Previously I had followed the path that the journalist is supposed to tread: begin gently with easy questions about the interviewee's life and career, keep things light and breezy, only venture towards darker places once trust has been built up. Conversation with David followed its own trajectory; it made for the shadowy places sooner, and I made no attempt to divert it.

The thought that the eagles were *anyone's* birds, far less his, made no sense to me.

'I know,' he said, when I voiced this thought. 'To even suggest they're the RSPB's would be a stretch. They might employ me as their officer here, but we don't have any reserves on Mull. In some senses, an "island officer" is an old-fashioned role.'

'How do you cope with the conflict?' I asked.

'You need a very thick skin – and I don't have one, I'm afraid.'

'You must be pretty resilient,' I countered. 'You couldn't have stuck at this otherwise.'

'Maybe,' he said, but without conviction.

And to my instant regret I saw that my crudely aimed assertion had flown wide of the mark. Thus far I had met only a handful of rewilders. Perhaps because each of those people had skin thicker than your average rhinoceros, I had come to believe that all of those who champion a species were built of the same stuff. David's muttered 'Maybe' triggered a swift reassessment of assumptions.

The true extent of lamb predation by eagles is very difficult to establish. Despite watching the birds closely for 20 years and once sitting for 13-hour shifts watching a lambing park where the farmer was claiming daily losses, David has never seen a kill. For him, the question was not *whether* it happens (he accepts that it does), but how frequently? So often, he explained, people failed to drill down and ask how the lamb died, who actually saw the kill, and whether it *was* actually killed rather than scavenged.

We spoke of the 2004 Scottish Executive report, *The Impact of White-Tailed Eagles on Sheep Farming on Mull*, which found that although some lambs were predated, the overall effect of eagles was minimal. When eagles grab a dead animal, they leave only puncture marks on the body. When they seize a live one, blood and bruising is evident around the wounds. Of 114 lamb carcasses found near eagle nests, 85 were deemed to have been scavenged and 29 killed. Most of the kills were made by a couple of pairs, which gave rise in farming circles to the notion of 'problem eagles', birds that were more prone than others to attack lambs.

Whatever side of the fence you stood on, the report provided validation. For farmers, sick of being told that eagles do not kill lambs, the findings showed that they do. For conservationists, tired of hearing that eagles decimate lambing parks, the figures indicated that most are far more inclined to scavenge than to hunt.

More recently, an analysis of prey remains found in 14 nests in Lochaber, Sutherland, Skye, Raasay and Argyll proved just how varied their diet is; over 400 prey items representing at least 42 different species were either hunted or scavenged by the nesting pairs. Each of these territories had been associated with or implicated in lamb predation, but the amount of lamb remains found in nests varied hugely. Some contained as few as two carcasses, one as many as 24. Due to the skeletal condition of the remains, 'the "killed or scavenged" question' could not be answered.[32]

Quite where any of these findings leave those farmers affected by predation (or by 'black loss', where lambs vanish for no obvious reason) is another question. NatureScot runs a sea eagle management scheme which offers support to those suffering from unwanted eagle impacts. Advisers will suggest suitable mitigation measures, and payments are available to those who are willing and able to adapt the management of their sheep and lambs. But as any farmer will tell you, financial payments do not make up for the loss of stock and depletion of the genetic strength of a hefted flock.*

Our talk turned to stories that hit the press in 2008 when west coast crofters in the Gairloch area said that 200 lambs had been killed in a year by eagles. It was a fundamental misunderstanding of their ecology, David insisted, to think that eagles were such active hunters.

My eyes climbed the hill, finding the eagle once more. For several minutes I had forgotten it was there.

'They can sit for hours,' David said. 'They're opportunists. Often, they'll follow hooded crows, ravens and great black-backed gulls into the lambing park and scavenge on their kills. Sometimes they attack those birds too.'

'So that could actually bring a benefit to sheep farmers?' I asked.

'Yes, because those birds can do real damage to newborn lambs. But it's the eagles which get the blame. I guess it's just easier. Even those studies which showed lambs having been apparently killed by sea eagles could be misleading. The lambs might well have already been incapacitated by other predators before the eagles eventually moved in and finished the job.'

'What are the farmers' views on golden eagles?' I asked. 'Don't they take lambs too?'

'Absolutely,' David said. 'But they were much harder than sea eagles for Victorian gamekeepers and farmers to find and kill. They were never wiped out, didn't have to be reintroduced, and farmers say they're OK because they've always been here!'

---

*Hefting is a traditional means of farming unfenced hill ground. In order to establish a heft, constant shepherding is required to keep the flock from straying away, but over time ewes learn their boundaries and do not require management. The knowledge of where to graze and where to shelter in inclement weather is also passed down from ewe to lamb, but this chain of knowledge can be broken if, for any reason, too many lambs are lost from the flock.

Different species, same issues, I thought to myself. It seemed less of a question now, more a statement of fact. Our anger at an animal and its impacts always seemed greater when said animal was reintroduced, when we could blame someone for it being in our lives.

I returned to the notion of 'problem eagles'. While I knew that some birds took more lambs than others, I couldn't help but wonder whether other factors influenced their feeding. Was predation more common in degraded habitats? If the landscape had been hard-grazed by sheep and deer, was there still much by way of heather, trees or scrub for shelter? And if not, were there many mountain hares or grouse left? Or were lambs the easiest meal the eagles had?

'Well . . . nobody has ever asked the question . . . Not in an official capacity.' From the way David was weighing his words, I had the sense that I'd taken us into controversial territory. No farmer wishes to hear that their own practices might contribute to predation losses. 'But land use must have an impact. Ecologically you could say that much of the west coast is pretty knackered.'

Down on the beach, the curlew trilled in an ethereal ascending scale, then launched into head-height flight, making for a point further along the shore. The wind coursed up, causing me to shiver. Even on this, the sunniest of Mull days, the western seaboard weather made its presence known. In this part of the world, farmers would always be battling the elements. And the weather was just one variable that they had absolutely no influence over. Food production costs had risen; farming subsidies were subject to politicians' whims; trade deals saw increasing amounts of meat imported from abroad; the value of wool had fallen through the floor . . . In these circumstances perhaps people clung to the things they felt they ought to be allowed to decide, such as whether or not to control animals on their land.

Questions on culling and species protection had certainly

come to dominate many farming conversations in recent times. Why can you shoot a fox but not a badger, a crow but not a raven? Understanding why some are protected and others not can be difficult. Knowing what a land manager is to do when a protected animal threatens their income is harder still. Deprived of the option to cull, some fear that their autonomy is being stripped. 'Let *country people* manage the countryside' has become a rallying call for those who feel disenfranchised by decisions made by urban politicians representing an urban electorate. Such arguments can be reductive and divisive, and though they perhaps have *some* basis in fact, one only has to look at the number of supposedly protected raptors illegally killed on shooting estates, or beavers indiscriminately blasted in Tayside, to understand why these laws exist.

These wildlife conflicts are not, of course, unique to Scotland. Similar tensions exist almost everywhere. To some, it may seem faintly absurd that we struggle to accommodate creatures like beavers here, yet simultaneously expect people in other parts of the world to coexist with dangerous animals. Living alongside wildlife can be challenging however, and certain statistics perhaps make tensions inevitable in our country. As a proportion of the overall population, relatively few people live in the Scottish countryside (according to the National Records of Scotland, 91 per cent of our population resides in just 2 per cent of its area). As has already been discussed, even fewer people own land. Farmers are also an ageing population – 64 per cent of male and 60 per cent of female farmers are over 55 years of age.[33] These people grew up in an era of agricultural intensification, when food production was prized (and incentivised) above all else. Some degree of pushback is to be expected when a small proportion of the population, unaccustomed to considering many priorities beyond production, is suddenly asked to coexist with animals which appear to make their job more difficult.

While eagles and beavers force us to confront difficult questions, this debate is not simply about those specific species. In a SCOTLAND: The Big Picture feature on the return of sea eagles and its implications for a west coast farmer, Pete Cairns wrote: 'If we changed the characters in this story from sea eagles and a proud farmer in Argyll to, say, seals and a salmon angler, or to beavers and a Tayside arable farmer, the same confused cocktail of science, economics, morality and pure emotion bubbles to the surface. This is about people: who they are, what they stand for, and what they believe to be right and wrong.'[34]

Right and wrong. Fair and unfair. We employ these words, see the world through these lenses, but as Pete concluded later in the same article, 'There is no black and white here; no definitive right and wrong. We are all learning to live with the challenges of change.'

My mind reverted to the topic of disenfranchisement. I remembered the conversation, held months earlier, where I'd complained to my cousin, Jock, at the pointlessness of consulting some people and organisations on beaver translocations, just so that they could say, 'No!'

Again, I heard his reply: 'But if you don't bother, they'll always be able to say that they weren't consulted, and they'll always be right.'

On this subject Jock knew more than most. Ten miles from his in-laws' west coast farm lies Loch Maree, where further sea eagles were reintroduced between 1993 and 1998. One of the crofting community's grievances was that they had not been consulted about that project, just as the wider farming community's views had not been solicited when the eagles were brought to Rum in the 1970s.

'I think the lack of consultation in the seventies compared to what would be done today will always be the millstone around the eagles' necks,' David said.

Different Species, Same Story?

I did too and felt certain that beavers carried a similar burden, thanks to the ad-hoc nature of their return. When discussing them with farmers, one could not fail to notice how frequently talk shifted to eagles. The sense that both had been forced upon the land management community was so powerful that the two species could seem almost interchangeable.

'But ...' I began, thinking that in these circular rewilding debates, where right and wrong were always a matter of conjecture, there might always be a 'but', 'would we have eagles back if there *had* been a lengthy and in-depth consultation? Ask any sheep farmer if they'd welcome a large predator being reintroduced on their doorstep and it's fairly clear what most would say.'

This drew a knowing smile. 'True,' David said. 'And even now, when each reintroduction is subject to an extensive consultation process, you won't please everyone. Some will forever claim they weren't listened to. It won't ever go away.'

'You don't think so?'

'Well, some things give me hope,' he said after a moment's reflection.

Several farmers, he explained, were adapting how they managed their flocks. Some were seeing the benefits of eagle tourism, too. Despite their differing views on sea eagles, many would tip him off when they found one injured or spotted a new nest. Diversionary feeding – supplying eagles with carrion to keep them away from farmers' fields – had also been found to work. As the population grew, they had some non-lethal tools to work with.

'And the population is growing remarkably,' I said. 'That's a positive too.'

'It is,' he agreed.

We turned again to look at the bird still standing sentry above us and David's expression turned grave.

'Their chicks succumbed to avian influenza this year,' he said. 'All season long we'd been watching them bringing fish in and then one day they flew right over the nest and kept going. At that point, you think, "Oh-oh, something's not right there."'

Highly Pathogenic Avian Influenza (HPAI) had devastated seabird communities that year. Thousands of dead or dying birds were being reported. Eagles had proved highly susceptible to it too, scavenging on the carcasses of infected birds and taking the disease back to their nests to feed to the chicks. Of 22 nests in Mull, over half had failed, several as a result of HPAI.

'We only have 150 pairs in Scotland now,' David said. 'A few very bad breeding years, HPAI getting into adults – suddenly that's a vulnerable population.'

The speed with which the mood of our conversation could jump, between happiness and sadness, hopes and fears, was quite striking. To what degree, I wondered, did this reflect the reality of the Mull officer's life? More than almost anyone, David had known real highs and lows. How did he reflect on it all? Had this work given more than it had taken away?

'Oh, without question,' he said. 'I've been able to live here, raise my family here. Spring can be tough, but then the Salen Show comes around and you realise another lambing season has passed and you've made it through. I owe everything – my family life, my career – to these birds.'

Two hours had passed since we arrived here. Though I could easily have stayed longer, discussing these matters, watching the eagle, the curlew and the world pass by, it was time to let David return to work. Besides, I had a boat to catch. One point was nagging at me, however. Earlier in the conversation, he'd described the Mull officer's job as 'an old-fashioned role'. At the time I'd thought nothing of that choice of words. Returning to them now, I wondered if I'd caught a hint of finality there.

'This role won't last forever,' he said when I put the question to him.

Sea eagles were faring well in Scotland, he explained. Limited resources had to be diverted to where they were most needed, namely towards those species that were teetering on the brink of extirpation. Going forward, the RSPB might employ a conservation officer who covered a much wider area and remit, but they could justifiably claim to have done their bit since establishing the first fledgling Mull officer post in the 1980s.

'Surely these birds still need an ambassador,' I said, silently wondering how far David was from retirement age.

And unlike earlier, this time I felt that my assertion had hit the mark.

'Absolutely,' he said. 'There's still too much opposition and misinformation flying around. They still need all the help they can get.'

'Will you leave Mull?'

'Oh no, I'm here for good. This is home. And who knows? If the threats from bird flu and elsewhere continue, maybe decisions will be delayed. I'll never stop fighting for them. I couldn't leave them like that.'

Sometimes the smallest of words can change an entire sentence. David Sexton did not say 'I'll never stop fighting for *the eagles*' or 'I couldn't leave *the birds*'. He said 'I'll never stop fighting for *them*', 'I couldn't leave *them*'. And that one word was the chord that changed the song, the one that struck you in the heart. For most of his working life he had lived alongside them. He had treasured them, fought for them and sometimes he had suffered for them. All those years of dedication, of love, had been folded carefully and sealed within that single tender word.

In July 2024, 23 months after this interview, David Sexton retired from RSPB Scotland.

*

Although the true impact of white-tailed eagles on sheep farms may always be the subject of furious debate, the economic gains that the birds had brought Mull were surely beyond question. The previous evening I'd enjoyed a wonderful tour of the island in the company of Ewan Miles, owner of the award-winning tour group Nature Scotland. Our journey had taken us to The Wilderness, a stretch of coastline on the Ardmeanach peninsula. Sheer cliffs hung above us, remnants of volcanic crags that fell sharply down to the shore. Old stretches of Atlantic hazel wood crouched at our side. We stood watching as dolphins and minke whales followed fleets of fish through the water, as riffles of smoke-coloured clouds stole across the sky and the setting sun fell and was swallowed by the sea. According to a recent RSPB report, wildlife spend supported between 98 and 160 full-time jobs on Mull. Ewan and his two rangers accounted for three of these. They were amongst a growing number of people demonstrating that nature tourism can be a viable career path, even in more remote parts of the country.

Now, having thanked David, I headed for the Ulva ferry port, ready to meet two other well-known beneficiaries of the eagles' return.

Martin Keivers was a Yorkshireman as one imagined Yorkshiremen should be: big, plain-spoken, amiable. While a younger version of him took to the helm of the *Lady Jayne* and steered us away from the Ulva ferry dock, Martin came to join the passengers on deck.

'How's your tourist season going?' he asked, sitting down beside me.

He knew who I was. Somehow, I wasn't surprised. Word must travel fast on an island.

'Your son?' I asked, looking towards the young man at the wheel.

'That's Alex, yeah.'

'Must be wonderful to have him out here, working with you.'

'It's the biggest thing for me. When he was finishing school, I told him to go off and get a trade. He's a bright lad. Could've gone to uni. But he said: "Dad, you know what I want to do." I told him, "OK – but *you* have to tell your mother!"'

The Keivers' business, Mull Charters, began in 2009 with an epiphany straight from Alfred Hitchcock's *The Birds*. One day Martin was fishing on his boat. Consumed by his efforts to free a freshly caught fish from a deeply embedded hook, he only realised that he had company when a huge shadow eclipsed the boat. An eagle had come to inspect the catch.

'In those days my kids were at school with David Sexton's,' he recalled. 'Next time I saw him I said: "Wouldn't it be great if we could make a thing of this?" And he said: "Well, why don't you give it a go?" So, I had to break the news to my wife that I was starting a new career.'

'What did she say?' I asked.

'Does it involve buying a bigger boat?' he replied, with a laugh so big it filled the air.

Martin bought his boat; he began his new career. The early tours were already proving popular, but appearances on television shows like *Springwatch* sent bookings through the roof. Before long he was running two to three trips a day, sailing up Mull's sea lochs, a bucket of fish stowed on the deck, seeking out the UK's largest avian predator. The Keivers' bed and breakfast, run by wife Judith, was thriving too. They were the ultimate example of a family that had spotted an opportunity and embraced it.

The morning's winds had died down and the waves were moving at a gentle jog as we sailed up Loch Na Keal. While the *Lady Jayne* shouldered her path through the water, we discussed eagles, beavers and reintroductions, and the conversation proved so engrossing that I failed at first to notice our entourage. Trailing behind us, like a fistful of balloons on a string, was a flock of gulls.

A bag of crushed bread, produced from Martin's pocket, was cast like confetti into the water behind us. One by one the gulls descended, grabbing, squabbling, retreating. The reason for feeding them was not clear to me. Not yet.

I didn't see the first eagle coming. The cloud of gulls parted and suddenly it was there before us, great wings thumping the air. From the bucket Martin grabbed a fish and pitched it skyward. Neck tilting, head cocked so that a wary eye remained all the time locked on the target, the eagle swooped. So delicately did it pluck its meal that the slate grey sea barely stirred from its slumbers. The bird made off in the direction of a stone and shingle beach. In the sun the trademark tail feathers shone so brightly they might have been dipped in fresh white paint.

From the *Lady Jayne* a squad of smiling faces stood watching the giant figure depart, and I was instantly transported home to Argaty. All summer long I'd seen the same looks of delight from our beaver tourists. The road to restoration can be rocky for reintroduced species. A vocal minority may always debate the merit of bringing animals back. What nobody can deny is the wonder that these creatures inspire, the joy that they bring. For all the hardships known along the way, sea eagle and beaver populations are growing magnificently. One day both will again be found throughout this country. Different species, same story? Perhaps. And that story looks set for a happy ending.

By the time we'd reached the eastern end of the loch, two more birds had come, sending the gulls scattering as they closed in. I saw the purpose of the bread now. Just as the ever-opportunistic eagles might shadow a flock of crows or gulls on land, so they followed them at sea. Birds cluster for a reason – at the head of the queue often lies food. The eagles knew this, and so they followed.

The last eagle had flown over the spot where, just a few hours earlier, David and I had stood talking. The moment that she had appeared in the sky I'd known she was the same bird we'd watched. She disappeared, heading for some hidden perch in the hilltops known only to people like David. Without him to direct me, I wouldn't spot her again. The sky felt suddenly very empty in her absence, and I felt sorry – sorry that she had gone, sorry that the return of her kind to Scotland had proved so contentious. To my mind they, like beavers, were a wonderful re-addition to our lives. Scotland was a better country for having both back.

We began the return journey to the ferry port and still the sadness gripped my heart. My Mull adventure was almost at an end. Tomorrow I would be heading for home. But just as that feeling threatened to overwhelm me, the world sent a gift to dispel it. A movement registered in my peripheral vision. It rose and fell, was there and then not. I turned swiftly, just in time to see a figure leap from the water.

'Dolphins!' someone shouted.

'Here, put this on and head up front,' Martin said, handing me a life jacket.

I returned him a blank expression.

Slowly, as if for the benefit of someone who spoke very little English, he said: 'Put that on. Hold onto that rail.' He gestured to the metal bar on the cabin's exterior. 'Sidestep to the front of the boat and lie down . . . Oh, and don't fall in!'

Avoiding eye contact with the other passengers, none of whom, I noted uneasily, had been handed a jacket, I did as I was bid. The *Lady Jayne* reared and plunged on the crashing waves and the dolphins raced alongside us. They jumped and they dived, they dipped beneath the stern and were carried forward by us. And lying on the bow, I watched and whooped, I smiled, I laughed.

19

'The Word "Whore" Gets Used a Lot'

In the first week of September, the rain finally came. For days on end, it fell. The second beaver family's pond rose again, the islands of mud disappeared beneath the waves. A new chill carried on the breeze. The year had turned bitter as she neared old age; her tongue was sharper than it had ever been in her youth.

With autumn drawing in we brought our season of beaver tours to an end. By the time they emerged from their lodge for the evening, it had grown too dark to see them. An archive of happy moments from the final evenings is stored in my mind. From time to time, I sift through them, delighting in the memories. In my head I hear the kits chattering and whining as they speed around the pond. I see the mother standing on a barely submerged mud island, stripping leaves from low branches, folding them into parcels and devouring them. I glimpse a shadow slip silently past as a tawny owl glides through the trees. I see contorting formations of geese passing overhead, their arrival heralding the change of season.

In mid-September I conducted what was to be my penultimate interview, meeting online with raptor conservationist Ruth Tingay. Although in recent times she'd gained additional renown for her work co-directing the wildlife campaign group Wild Justice, she was best known as the author of Raptor Persecution UK, a blog created to raise awareness about the illegal killing of birds of prey. From the Ramsays and David Sexton, I'd gained an insight into the societal strife that advocates of reintroduced species can face. Ruth's work focussed on a separate strand of rewilding – protecting the animals that we already have. From the outside, that campaign might seem largely uncontentious. All she asked was that people uphold the law and refrain from killing birds of prey (all of which are protected in Scotland). Could this possibly incite the same degree of heat as the previous interviewees had experienced? Unfortunately, I suspected I already knew the answer.

Although Ruth and I had met briefly in 2019, at a parliamentary reception held for the Scottish Raptor Study Group, it was in 2021 that we'd got to know one another better. That summer she'd brought a group of friends to Argaty to watch the kites. I'd noted how they'd kept themselves apart from the rest of that day's visitors, standing several metres away for the entirety of the afternoon. In her group had been another lady, referred to as a 'mental health coach'. These clues alone were enough to show that Ruth had known troubles, but I couldn't have imagined the extent of them. To hear Ruth Tingay's tale was to put one's own minor issues in their rightful place.

Her career had taken many unexpected twists and turns. Raised in Chesterfield, she left school at 16, working at Battersea Dogs Home for a couple of years before taking a job at the Animal Quarantine Centre at Heathrow Airport. When domestic pets being shipped around the world came through Heathrow in transit, centre staff had to unbox, feed and water them, ensure they were in good health, and hold them until their ongoing flight. Alongside domestic animals, the team also monitored the wildlife trade.

In the late 1980s, wild bird trading was still in full swing. Crates of birds came either for the UK pet trade or to transit on to other countries. Often transportation boxes were deemed inadequate and charges were brought against the airline for accepting them. Ruth and her colleagues also had to identify the birds because traders would attempt to smuggle in species that they weren't allowed to have.

Though the work was often hard, the team was tightknit, the job was exciting and she felt they were doing something worthwhile, not just for people's pets but wild animals too.

'For a time,' she told me, 'life was pretty good.'

But that would change. Through a tip-off the team learned that a big shipment of wild caught birds was in the warehouse of a well-known airline, waiting to be transported to the United States. Immediately, this raised alarm bells as all birds in transit were supposed to come to Heathrow for a welfare check.

'There were probably about 150 boxes and the moment you went into the warehouse this smell hit you – you could just smell death,' Ruth said. 'It was overpowering. We walked towards these crates and we could see immediately ... These wooden boxes had ventilation panels, and they were all stacked on this pallet, but instead of facing the panels outwards they'd faced them inwards. There was this massive heat being generated from these birds. They couldn't breathe properly. We started working our way through boxes, pulling out hundreds of dead birds. Really horrific stuff.'

She recalled holding a flamingo that had been forced into a tiny box. Its legs had been folded up, perhaps for days, causing the blood vessels to constrict. She was rubbing them, trying to help the bird stand, when the office phone rang. A journalist from the *Daily Mail* had got hold of the story.

'Because we were Civil Service we weren't allowed to talk to the press and had to deny everything,' she recalled. 'But I was so moved by the experience ... I was saying: "I don't know what you're talking about, I can't comment," and it just felt wrong. I wanted to say "Get your camera down here!"'

At the time, airlines were being pressured to cease the transport of wild caught birds. Several claiming to have already given it up were still very much involved.

'It just felt so wrong,' Ruth said. 'Airlines were going to get away with this and keep doing it because nobody was allowed to know about it and that sat with me. I didn't want to be part of this game any more.'

That feeling of injustice would remain with her, fuelling her fire later in her career.

Disillusioned with life at Heathrow she took a three-month sabbatical, travelling to Mauritius to work with Carl Jones, the conservationist famed for saving the echo parakeet, pink pigeon and Mauritius kestrel from the brink of extinction. That experience proved formative. On Ruth's first day back at Heathrow, she realised she no longer wished to be there; her heart lay in conservation. She returned to Mauritius to volunteer with Carl for a further six months and never looked back.

So began a peripatetic career in raptor conservation, a 30-year journey that took in such diverse locations as Mexico, Madagascar and Hawk Mountain in the USA. In the early 2000s the chance came to study golden eagles in Scotland.

'Up to that point I hadn't been interested in working in the UK,' she said. 'I thought UK raptors were fine. In a civilised country, why would there be an issue?'

She spent time on Lewis and Skye before beginning a research project collecting and DNA-testing feathers from raptors. It was then that she met Scottish Raptor Study Group field workers and first heard tales of persecution on driven grouse moors. On driven shoots, beaters walk in a row, flushing red grouse from cover and pushing them towards the waiting guns. Shooters pay handsomely to take part in big bag shoots and high numbers of grouse are required to satisfy that demand. As a result, certain estates show little tolerance for predators that might reduce those numbers and, consequently, their income.

'The thing that struck me was that the persecution wasn't mainstream news,' Ruth remembered. 'I kept hearing about it from field workers. They were adamant that this was a massive deal. And I thought: "How can it be? I've worked in raptor conservation for a long time now and I haven't heard about this."'

The reasons why she hadn't seemed clear enough in hindsight. Firstly, driven grouse shooting is a very British pastime and much of her career to that point had been spent abroad. Secondly, few people or organisations were publicising the problem. Each year birds like hen harriers and golden eagles were illegally killed on driven grouse moors and next to nothing was said about it.

'It got to 2010, and I thought, "I need to do something about this,"' she recalled. 'I couldn't just walk away because if people knew about it they'd be as astonished as I was that this was going on in this country.'

She decided to write a blog highlighting the issue. Initial progress was slow, but gradually her audience began to grow. As one might expect, not everyone was thrilled that a spotlight was being shone on criminality in the shooting community's ranks. However, in the early years those opponents were flailing blindly.

'I was writing anonymously,' she explained. 'I wanted it to be about what was going on, not about me. And because they didn't know who was writing it, it was difficult for them to have a go.'

She paused, sucked in a quick breath, and I held mine. We had taken a sudden step forward and now stood on the edge of something. I knew, of course, that she had lost the mask of anonymity – were it still in her possession we would not be holding this meeting. And now that I thought back to her visit to Argaty, to the mental health coach and the way her group had held themselves away from the crowd, I thought I knew what had happened.

'One of the trolls found out who I was,' she said, confirming my suspicions. 'My phone number and address were shared online, a barrage of hate started, and it's never gone away.'

The experience had, she admitted, made her 'a completely different person'. She had moved house and kept her new address private. She only answered the phone to numbers she recognised.

'I'm a lot more wary of my surroundings, of who's near me,' she said. 'I find it really hard to trust people. And I was never like that. I was quite carefree.'

'Did you always have some idea that you might be unmasked?' I asked.

'It was a shock, really, because I didn't expect the vitriol. I wasn't ready for it – didn't understand it at the time. When I first started, I didn't want the blog to be about me, so I didn't expect it to be vitriolic about me. I don't think anything could have prepared me for that.'

'What sort of things do people say?' I asked.

'It's rarely about the arguments or my qualifications. They don't try and get at that, I guess, because you can't really knock them. So, it tends to be about personal appearance. They use some words that I'm not used to hearing in everyday language – the word "whore" is used a lot. And "bitch". When you look at the stuff other females get online, whatever field they're in, it's the same thing. So, you realise that those words aren't really about me. It's just language those people use about women they don't like. And in this field it's mostly men I'm fighting against, so you have to expect it.'

Those final five words told me a lot. Contemplating them, a comment made by Sarah as I'd prepared for this interview came back to me: 'If you think people gave you a tough time, imagine how much harder it would be for a woman.'

As usual, my wife was absolutely right. Next to Ruth, any hardships I – a middle-aged, white, landowning male – felt I'd faced no longer felt quite so hard.

My thoughts reverted to the questions I'd asked myself while boarding the ferry to Mull. Why was it so difficult to move beavers a few miles? Was the conflict peculiar to beavers, or did all rewilders have to expect such opposition?

From what I'd since learned, it seemed that opposition was very much to be expected, whether one wished to reintroduce a species or simply protect those we already have. If moving beavers a few miles had seemed hard, it was surely because of this existing backdrop of division, because people have such wildly different views on what our countryside is and should be. And so, conflict could not be unique to beavers. In fact, the fight to protect them seemed little different from the fight to protect Scotland's raptors. The same sort of people were arguing over broadly similar issues, the only difference being that the two wars were being waged on different fronts: one in the water, the other on land.

'Did you ever think about giving up?' I asked.

'Mmm, that's a good question.' While she considered the point, Ruth's gaze fell away from the screen. Light, presumably from a window, illuminated her face.

'I went to get some mental health coaching a couple of years ago. When Wild Justice started, the level of abuse had got to a stage where I really didn't know how to deal with it.'

In 2019, Ruth, Chris Packham and Mark Avery formed Wild Justice, a non-profit organisation which took legal cases on behalf of wild animals when public bodies failed in their legal duty to protect them or their habitats. They quickly drew the admiration of many and the ire of some by successfully challenging Natural England's general licensing system, which allowed birds including wood pigeons, crows and jays to be shot as pests without shooters having to apply for a licence. The system has since been partially reformed and the number of species that can be killed greatly reduced.

'Did coaching help?' I asked.

Returning her gaze to the screen, she smiled. 'It was brilliant. It turned my perspective around and now I'm just not fazed by the abuse at all.'

For all that she had suffered, she remained committed to the fight.

'I know what it takes, how long change takes, but it's achievable,' she said. 'In terms of what's going on in Scotland now, that's a massive result for us.'

A huge moment of history was indeed unfolding in Scotland at the time of our interview. As part of their 2022–23 Programme for Government, the Scottish Government had proposed to implement a licensing system for grouse shooting estates to 'tackle wildlife crime and address the environmental impacts of grouse moor management'. Although the link between certain shooting estates and wildlife crime had been clear for years, one piece of evidence had finally forced the government to act: the 2017 SNH-commissioned report 'Analyses of the Fates of Satellite Tracked Golden Eagles in Scotland'. Between 2004 and 2016, 131 juvenile golden eagles had been fitted with satellite trackers that showed their location at any moment. When birds died of natural causes the tags continued to transmit, allowing bodies to be recovered. But of those 131 birds, 41 had vanished under suspicious circumstances on or around driven grouse moors. Their tags suddenly went offline. Their bodies were never found.[35]

In response to the findings, the Scottish Government ordered a review of how grouse moors were managed. An external taskforce was established to assess the environmental impact of moorland management and consider the implementation of a licensing system. Under the proposals, estates wishing to shoot grouse would have to apply for a licence, which could be permanently revoked if there was sufficient evidence to suggest that, on the balance of probabilities, a wildlife crime had been committed.

(In March 2024, 18 months after my interview with Ruth, the

Wildlife and Muirburn Management (Scotland) Bill would be passed by the Scottish Parliament. Grouse shooting was licensed, the use of snares was banned, the SSPCA (Scottish Society for the Prevention of Cruelty to Animals) was given increased powers to investigate wildlife crimes, and those wishing to burn heather moorland or use wildlife traps would have to apply for a licence.)

'Do you ever look back to your early days in conservation and think: "I've come a long way?"' I asked Ruth. 'It's quite a journey from where you began to challenging Natural England and leading on grouse moor reform.'

'I guess,' she said. 'But it's the injustice thing again. You care, so you do it. You know that.'

An on-screen message warned that our call had only five minutes remaining. Time enough for the biggest question of all. I put it to her, realising as I spoke that, more than in any previous interview, I had no idea what answer I'd receive.

'Has it given more than it's taken?' she repeated. 'Oh... that's a tricky one. It's taken away a lot. The sense of trust. What's it given me?' She stopped, frowning in thought. 'A sense of achievement. It's quite rewarding in a lot of ways. It's really hard to answer because if I wasn't doing this, I don't know what I'd be doing. I don't know if I'd be as driven. I might have a completely different life... I don't know if I'm answering your question.'

I nodded, but remained silent, fearful of losing even a fragment of this already fascinating answer.

'It takes...' she resumed, haltingly. 'It definitely takes from you. But the friendships you get from it, working with people in your field and your cause. Those are really powerful relationships that are cemented because it's such a difficult job to do. That's a plus. I'm not sure if I've answered...'

The sentence fell away to nothing. She looked enquiringly at the screen and found me smiling. Not only had she answered, but she had also revealed some truths that I'd hitherto been blind to.

Quietly chastising myself, as we do when something we've been searching for turns up right under our noses, I saw that the *either/or* premise of the question had been utterly flawed. While some could answer it easily enough, for others life could never be distilled down to so binary a choice. Life gave *and* it took. A person could be in credit *and* debit. Ruth was one of those people. Since that day I've often wondered if I might be too.

20

All Roads Lead to Roy

Some minutes earlier I'd left the Moray town of Forres behind. Now a vast expanse of heather-floored pinewood stretched out beside the road. Approaching Half Davoch Cottage, home of Roy Dennis, I felt like a moth flying towards a light, a migrant bird drawn north for spring. That my path should lead me here for what would be the final interview for this book seemed somehow inevitable. I could not hope to understand anything about rewilding and those who do it without making this trip.

Often, I think of my generation as the first children of rewilding. We grew up in an era when the word itself was coined, when the concepts of ecological restoration at landscape scale and reintroductions of wiped-out species were slowly becoming normalised. For someone of my age, looking to the skies and seeing red kites soaring there, the people responsible for their return, people like Roy, seemed like the founding fathers of this exciting new movement. The list of species he had helped to restore appeared endless – it had come as no surprise when I'd learned from the Ramsays that he had been one of the driving forces behind the first enclosed beaver reintroductions. Simply put, all roads led to Roy.

His career is still very much alive and kicking. (In July 2023 – nine months after our interview – a white-tailed eagle chick hatched in England for the first time in 240 years. Its parents had been reintroduced by the Roy Dennis Foundation and Forestry England.) I was most keen to learn about another phase of his working life, however: the beginning.

Roy's career started decades before the R word was invented. He restored missing species when it was far from an accepted practice. I wondered what it had been like to work in that era, what challenges he'd faced, whether those obstacles had been consigned to the past or whether they still had a bearing on today's conservation landscape.

Roy stood waiting at his door. Though it was late October, one would not have known it to see him. Shirt sleeves rolled up, he might have been heading out for a summer's stroll.

'Good to see you,' he said, proffering his hand. 'Warm, isn't it? When I think back to the early sixties, when I lived in Strathspey, the idea of walking out in just my shirt, on the last days of October! We were usually snowbound from now until March. Anyway, come on in.'

He led me through the house and upstairs to a sunlit study where a pot of coffee sat steaming on the table.

'So, this is where you write, is it?' I said, certain that I sensed a scholarly aura in the room.

Roy is a prolific writer – of letters, articles and books. His most recent work, *Restoring the Wild*, told of his six decades in rewilding. For anyone interested in the ecosystem recovery, the book provided the blueprint.

'No!' He laughed, dashing my illusions just as I had begun to bask in them. 'I was evicted from that room. My daughter wanted it for her bedroom.'

'Same thing happened to me,' I said, thinking of the (now) purple-walled bedroom which once served as my (white-walled) writing base. In a house of strong-willed women, a man's study is always deemed expendable.

As he poured the coffee, Roy told me about his childhood.

Born in 1940, he discovered nature at an early age. From the woods to the marshes, he and his friends went everywhere. They caught newts and collected birds' eggs, in the days before it was illegal. By the age of 16 he knew every bird in that area of southern Hampshire, and its song.

Come 1958, he'd reached his final year at school and was considering applying to study atomic engineering when a field assistant job came up on the island of Lundy. Within a week he was living a 'brilliant but spartan' existence in a lighthouse in the Bristol Channel. Island life allowed him to gain further experience in bird ringing and identification and would lead to another incredible opportunity.

'I wrote to Fair Isle Bird Observatory in Shetland,' he told me. 'The warden had been on Lundy some years before, so in 1959 he appointed me as his assistant. That was just mind-blowing. I spent a year working there and decided that was me.'

'You knew this was what you wanted to do for life?' I asked.

'I knew,' he said simply.

That autumn the observatory's founder, RSPB director and Scottish Ornithologists' Club Honorary Secretary, George Waterston, visited Fair Isle. The timing of that meeting was to prove fateful. Ospreys had been pushed to extinction in Scotland in 1916, but in 1954 a pair of Scandinavian birds had flown to Loch Garten, near Aviemore. Realising that the best means of protecting their nest from persecutors and egg collectors was to put them in the public eye, in 1959 the RSPB had begun allowing people to visit the site. Thanks to that meeting with George, Roy would spend the subsequent four summers working as assistant warden at Loch Garten.

'It was special then,' he recalled. 'There were so few of us working full time on birds. Less than a handful. Those ospreys meant so much that all sorts of great people in wildlife came to Loch Garten. So, I met the heads of the Nature Conservancy

Council (NCC)* and RSPB. I made friends, asked what was going on. There was a lot of encouragement.'

Already he was making strides, the lack of an academic qualification proving no barrier to progress.

'I don't think you need a degree,' he said, when I made this observation. 'But you need to always be out there doing stuff. And then people see that that young person is knowledgeable. That's where you get help.'

One opportunity led to another, and another – from grey seal research on North Rona with John Morton Boyd to duck catching in Essex and bird ringing in the Moray Firth. At last Fair Isle beckoned him back. He returned as the observatory's warden. It was there, in 1968, that he would take a decisive step into a career in species reintroduction, thanks once more to the man who had fast become a mentor figure.

'There was a phone call from George Waterston,' he remembered. 'He said, "We want to bring white-tailed eagles to Fair Isle and I want you to sort out how we do it."'

Lit by both the memory and the stream of sunlight which poured in through the window, Roy's whole face seemed to glow in that moment.

'That was just fantastic,' he concluded, grinning widely.

Roy set to work, consulting the island's crofters, building aviaries. They brought in four Norwegian birds. Though one disappeared quickly, the others stayed the year and through the following spring. Eventually one died, having been sprayed with oil by fulmars, and the other two disappeared.

---

*The NCC was the government agency responsible for managing National Nature Reserves and conservation areas. In 1991 it was disbanded and separate devolved nature agencies, including SNH, were formed.

'I like to think that they went back to Norway – later releases showed that some did go back,' Roy said.

Convinced that greater numbers of birds would be required were they to make a success of the reintroduction, he suggested bringing more the following summer. But the idea met with resistance from an unexpected source. Objections did not come from farmers or landowners, but from the conservation community.

My ears pricked up at this. Until that moment my interviews had focussed upon the external opposition one receives. Now we were set to place conservation itself under the microscope.

'What was their issue?' I asked, leaning in so as not to miss a word.

'George...' he began, then stopped, considering. 'I didn't realise till afterwards, but he had had a great problem persuading people to allow him to bring those first birds over because everyone in the ornithological world was against it. They didn't like the idea of manipulating and reintroductions, and that sentiment carried on for a very long time.'

For several years, sea eagle reintroduction would sit on conservation's back burner. Roy moved to the mainland and took a role as the RSPB's Highland officer. Then, in 1975, the plan was resurrected. As is so often the case, having the right people in positions of influence at the right time made all the difference. John Morton Boyd (by then director at the NCC in Edinburgh) wanted to do it, and so Ian Newton started the new reintroduction on the island of Rum. Though Roy helped, he couldn't do so in an official capacity as a staff member of the RSPB because they still opposed the plan.

Thankfully, once white-tailed eagles began to breed on Mull and it became clear that the reintroduction had been a success, attitudes started to change. As eagles moved around the mainland, monitoring became a regular part of Roy's RSPB workload.

'Was it inevitable once you had started on the journey to restore species that you would go on and try to do more?' I asked.

'Oh, I knew I wanted to do far more. And I wanted to do far more with the big ecosystem recovery,' he said, his smile growing again.

The next species in his sights were red kites. Persecuted by gamekeepers, kites had been wiped out in England by the 1870s, while in Scotland their last record came from 1917 at Glengarry, Inverness-shire. From that point onwards the only survivors to be found in all of Britain were a tiny handful living deep in the Welsh valleys. Guided by the belief that if human persecution was the sole reason for a species being absent then we had a duty to rectify past mistakes, Roy and colleagues set to work on returning the birds to Scotland and England.

'And as I recall, you didn't have much support from the conservation community then either,' I said.

This part of the story I already knew something of. When researching for my previous book I had spoken to Roy and learned of the hurdles he'd had to leap in order to bring kites back.

'That was really difficult,' he said. 'I think the opposition was partly due to the fact that the red kite was such a flagship species in Wales, with a population so small. The RSPB had spent oodles of time and money protecting those last kites, from egg collectors and so on. And slowly they'd got on top of that and the population rose.'

That small, isolated group would always be vulnerable, however. Reintroductions to select sites across Scotland and England offered the best means of growing and safeguarding the UK population. Again, sceptical bosses lined up to throw spanners in the works. This time Roy made sure to anticipate their concerns and have answers ready.

'When they said, "Where are you going to get kite chicks from?" I replied, "Contacts in Sweden have already agreed to supply us." When they said, "But how are you going to get them here?" I replied, "It's all sorted. The RAF will fly them over."'

He and his colleagues achieved their goal. The first kites were reintroduced to the Black Isle, in the Scottish Highlands, and to England's Chiltern Hills in 1989. Those projects spawned a series of others, and today Britain has an estimated 8,000 breeding kite pairs, equivalent to 20 per cent of the birds' global population. When one considers that at their lowest point, in the 1930s, only ten pairs are said to have remained in the Welsh valleys, the restoration of this species might represent Britain's greatest conservation success story.

In 1990, Roy took a decisive leap. Tired of bureaucracy, 'which was only going to get worse and worse', of bosses who thought he 'should be in the office working out a budget, not out doing fieldwork', and of the conservative nature of big organisations that 'don't want someone doing something that's going to get them into trouble', he left the RSPB. Five years later he established a non-membership charitable trust, the Highland Foundation for Wildlife (later renamed the Roy Dennis Wildlife Foundation). From that day to this, his work has focussed upon wildlife research, species recovery and ecosystem restoration. The Foundation has led on the restoration of ospreys to Rutland Water in the East Midlands and Poole Harbour in Dorset, of red squirrels to areas of the Highlands where they had been extirpated, and, most recently, of white-tailed eagles to the Isle of Wight. Now in his 80s, any thought of stepping back and sinking into cosy retirement was far from Roy's mind.

'I'm always working on several projects,' he said. 'I'm a great believer that you've got to just get on with it.'

Just get on with it. This five-word salvo, anathema in the plodding world of conservation, was a mantra in the Dennis household. Over the course of our two-hour interview he would utter it often, his conviction increasing each time. Life had neither doused his fire nor made him fearful of failure.

As he explained, 'Whenever you try something, you might fail.

And there's far too much emphasis on worrying about that and then never doing anything. So, I say the damaging thing is never to try, not that it may have failed.'

Since leaving the RSPB he had kept himself apart from the conservation mainstream and appeared to maintain a healthy scepticism for it.

'Organisations do their best work when they're about here' – he raised a slanted hand as if to demonstrate the early stages of growth on a graph. 'I was in the RSPB when it was there. And then they get too big.' His hand rose, its trajectory levelled off. 'Their bosses get high up in their position because they're not going to rock the boat. Organisations should be killed off then. Let some young people start another one.'

We fell into momentary silence while I considered the point. Having seen the power and influence that the older conservation order could wield, if and when they chose to, I couldn't agree about killing them off (especially not the RSPB who, to my eye, seemed one of the most effective of the larger organisations); I wondered if Roy really meant it either. But the barrier he'd mentioned most frequently was conservatism and faintheartedness (past and present) within the community. He'd faced it when trying to reintroduce species and clearly felt the problem still existed. Even I'd noticed it since my beaver story began (the organisations leaving the Rewilding Alliance over the Move Don't Kill campaign being the most obvious example). While I wouldn't call for their demise, I think Roy's other points were on the nose. In the face of environmental collapse, when bold action is needed and radical opposition to that action is guaranteed, a conservationist's job will always be hard, but it will be harder still if they allow fear to paralyse them. To paraphrase Roy, they must never be afraid to take risks, to rock the boat, to just get on with it.

Outside, the sky had suddenly grown darker. The warmth had seeped from the room.

'Bugger it,' Roy said, turning in his seat and looking out to the garden. 'I put the washing on the line. I wonder if that was a mistake...'

The heavens opened in immediate answer. Appearing not at all concerned, he turned back towards me.

'I wanted to discuss mentoring,' I said, raising my voice to make it heard over the rain, which was now lashing against the window. 'Do you remember when I was beginning our beaver project? You gave me all that time to talk through running a consultation, telling me what would work and what wouldn't. In conservation I've found there is a real divide. Some people are really generous with their support. Others...' I broke off, uncertain how best to finish the thought. The truth was that some organisations had been less than helpful along the way, and others less than kind about us since we gained the licence. 'We've enough problems to deal with without fighting with those we're supposed to agree with,' I remember thinking at the time.

'I think you'll find there's some that don't want to help you because they don't want you to be successful,' Roy suggested. 'Might be a bit envious.'

'I don't know what anyone would be envious of,' I mumbled, as a heat that had certainly not come from the rapidly cooling weather rose to my face.

'You're getting on and doing it.'

'Well, it's a small thing that we did really,' I said, bumbling and blustering. 'But I suppose after you and I last spoke, I always wanted to know what it was that you looked for in young people that made you think: "I'll help them."'

'I think it's if that guy or girl has got a real commitment and they're going to get this done,' he said. 'And if I can help them do it more easily, then I want to do that.'

'There was a point at the end of our call when you said to me that you thought that if NatureScot had given me the time of day to that point, then I would get the beavers. And that ended up being a light in the dark later on, because there were times when it really looked like other political pressures would prevent it from happening. Remembering that *people* thought that we could do it meant a lot.'

People. Why had I picked that word? I wanted to say *you*, but some strange sense of propriety held me back. Though he was too discreet to say it, he seemed to understand my true thoughts anyway.

'One thing I try to do is make people feel more confident. And I always say: "If you run into a snag, get back in touch because we've got to make it work." A project should never fail because someone's not willing to help you.'

Had Roy ever experienced jealousy from people who ought to have been on his side? I could imagine many would look at his work restoring species and think he was living the good life.

'No, I don't see that,' he said. 'I think most folk recognise that we did our best, and that the reason you're seeing these things flying about or climbing up trees is because we did it. And it was hard. In the seventies and eighties, I was working a hundred hours-plus a week. My emphasis all the time was on helping nature. It probably wasn't good for my family at times, but this job was just ... well, it's more than work.'

An unwelcome sensation came over me upon hearing these words. How often, I wondered, could my family say that my work had been good for them? For every soldier who has ever told their tale, there's a partner and family whose voices will never be heard.

Keen to usher the conversation along to less uncomfortable surroundings, I mentioned the opposition one faces, particularly from farmers, when trying to restore a species.

'In the farming community,' Roy said, 'what you have to remember is if you're friends with Jock, then Stan will hate you, and if you're friends with Jimmy, then Hamish won't like you. To think that they're all friends, by God they scrap. Just like everyone else. But these people recognise a common enemy.'

'And when you get them together they're bloody hard to break up,' I said.

'They certainly are,' he agreed, laughing.

'Do you sometimes think that conservation can be a lonely profession? You know, when you're dealing with people that really don't like what you're doing?'

'No,' he replied instantly. 'Because you have this marvellous relationship with nature. Whenever they talk about stakeholders – my stakeholders are birds and mammals and nature. So, I never feel lonely. I'm alone, but I'm never lonely.'

'Even when you have to consult people who oppose you, and you're on your own. . .?' I pressed.

'I think being on your own is an advantage,' he replied, his tone even more certain now. 'If you're talking one-on-one with a farmer or a politician, you've got each other's full attention. You can have really meaningful discussions.'

Aware that I would only hit rock by continuing to dig in this spot, I moved on. A month earlier he and I had both spoken at SCOTLAND: The Big Picture's rewilding conference. Roy was the event's keynote speaker. Although his body of work was unrivalled by anyone in Britain today, I remember finding it strange that this one man was the exception rather than the norm. Why weren't there more Roys? Why was it him and not the head of a large wildlife charity on stage, talking about all the things they'd achieved?

'I've thought about that too,' Roy said. 'I think most conservationists are within an organisation and those organisations are risk averse.' He paused, considering his words, then continued: 'I've got an old friend who was on the board of SNH when I was. We were talking one time, and I said: "Do you think nature has affected my brain and made me fight for it? You know, so . . . somehow I'm very involved with nature, but it's made me responsible for it? It's kind of... telling me to get on with it?" And he said: "You know, that's possible."'

He stopped, looked at his hands, which lay knitted across his chest. 'What was it that Shankly said when someone asked him about life and death?'

Given a chance to throw some football knowledge into the mix, I would never be found wanting. I quoted Bill Shankly's famous saying: 'Somebody said that football's a matter of life and death to you. I said: "Listen, it's more important than that."'

'Yeah.' He chuckled. 'That's the one. And that's how I feel. It's been my life. And I'm determined to try to keep it going as long as I can.'

We brought the interview to a close soon after. And I didn't ask him if this life had given more than it had taken from him, because I knew what the answer would be. Nor did I give the question much thought after that, because I knew what my answer was too.

21

Fig

The rains that drenched Roy Dennis's laundry that day were just some of many that would fall upon Scotland during the back end of 2022. Winter would not feel like winter at all but one long, wet autumn. On the Carse of Stirling, less than ten miles downstream of Argaty, entire fields disappeared in the floods. The only evidence that grass lay beneath the waves was the fenceposts, which poked up like the flailing hands of drowning sailors.

At the top beaver pond, water scaled the walls of the dam, sluiced around the edges and made a bid for freedom. Thirty metres downstream it met a dry-stone dyke and began to leach through it. That night the beavers set to work, dredging up mud and plastering the wall. For several days their repair job kept the flood at bay, but soon a large pool had backed up. Eventually it catapulted forward, vaulting the barrier. The beavers built dam after dam. They kept every drop that they could upon the land. At last, at the very edge of their territory, the outflow stream escaped, slipping over the final wall and off towards the farm. Like victors in a battle, allowing a few surviving opponents to flee, the beavers let those last drops go. A few litres lost meant nothing when so many had been captured. Through these tireless efforts, the beavers achieved their aim, slowing the flow sufficiently that a large cache of sticks, dug into the pond's floor outside a recently built lodge, would not wash away in the spates. Whatever the weather brought, their provisions would see them through to the spring.

They did not know it, but in those sodden months their engineering saved my family a great deal of inconvenience and expense. The outflow stream regained momentum as it sped away from the final dam; as in previous years, it burst its banks. But the marathon run through the wetland had sapped so much of its strength that when it attempted to attack our farm track it could only scratch the skin, nothing more. For the first time in five years, the track did not wash away, our yard did not flood. Only beavers could have achieved this feat – working in the dead of night, in places so wet that no person could walk, no machine approach. In their paws beavers hold powers that we can only dream of. Stirling University's Nigel Willby and Alan Law would later measure the size and depth of the pond and calculate that the main and subsidiary dams had increased its volume from 1.5 to 2.5 million litres – '5,000 free-standing Victorian bathtubs in old money,' as Nigel is fond of saying.

That winter found me on the evening speaker circuit, travelling Scotland, from north to south, east to west, telling our beaver story to audiences big and small. And late at night, in faceless travel hotels, I put words down on paper, laying the foundations of what would, in time, become this book.

Life on the road provided time to reflect on the journeys I'd made and the lessons I'd learned from those people who'd been kind enough to share their experiences with me. As the last town shrank to nothing in my wing mirrors and the next one loomed large in the windscreen, I considered again how I might respond should someone ask what our efforts to bring beavers to Argaty had taught me about the wider world of rewilding.

I would say that this is a messy business, an *all's fair in love and land management* brawl.

I would say, as David Sexton had, that those attempting to

reverse nature's decline need a thick skin. I would admit, as he had, that I didn't have one. Like David, I could also imagine the day when I might say that I owed my career to an animal. Already I had signed a book contract, I'd travelled, had met many people and seen many places. I would say, as David had, that this life gave.

I would say, as Ruth Tingay had, that it took. It definitely took. I would say, as she had, that those who choose to fight an injustice have to expect unpleasantness from those who support the status quo.

But I also knew that, difficult though I'd found certain experiences, at least nobody had waved dead lambs in my face, trolled me online or forced me to abandon my home. And so I had to conclude that this life had taken considerably less from me than it had from either of them; in fact, it had taken very little at all.

Of the things it had given me I could say, as Louise Ramsay had, that beavers had brought me many friends. And as these incredible animals worked and reworked Argaty's watercourses, I realised, as Sophie Ramsay had, that I had to change inside, and that changing was a relief. I had never been in control anyway. I stood back and watched as my new neighbours restored this landscape. I let go and welcomed a new world of possibilities.

Should anyone ask whether this life gave more than it took, I might once have shrugged my shoulders, as Derek Gow had, and said that it just became something that you did. But time had a healing quality. The further I travelled from those people and organisations that had made parts of this journey so hard, the less they seemed to matter. One day I glanced in my wing mirrors and realised that they, like the towns just-departed, had vanished. Asked today, I would not say that this just became something that you did. Today I would say that I was glad that we had done it.

And though at times in this journey I was both alone and lonely, though in the future I may find myself alone again, I, like Roy Dennis, can say that I enjoy a marvellous relationship with nature. My stakeholders are the beavers. With them here I'll never again be lonely.

*

November arrived. The anniversary of our first translocations came and went without fanfare. Ellie took her first steps and would spend the rest of that winter charging towards any danger she could find, hapless parents and sister trailing in pursuit.

With the first frosts of December there came good news. James Silvey and his colleagues at RSPB Scotland had succeeded with their licence application. Six weeks later a family of beavers was relocated to their Loch Lomond reserve.[*]

Days and weeks passed. One by one, in supermarkets and petrol stations, at farm shows and agricultural stores, I ran into the neighbours who'd opposed our translocations. Heart in mouth, uncertain whether they would greet me or hit me (some did the former; none, I'm glad to say, did the latter), I approached them, said hello, asked after their families. We were friends with these people before all of this. In the future I hope that we may be again.

In February 2023 our second beaver family attained an unlikely form of fame. Logging in to our trail camera one morning we were surprised to note that the view (beamed through an app to our phones) showed nothing but sticks and mud. In mounting the device upon a wooden stake we had made a fatal error. The beavers had plucked it like a flower from the ground and added it to the growing number of sticks thatching the roof of their lodge. The story went viral, making the press in five different countries: 'wood you believe it' jokes followed us at every turn. Fame is not always what it's cracked up to be.

---

[*] In an encouraging development, although the consultation costs still fell upon the applicant, NatureScot footed the bills for health screening, zoo care and carriage.

As spring drew closer, the beavers' world came back to life. With rising temperatures, pools that had formed downstream of the main dam slowly disappeared, the water leaching into the ground. Rendered unemployed, the smaller dams grassed up and melted back into the landscape. At the same time, gnawed trees we'd believed dead began to coppice. Each time we visited the ponds we noticed another change, and we came to see that this was how it would always be. With beavers in the saddle, the landscape would forever be in flux.

In March, the Cairngorms National Park Authority began public engagement on their translocation proposal, hosting a series of public drop-in sessions. Employed as a beaver consultant – a new hat, which I found I rather liked wearing – I attended several of these wonderfully titled 'Beaver Blethers', sharing my experiences as a landowner who lived alongside the animals. Although the farmers who attended evinced some wariness, the proposals were overwhelmingly well-received by the wider public. How thrilling to think that beavers might be relocated to an entirely new part of Scotland when, just a few years earlier, moving them any distance at all was prohibited.

With several release sites identified, the Cairngorms project represented Scotland's greatest translocation hope. We in the beaver community would support them as best we could, but the baton was theirs to run with now. I left the Highlands certain that my part in the story was at an end. And if some things remained unresolved, if translocation was yet to become an established mitigation tool and beavers were still being killed in ways that few of us would wish to contemplate, I told myself that I had done what I could.

And both my story and this book might have ended there, on that somewhat unsatisfactory note, had Sarah and I not taken the girls on a short holiday to St Fillans in north-west Perthshire, had I not made the two-mile trip to Comrie for a cup of tea with James Nairne, had he not said the fateful words:

'I suppose you heard about the SSPCA's beaver?'

*

'A gamekeeper found him wandering the side of a road,' April Dodds, assistant manager at the SSPCA's National Wildlife Rescue Centre, told me when I called her later that week. 'Poor thing was dazed... covered in dirt. God knows how long he'd been walking around like that.' The beaver's hip bones were clearly visible; he'd been struggling to eat for a while. Blood was trickling from his mouth too. 'The obvious conclusion, because he'd been found at the side of the road, was that he'd been hit by a car,' April said.

However, something told her that all was not as it seemed.

'I just had this feeling,' she said. 'This voice inside my head was saying "What if..."'

By the following morning the beaver, named Fig by the centre's staff, had not touched any food. He was put under anaesthetic and April's worst fears were confirmed. This was no car accident. Fig had been shot, and shot poorly. His mouth and head were peppered with shrapnel; his upper incisors had been blown clean off.

April and I were old friends. For years we'd been working together, releasing rehabilitated wildlife on Argaty, always hoping that one day government policy would allow us to bring beavers here. Neither of us could ever have foreseen it happening in such a way, because of such an act.

'It was just awful,' she said. 'The skin around his mouth had turned rotten. We'd find bits of flesh that had fallen off in his pen. Honestly, we were sure he'd have to be euthanised. Without his teeth how would we ever feed him? How could he survive in the wild?'

Already, I could hear the strain in her voice. I knew that she was fighting tears.

Fortunately, rodent teeth are always growing and when X-rays showed that the roots weren't damaged, the SSPCA staff realised that Fig had a chance of pulling through. Provided that they could keep him alive, his teeth would regrow.

'How on earth did you do it?' I asked.

'We had to plane bits of wood and grate veg for him. It took us an hour every day. We've been doing it for nearly three months.' She faltered, her voice cracking as all those long hours of exhaustion and stress came to bear. 'Every two to three weeks the vets had to put him under anaesthetic so they could file down his bottom teeth, otherwise . . .'

'Yeah,' I cut in, sparing her from having to say the words.

Had he not been rescued, had the vets not done as they had, the lower teeth would have kept growing until they punctured his upper palate. I tried to close my mind's eye, tried not to picture that appalling alternative, which would have been Fig's fate had he not been rescued. A rawness hit my throat. Sadness was leaching through my body, spreading to my chest, my lungs. To my horror, I realised that I was going to cry

'Christ,' I burbled, as a sob escaped my lips. 'Sorry. I– It's just . . . You think you're making some progress and then . . .'

'I know,' she said, saving me as I floundered, grasping for words with which to explain a reaction that required no explanation.

'I'm glad we can help him,' I said, finding my voice at last.

Thanks to the SSPCA's dedicated care, Fig's condition had improved. He'd begun swimming in the water trough and damming the drain in his pen. Shaped by vets Liam Reid and Joe Heaver, his incisors had fully regrown and were knitting together. At last, he'd begun to strip wood.

'That was the first time I thought this was going to happen – he was going to pull through and be released.' Tears from a happier source began to flood April's voice again.

*

The pressure was back on NatureScot. Concerns had already been raised about the lax nature of their lethal control licensing policy which, critics argued, risked compromising animal welfare. In order to gain a licence, prospective beaver controllers had only to attend a training course at which they'd learn best culling practice. At no stage, however, were they required to prove their shooting proficiency. There was no prohibition on shooting beavers in water, or on shooting them with a shotgun* and, to make matters worse, the lethal controllers still weren't handing in cadavers so that the agency could ensure that the animals had died swiftly.

Fig's story raised several uncomfortable questions. How often did incidents like this happen and go unreported? How often were beavers shot at half-light over water, when the chances of a quick kill were slim? How often were they left either to drown or to die in pain from their injuries? Why, when many beavers were shot in shallow agricultural drainage ditches, were NatureScot still blithely accepting excuses that recovery of the body was too dangerous? What was happening to the bodies? Were they buried, or incinerated perhaps? Few people, least of all anyone at NatureScot, could answer these questions. The only ones who knew were those who pulled the triggers.

The Fig situation put the SSPCA in a bind too. Never before had their staff cared for a beaver that had been shot and lived. Now they had one such survivor on their hands and he desperately needed to be released. Had this been any other species, they could, with landowner permission, have simply released it in a site with suitable habitat, but the Scottish Government still treated beavers differently to other animals. Official translocations remained the only method of rehoming them, but no release sites were on offer. (The RSPB had completed their relocations; the

---

*Shotguns are inevitably less accurate than high-velocity rifles, and the chances of pellets ricocheting off water and causing non-fatal wounds are greater.

Cairngorms National Park were only in the engagement phase of their proposals. No other applicants had come forward.) The only apparent option was to send Fig to an enclosed project in England, but deporting victims as though they were criminals would set an alarming precedent when a new strategy was in place to help grow Scotland's beaver population. A solution was urgently required.

On Argaty there remained one other pond which Roisin had deemed suitable, but which I had not included as a prospective release site in our original application. It lay beside the only access road to the houses here. While everyone living on the estate had been hugely supportive of our project, I imagined their goodwill would have dried up if beavers felled trees and blocked the road. Time spent living alongside the animals, observing how they worked, had since taught me that the large trees that skirted the roadside would not be felled in one bite, but instead be worked on over the course of several nights. Provided that we kept a wary eye upon them, they could be wrapped with mesh to prevent further gnawing. Confident that we could handle whatever the beavers threw at us, we contacted NatureScot, offering to release Fig here.

While I have been critical of the agency at times in this book, where deserved, it's only proper to offer credit too. We were not forced to apply for a new licence and go through further rounds of consultation. All that work had been done and the question of whether Argaty represented a suitable release site had already been satisfactorily answered. Within the week, we were granted permission. To encourage Fig to remain and not to unsettle our other families by rampaging through their territories in search of a mate, he was to be given a female for company. (Roisin would source the lucky lady from another lethal control area in Tayside.) NatureScot's beaver team were utterly pragmatic. I was grateful for that.

And so, just as we seemed to be reaching the end of our beaver story, we were to bear witness to one last new beginning. On 19 March 2023, Fig the beaver came to Argaty.

As we carried his crate to the water's edge a buzzard arched overhead, its clipped cries punctuated by the occasional whistle of a distant kite and the churring of a wren. A small group of onlookers had gathered for the release. April was here with the team from the SSPCA. Roisin and her Beaver Trust colleague, Sheelagh McAllister, had Fig's prospective partner in a crate. Elliot McCandless was there to photograph the action.

Keen to catch a glimpse of Fig, I crouched beside his cage. Alerted by the swish of my waterproof trousers, he turned and pressed his face to the grate, quizzical yet unafraid. He had quite the boxer's nose. Some shrapnel, deemed too dangerous to remove, remained lodged within the skin. He would travel with it for life – a reminder of his brush with death.

All eyes fell upon me when I rose to a stand. From the expectant expressions I gathered that I was supposed to open the door. But these beavers were being released because of the SSPCA's hard work rather than mine. I had had my moment; now I was happy to slip into the crowd. I watched as Juanita Zaldua from the SSPCA's large animal team slid the bolt and set their patient loose.

Fig did not charge towards water as other beavers had. Nor did he make for the rushes and vanish from view. Instead, he rose on his hind legs, lifted his head and breathed in the fresh air of freedom. Sinking down to all fours he slid unhurriedly into the pond, but after a quick dip he was back on the bank, walking within feet of us, battered nose still twitching; he had caught the scent of food.

At the foot of a nearby willow he reared again, set new teeth into the sweet flesh of wood and began to bite.

Epilogue

I park the All-Terrain Vehicle midway across the field, 20 metres from the gate, and quickly kill the engine. We close the doors gently, wary of slamming them shut. The sharpened stumps of willows and cherries flank the now well-worn path down to the water's edge. I eye each tree as we tiptoe past, marvelling at the regrowth sprouting from them.

It's September 2023. Nearly two years have passed since the first beavers arrived here, an incredible three years and nine months since the unexpected phone call that set the events of this story in motion. How long ago that seems. What changes we've witnessed in that time.

But for the tiny rings left by insects flitting from its surface, the water before us is motionless; tonight we have arrived before the beavers. Still, we talk in whispers. Are such precautions still necessary? I no longer know. They barely turn their heads at our smell or sound now. This realisation always leads to panic, for who knows what sort of people the sub-adults will meet when they move on from here? These days I feel more and more like a concerned parent. My neck and shoulders are tangles of knots that only ever pull tighter. When I sleep I grind my teeth, working them to dust. Last month I turned 40. Forty. For a small word it sounds huge. I see my father's hair loss reflected in the thinning on my own scalp, his greying on my temples. Some things we expect with age, but others have come as a shock. Nobody told me that I would worry about things so much. I worry for the beavers, worry that they accept people more than they ought to. Like that concerned parent, I fear that I may be to blame.

And yet, as I tell myself repeatedly, it must be this way. They must become familiar with us if we are to become familiar with them. Familiarity is key. People must see these animals if they are to understand them and care for their survival. I repeat these reassurances again and again, but still the neck knots tighten.

Water is lapping at the tips of my boots. Recent rains have caused the pond to rise and swell. It bulges in the middle as though suffering from middle-aged spread. Several metres inside the dam two tall alders are now paddling. They look like tentative tourists, testing the water at a frozen seaside resort. Those trees once marked the edge of the pond. I wonder if their roots will drown this year, if the leaves they cast this autumn will be their last. This is a landscape in transition, leaving its past behind, moving towards new worlds of possibilities. And its identity will forever be as fluid as the waters that flow through it. The view I enjoy tonight will not be the same in a year's time. To live alongside beavers is to learn the true meaning of rewilding. It is to embark upon a journey without an end.

Much has happened in this, our second full year with them. Fig and his partner remained on their pond for a month. They took tentative nibbles from the willows, were photographed together on our trail cameras; we thought they were settled. But when days and then weeks passed without them touching food or further sampling the vegetation we knew that they had chosen the wild. We never saw them again.

Beavers are sexually mature from 18 months old, and as they reached two years of age the sub-adults of both translocated families dispersed in search of territories and mates of their own.

Worn patches of earth beneath fence lines told of their trails. Where any of these animals is now is anyone's guess. Had they caused any mischief with our neighbours I suppose we might have heard. Dispersing beavers can travel as far as 50km downstream.[36] My hope is that they went as far as they could, that they found the river and kept going.

Autumn is fast approaching. Swallows sit in congregation on the wires. The trees are shedding their leaves. Around the beaver ponds all is wilting now, but summer was glorious here. From unseen places in the undergrowth, willow warblers trilled in descending scales. Water shrews were spotted on the banks. A mandarin duck swam here for a time. Mallard and teal remained longer. A moorhen family was ever-present. Foxgloves sprouted in the places where trees once stood. Water incarcerated behind dams sank down into the soil, the nettles which had once dominated these places withered as their roots grew wetter. Great bouquets of forget-me-nots, marsh woundwort and meadowsweet appeared in their stead. And plant-growth was not confined to dry land. Until the beavers came, the pond had been an unsightly shade of muddy brown. For years leaves had dropped into the water, covering and eventually smothering its plant-life. When the beavers pushed up their islands of mud the previous summer, that leaf litter was forced to the surface, where it began to oxidise. Freed at last from their choking grasp, seeds that had lain dormant for decades began to grow. Water pondweed and water starwort bloomed. Finally oxygenated, the water turned clear as glass.

'Conventional wisdom would say that the only way of restoring that pond would've been diggers and chainsaws,' Nigel Willby would later tell me. 'The beavers saved it.'

Each time I visit this growing wetland I see bubbles rise as frogs flee my feet and plunge for deep water. I see rain-glistened cobwebs strung in the cracks of felled trees, hear the tinnitus-inducing alarms of flies caught within them. Every minute of every day, small explosions of life are detonating all around. And thanks to Nigel, Alan Law and their brilliant team of Stirling University PhD students, these changes are being measured. In the fullness of time, when results are collated and projects published, we will have a body of evidence demonstrating the benefits beavers bring to water temperature and quality, to biodiversity and more. For anyone still doubting why we brought beavers here, these results will provide answers.

Recently James Nairne lent me a well-thumbed copy of Eric Collier's *Three Against the Wilderness*. Published in 1959, the memoir tells of fur-trapper Collier's 26 years living off the land with his Native American wife and their son in Meldrum Creek, British Columbia. In former times herds of elk had visited the creek, thousands of migrant Canada Geese rested in the lakes, the water below the beaver dams 'teamed with monstrous trout', resting a moment before moving upstream. By the time of Collier's arrival in the 1930s, the elk are gone, no trout stop, the creek is a shadow of what it once was. The only person who remembers that time of plenty is Lala, the elderly grandmother of Collier's wife.

'Until white man come,' she explains, 'Indian just kill beaver now an' then s'pose he want meat, or skin for blanket. And then, always the creek is full of beaver. But then white man come and give him tobacco, sugar, bad drinks every tam' he fetch beaver skin from creek Indian go crazy and kill beaver all tam' ... What's matter white man no tell Indian – s'pose you take all beaver, all water go too. And if water go, no trout, no fur, no grass, not'ing stop?'[37]

At Lala's suggestion, Collier sets out to bring trout, ducks, geese, muskrats, mink and otters back to Meldrum. He does so by giving the creek back its beavers. Each of the new, exciting discoveries our generation makes about this animal are not in fact new at all; Collier's story serves as a pertinent reminder of that. Every small detail of beavers' lives would have been known to our ancestors, just as they will one day be known to our descendants, as we learn to live alongside these animals again.

Much of our year has been spent sitting high on the banks of the amphitheatre pond, watching the second beaver family; however, we do still check in on our other residents from time to time. Around the farm I find new dams and pointed stumps in places to which I thought no beaver had ventured. Word reaches my ears of similar sights being uncovered around the local area: gnawed trees at Loch Mahaick, territories stretching west across the Carse of Stirling, a dam beneath a bridge in Aberfoyle. Hundreds of miserable years of history are being undone. The beavers are writing their own tale now.

A gentle sloshing sounds from the far bank. A ripple is spreading like a rumour. We sit stock still, breath held, following its path.

'There,' Sarah whispers, gesturing across the water.

I follow the direction of my wife's pointing finger. It's her first night of beaver watching and already she has her eye in. In the shallows beneath the shade of an overhanging tree, an adult sits chewing on a newly severed branch. I suspect it's the mother. She always seems to emerge first.

Soon she casts out, diving, resurfacing, paying us no mind. Somewhere below her, buried beneath the waves like the ruins of Atlantis, are the trenches she and her family dug during the worst of last year's heatwave. In those hard times the beavers created their own civilisation and kept untold numbers of species alive. We need beavers like never before. We need them for the insects, the birds, the bats, the amphibians, even for the trees. We need them for us.

Short forearms heaving, the mother bench-presses herself back up the bank. She finds another branch and, holding it like a flute, begins to nibble.

'I can't believe how big they are,' one of our guests remarks over the rising sound of crunching.

'Nobody can when they first see them,' I reply, smiling.

A smile is playing at the corner of Sarah's mouth too. That grin expands to full form as a kit emerges from the lodge with an ungainly splash, as it climbs the bank and joins its mother, as it cocks its neck then begins to preen her coat. Binoculars pressed to her eyes, Sarah takes this all in. She doesn't know that I am watching her, revelling in that smile. These years have been hard on her. I know that, and my heart hangs heavy with guilt. How does one strike the balance between the people and causes one cares about? I don't know. I don't suppose that many of the people in this story do either. Watching her as she watches the beavers, I want to ask if this journey gave more than it took. But I can't. Because I'm afraid of how she might answer. I want to tell her that she is my best friend, my rock. I want to say sorry, because often I took more than I gave.

Branch in mouth, another beaver emerges to our left.

'In autumn, they cache food,' I tell the visitors. 'They create the caches by—' As if on cue, the beaver makes a perfect dive, carrying its stick to the pond's muddy floor. 'By doing that,' I conclude with a chuckle as the animal rises, stickless, and resumes its swim.

On the opposite bank a third family member has appeared. Last night they took down the alder that stood behind their lodge. Sap flows in a bloody shade of orange where it was chopped. Like a gang of thieves, the beavers loot the body, picking pockets before the police show up. One hastily shoves leaves into its mouth, the others make off with armfuls of branches. Though the weather remains stubbornly warm, they have felt the change in the season, noted the darkening nights. Their preparations for winter begin now.

Watching the team at work, my thoughts move, as they so often do, to another team: the friends who helped make these translocations possible. Nobody in this story is especially famous. Our names mean little to the average person on the street. That might sound like a weakness, but actually I think it's our strength. Our story shows what people can do if they are coordinated enough, determined enough, if they care enough.

If there's one message I hope readers of this book will take away, it is this: We don't have to sit idly by, watching as the natural world collapses before our eyes. We can make change happen. It's not always easy, it's not always fun, but it can be done. I hope this story will give others the courage to make a stand for the incredible creatures that we share this planet with. They need us.

*

These days I dwell less and less on matters of give and take. As we move further from conflict, I find that I need answers less than I once did.

Curiosity would move me to ask the question one last time, however.

'Wow, that's a good one,' James replied. 'I wouldn't go as far as to say that beaver advocacy has *impacted* upon my mental health – that's too strong a word. But there are times, particularly when fighting with opponents, when I definitely feel it impinging. I honestly don't know if it gives more than it takes. But Tom, did you ever hear the Chinese curse?'

He stopped, waiting. I thought I'd heard mirth in his voice.

'Which one?' I asked, dutifully fulfilling my role as the 'Who's there?' guy in the knock-knock joke.

'May you live in *interesting* times,' he said.

'Interesting times?' I repeated, mulling the thought over. 'We'd take that, wouldn't we?'

'We would,' he agreed. 'Now I need to ask you something in return.'

A new note had entered his tone. My neck muscles tensed, my jaw clenched. They always would when he uttered words like this.

'Go on,' I said, against my better judgment.

'I want to know . . .' He stopped, waiting several seconds before the big reveal. 'Has it all been worth it?'

Without warning, I felt the water rising. Dams were breaking behind my eyes.

'Yes,' I replied in a voice not quite my own. 'Every second.'

*

Night is falling on the beaver pond now. Bats are swerving between the trees, replacing the swallows which dived, cackling like deranged bomber pilots, over the water not half an hour earlier. Autumn will soon be upon us. This will be our last visit here, the last we see of the beavers till spring. I miss them already. These friends have been part of my life for so short a time, yet are now a part of it forever.

The events of these past three years have changed me a great deal. I think of who I once was: a younger man, burning with a desire to make his mark on the world. Ambition can be an ugly thing, but we'd be nothing and nowhere without it. The younger me believed that people were, in broad terms, either content or discontent, and that achieving one's goals was the key to finding happiness. I'm not so sure of that now. It seems to me that most of us will forever walk a fine line, holding happiness and sadness in the same hand at the same time, trying to keep as much of one cupped as we can whilst letting the other slip like water through our fingers. Who can say whether life takes more than it gives? Who can say whether it gives more than it takes? Not I. But when the last light fades and darkness douses the sky, when trees and stars and moon look down upon the kin they thought they'd lost forever, when the bats wheel and blackbirds conspire and water laps against a wall built of mud and stick and stone, of teamwork and intelligence beyond anything we humans can comprehend, the sounds of splashing and diving fill my ears. Four beavers are swimming before me, and I can only feel glad for every second of these happy, sad and always interesting times.

Postscript

Much has happened – on Argaty and across Scotland – since the completion of this book.

Thanks to a Scottish Government Nature Restoration Fund grant, from late 2023 we began to fence off Argaty's waterways to exclude grazers. Within these wildlife corridors we planted alder, aspen, birch and willow. We sowed yellow rattle to parasitise grasses and encourage wildflower growth. In the not-too-distant future, when these habitats have established, beavers will be present throughout these waters. We'll make Argaty an incredible home for them, do all that we can to demonstrate that farmers can live alongside them. It's the least that we can do to thank them. They have opened so many doors for us.

We've featured on Gordon Buchanan and Jamma International's *Beneath the Baobab* podcast, discussing the importance of overcoming conflict and coexisting with wildlife. BBC *Springwatch* spent two days broadcasting live here – a ravenous mother beaver (nursing a litter of four kits) treated presenter Megan McCubbin and the team to some fantastic carrot-munching action. Hamza Yassin filmed the family for his BBC One series, *Hamza's Hidden Wild Isles*. Our winter wetland tours and summer beaver-watching experiences sold out almost as soon as they were advertised too. Interest in our rewilding work has never been greater. All of that is down to the beavers. They have been the making of this place.

At national level there have been further exciting developments on the translocation front. From October 2023 Forestry and Land Scotland at last began to rehome beavers to sites they manage in Tayside, Knapdale and the Trossachs. (From contacts close to the agency we later learned that a combination of ministerial and public pressure had forced reticent forestry chiefs to act.) In November 2023 RSPB Scotland released a further pair onto their Loch Lomond reserve. But by far the most exciting news came in December 2023 when Cairngorms National Park's translocation application was approved. The five-year licence allowed up to 15 families to be released. In December of that year, two pairs were released into the Upper Spey area. They were the first beavers to grace the Cairngorms for over four centuries, the first to be relocated to an entirely beaver-free river catchment.

Thanks to these releases and to continued demand from enclosed projects in England, 74 beavers were translocated from Tayside between January 2023 and April 2024. In that same period only eight beavers were recorded as having been shot under licence. (These figures make impressive reading compared to the 2022 totals, where 108 animals were removed, 45 by trapping, 63 by lethal control.) With a programme of wild releases having begun in England in March 2025 and the Welsh Government also pledging support for managed reintroductions, demand for beavers south of the border should, we hope, keep Scotland's death toll at a low level for years to come.

Meanwhile, Fig became a near-martyr, the hero that didn't quite die for the cause. For every action there is an equal and opposite reaction, and his story brought widespread condemnation of NatureScot's lethal control accreditation system. The scrutiny brought some degree of change. As a condition of receiving a licence, shooters will have to hand in bodies for autopsy. Only in exceptional cases, when retrieval is *genuinely* too dangerous to attempt, will failure to produce a carcass be accepted.

We are not out of the woods yet. Although much has improved for beavers, the fight is far from over. The translocation process remains onerous. Without a future pipeline of receptor sites, government's desire to grow the population and see them translocated to new Scottish catchments cannot and will not happen. Lack of any official oversight also means that we still have no idea what is happening at night on those Tayside watercourses, how many beavers are unofficially killed. To make matters worse, the authorities have thus far resisted calls to ban the shooting of beavers over water. There will be more stories like Fig's before the fighting is over.

But for all of that, the progress made in recent years remains very encouraging.

Sometimes I wonder what would have happened had the people in this book not done as they did. Success was a fragile thing. Had we turned him down, would James have found another landowner willing to apply for beavers? Had Trees for Life not taken NatureScot to judicial review, might someone else have? Had the Greens not entered the coalition at the precise moment that they did, would the Scottish Government have softened their stance? Or would translocations remain prohibited, and 100 beavers still be culled under licence annually? I don't know. All I can say is that I hope we helped them.

Scotland's beaver population continues to grow. With each dispersing kit, each translocation, they are reclaiming these waters. They are coming home.

Notes

1. Rosell, F. & Campbell-Palmer, R. *Beavers: Ecology, Behaviour, Conservation, and Management* (Oxford University Press, 2022), p.3.
2. Grey Owl, *Pilgrims of the Wild* (Voyageur Classics, 1934).
3. Halley, D.J., Saveljev, A.P. & Rosell, F. 'Population and distribution of beavers Castor fiber and Castor canadensis in Eurasia', *Mammal Review*, 2020.
4. Giraldus Cambrensis, *The Journey Through Wales The Description of Wales* (Penguin Classics, 1978), p.174.
5. Kitchener, A.C. & Conroy, J.W.H. 'The History of the Eurasian Beaver Castor fiber in Scotland', *Mammal Review*, 1997, p.102.
6. Crumley, J. *Nature's Architect: The Beaver's Return to Our Wild Landscapes* (Saraband, 2015), p.53.
7. Gow, D. *Bringing Back the Beaver* (Chelsea Green, 2020), p.6.
8. 'Scots Wildlife Officials Stalk Beaver on the Run', www.reuters.com.
9. Gilvear, D. & Black, A. 'Flood-induced embankment failures on the River Tay: Implications of climatically induced hydrological change in Scotland', *Hydrological Sciences Journal* 44(3), 1999, pp.345–62.
10. Law, A., Jones, K.C. & Willby, N. 'Medium vs. short-term effects of herbivory by Eurasian beaver on aquatic vegetation', *Aquatic Botany*, 2014, p.116.

11. Puttock, A., Graham, H.A., Ashe, J., Luscombe, D.J. & Brazier, R.E. 'Beaver dams attenuate flow: A multi-site study', *Hydrological Processes*, 2021.
12. UK Government. https://assets.publishing.service.gov.uk/
13. CBS News. www.cbsnews.com
14. Law, A. McLean, F. & Willby, N. 'Habitat engineering by beaver benefits aquatic biodiversity and ecosystem processes in agricultural streams', *Freshwater Biology*, Vol. 61, Issue 4, 2016.
15. Puttock, A., Graham, H.A., Cunlifee, A.M., Elliott, M. & Brazier, R.E. 'Eurasian beaver activity increases water storage, attenuates flow and mitigates diffuse pollution from intensively managed grasslands', *Science of the Total Environment*, 2017.
16. Crumley, J. (2015), p.36.
17. Webster, H. 'Friends with Benefits?' SCOTLAND: The Big Picture. scotlandbigpicture.com/rewilding-stories/friends-with-benefits
18. Trees for Life. www.treesforlife.org.uk
19. Judge Carmichael's verdict can be read in full at: https://www.scotcourts.gov.uk/
20. Crumley, J. 'Beaver Ruling is a Victory for All Scottish Wildlife', *The Courier*, 26 October 2021.
21. The Wildlife Trusts. https://www.wildlifetrusts.org/water
22. WWF-UK 'Hidden waste: The scale and impact of food waste in UK primary production', 2022.
23. The Trussell Trust. www.trussell.org.uk/
24. Scottish Environment LINK
25. NFUS:https://www.nfus.org.uk/farming-facts/what-we-produce.aspx
26. Summary Report, 'Analysis of the Future UK FTA Scenarios on Scotland's Agricultural Food and Drinks Sector', 2023.
27. Rosell, F. & Campbell-Palmer, R. (2022), p.131.

28. Soga, M. & Gaston, K.J. 'Shifting Baseline Syndrome: Causes, consequences, and implications', *Frontiers in Ecology and the Environment*, 2018, p.16(4).
29. 'The Land of Scotland and the Common Good: Report', the final report of the Land Reform Review Group, 2014.
30. Rosell, F. & Campbell-Palmer, R. (2022), p.187.
31. Fairfax, E. & Whittle, A. 'Smokey the Beaver: Beaver-dammed riparian corridors stay green during wildfire throughout the Western United States', *Ecological Aspirations*, Vol. 30, Issue 8, 2020.
32. Grant, J. 'Prey Remains Analysis Report – Report to Nature-Scot on White-Tailed Eagle work with respect to collection and analysis of prey remains from territories associated with, or possibly implicated in, lamb predation in 2021', www.nature.scot.

    In December 2023, 16 months after my visit to Mull, a peer-reviewed paper, 'The Breeding Season Diet of White-Tailed Eagles in Scotland', was published. The study assessed the diet of breeding pairs of sea eagles between 1998 and 2017, and found that fish and marine prey were their most important food source, with occurrences of lamb in their food decreasing as more pairs established in Scotland. It reported 11,375 different food items from 92 nests, with 70 species of bird, at least 30 fish species and 17 species of mammal. Between 1998 and 2002, 15 nests were sampled and lamb accounted for more than 30 per cent of the items in five nests. As the population of eagles grew, lambs accounted for 30 per cent or more of items at only five of 58 sampled nests. Reid, R., Grant, J.R., Broad, R. A., Carrs, D.N. & Marquis, M. 'The breeding season diet of White-Tailed Eagles in Scotland', *Scottish Birds*, 43(4), 2023.
33. Scottish Government, 'New Entrants and Young Farmers Start-Up Grant Schemes: Evaluation', www.gov.scot, 2022.

34. Cairns, P. 'The Wings of Change', www.ScotlandBigPicture.com
35. Whitfield, D.P. & Fielding, A.H. 'Analyses of the fates of satellite tracked golden eagles in Scotland', NatureScot commissioned report 982, 2017.
36. Warwick, H. *The Beaver Book* (Graffeg, 2021), p.37.
37. Collier, E. *Three Against the Wilderness* (Classics West, 1959), p.20.

Select Reading

Articles & Reports

Conroy, J.W.H. & Kitchener, A. 'The History of the Eurasian Beaver Castor fiber in Scotland'. Published in *Mammal Review* (1997)

Fairfax, E. & Whittle, A. 'Smokey the Beaver: Beaver-dammed riparian corridors stay green during wildfire throughout the Western United States'. Published in *Ecological Aspirations*, Vol. 30, Issue 8 (December 2020)

Halley, D.J., Saveljev, A.P. & Rosell, F. 'Population and distribution of beavers Castor fiber and Castor canadensis in Eurasia'. Published in *Mammal Review* (2020)

Law, A., Jones, K.C. & Willby, N. 'Medium vs. short-term effects of herbivory by Eurasian beaver on aquatic vegetation'. Published in *Aquatic Botany* (2014)

Law, A., McLean, F. & Willby, N. 'Habitat engineering by beaver benefits aquatic biodiversity and ecosystem processes in agricultural streams'. Published in *Freshwater Biology*, Vol. 61, Issue 4 (2016)

Puttock, A., Graham, H.A., Ashe, J., Luscombe, D.J. & Brazier, R.E. 'Beaver dams attenuate flow: A multi-site study'. Published in *Hydrological Processes*, Vol. 35, Issue 2 (2021)

Puttock, A., Graham, H.A., Cunlifee, A.M., Elliott, M. & Brazier, R.E. 'Eurasian beaver activity increases water storage, attenuates flow and mitigates diffuse pollution from intensively managed grasslands'. Published in *Science of the Total Environment* (2017)

Whitfield, P. & Fielding, A.H. 'Analyses of the Fates of Satellite Tracked Golden Eagles in Scotland': SNH Commissioned Report 982 (2017)

WWF-UK 'Hidden waste: The scale and impact of food waste in UK primary production' (2022)

Books

Bellenden, J. *The History and Chronicles of Scotland* (W. & C. Tait, Edinburgh, 1821)

Campbell-Palmer, R., Gow, D., Needham, R., Jones, S. & Rosell, F. *The Eurasian Beaver* (Pelagic, 2015)

Coles, B. *Beavers in Britain's Past* (Oxbow Books, 2006)

Collier, E. *Three Against the Wilderness* (Classics West, 1959)

Crumley, J. *Nature's Architect: The Beaver's Return to Our Wild Landscapes* (Saraband, 2015)

Dennis, R. *Restoring the Wild: Sixty Years of Rewilding Our Skies, Woods and Waterways* (William Collins, 2021)

Gerald of Wales (Giraldus Cambrensis) *The Journey Through Wales and the Description of Wales* (Penguin Classics, 1978)

Goldfarb, B. *Eager: The Surprising, Secret Life of Beavers and Why They Matter* (Chelsea Green, 2018)

Gow, D. *Bringing Back the Beaver: The Story of One Man's Quest to Rewild Britain's Waterways* (Chelsea Green, 2020)

Grey Owl *Pilgrims of the Wild* (Voyageur Classics, 1934)

Rosell, F. & Campbell-Palmer, R. *Beavers: Ecology, Behaviour, Conservation, and Management* (Oxford University Press, 2022)

Acknowledgements

So many people helped in so many ways, both in getting beavers to Argaty and in the subsequent creation of this book.

Huge thanks are due to:

All the many people who have supported our beaver project and made it a reality.

The following amazing people, all of whom provided us with supporting statements on behalf of the organisations they represent: Andrew Clark (Doune Primary School), Anna Clark and Jayne Whitehead (Kilmadock Climate Action), Bob Elliot (OneKind), Deborah Long (Scottish Environment LINK), Guy Harewood (Stirling Council), Helen Senn (Royal Zoological Society Scotland), Kevin Duffy (Scottish Wildlife Trust Callander members' group) and Moira Lawson (Kilmadock Society).

Alan Jones, still sorely missed.

Alan Law and Nigel Willby from the University of Stirling. Their pioneering scientific studies of beavers in Britain have taught us to consider the benefits that the animals bring, where once we were so focussed on the issues they posed.

Alan Puttock and his colleagues at the University of Exeter, of whom the same must be said.

Alan McDonnell and Steve Micklewright of Trees for Life, for their brave defence of these animals.

Alex and Martin Keivers and Ewan Miles, who treated me to some unforgettable wildlife experiences while on Mull.

April Dodds and the team at the SSPCA's National Wildlife Rescue Centre, for the amazing work with Fig.

The incredible team at Beaver Trust, for financing our translocations and for their tireless work to restore beavers across Britain.

Everyone at Birlinn Ltd for their great support with this project. Special thanks are due to Andrew Simmons, Deborah Warner and Hugh Andrew for their helpful and constructive feedback.

Bryony Coles, whose incredible research massively increased my knowledge of the history of beavers in Scotland.

Cian O'Driscoll, for helping to shape so many thoughts on books and on life.

Dave and Katy Anderson: great friends and great champions of wildlife.

David Sexton, for a very open and honest interview, and for the many years spent advocating for white-tailed eagles. 'They' are lucky to have people like him.

Derek Gow, a great champion for beavers and a great friend through the most trying of times.

Duncan Orr-Ewing, who provided support and sensible advice during our consultations.

Elliot McCandless and Kirsten Brewster, Scotland's beaver power couple. Two of the most knowledgeable and passionate advocates these animals have.

Elsie Blackshaw-Crosby and the legal team at The Lifescape Project, for their brilliant work on the beaver judicial review (and for patiently answering so many basic questions I had on legal issues).

Gary Curran, Romain Pizzi and everyone at Five Sisters Zoo who care superbly for these animals before they are moved to their new homes.

Acknowledgements

Hugh Chalmers, for an excellent interview about the return of beavers to Scotland.

James Leonard, whose help sourcing and installing trail cameras helped us to monitor beavers effectively.

James Nairne. In the words of his mother, he 'got that boy into a lot of trouble', but he had the good grace to guide him through it too.

James Silvey, a great friend throughout this process and a real leader in RSPB Scotland's beaver relocations.

Jock Gibson, who may only agree with 50% of this book (at best), but who has been an excellent cousin, friend and sounding board for many years.

Louise, Paul and Sophie Ramsay: Scotland's first and greatest beaver supporters. Tayside's beavers may well have been extirpated for a second time were it not for their bravery.

Our contract farmers, Mark and Harriet Donald, and Donald Heads, who've been wonderfully supportive and accommodating of our newest residents.

Mark Ruskell and his colleagues in the Scottish Green Party. What a difference the Greens made for beavers.

Nicky Downing, whose thoughts on biodiversity and food security helped shape big sections of this book.

Pete Cairns, James Shooter, Mark Hamblin and Mat Larkin. SCOTLAND: The Big Picture have made many things possible for us, and their glorious visual communications work helped us to tell our beaver story in ways we simply couldn't.

Philip Price, who first sparked the flame of beaver-enthusiasm in this writer.

Polly Pullar, who made these books possible and has been a great supporter of our project ever since.

Richard Bunting, a PR genius and an unsung hero of the beaver story. His thoughtful and intelligent media communications work helped us (and Scotland's beavers) on so many occasions.

Roisin Campbell-Palmer, to whom Argaty's (and Britain's) beavers owe their lives. Of all the heroes in this story, Roisin is surely the greatest.

Roy Dennis, for all the support, for the fascinating interview and for a lifetime of pioneering rewilding work.

Ruth Tingay, who has fought so bravely in the battle against raptor persecution and knows, more than almost anyone, what this life gives and what it takes.

Sarah Henshall, Sally Mackenzie, Lewis Pate, Jonathan Willet and everyone involved in the Cairngorms Beaver reintroduction. Beavers are now swimming free in an entirely new part of Scotland. What an achievement.

Steve Evison, who provided crucial advice at key times during our consultations.

Andrew O'Donnell, Annette Sproul, Clare Harte, Ettie Shattock, Fiona Brims, Gavin and Gillian Thomson, Gwyneth Campbell, John Wells, Keith Burgoyne, Marion Moore, Mark Taylor, Michael Yuille, Oliver Dalby, Richard Cuthill, Sandra McDerment, Steve Marshall, Roger Stewart and Vicki Nash – our incredible team of rangers and volunteers at Argaty, whose support and enthusiasm keeps the rewilding project going.

And lastly . . .

To Mum and Dad, for your love and support.

To my wife and best friend, Sarah. Thank you for guiding me through this, for the many ideas you've allowed me to 'bounce off you', for being the strongest and most intelligent person I will ever know.

And to our beautiful girls, Rowie and Ellie. You are my life and my joy.